M000034822

Presented to

Debb ♡

on

January 18, 2017

by

Brenda

Love you my friend!

"God does not give us everything we want, but
He does fulfill His promises, leading us along
the best and straightest paths to Himself."
DIETRICH BONHOEFFER

SPIRITLED PROMISES FOR

EVERY DAY and

EVERY NEED

SPIRITLED PROMISES FOR

EVERY DAY *and*

EVERY NEED

PASSIO

THE ART OF AUTHENTIC FAITH

Most CHARISMA HOUSE BOOK GROUP products are available at special quantity discounts for bulk purchase for sales promotions, premiums, fund-raising, and educational needs. For details, write Charisma House Book Group, 600 Rinehart Road, Lake Mary, Florida 32746, or telephone (407) 333-0600.

SPIRITLED PROMISES FOR EVERY DAY AND
   EVERY NEED
Published by Passio
Charisma Media/Charisma House Book Group
600 Rinehart Road
Lake Mary, Florida 32746
www.charismahouse.com

This book or parts thereof may not be reproduced in any form, stored in a retrieval system, or transmitted in any form by any means—electronic, mechanical, photocopy, recording, or otherwise—without prior written permission of the publisher, except as provided by United States of America copyright law.

Scripture taken from the Holy Bible Modern English Version. Copyright © 2012 James F. Linzey. All rights reserved.

Copyright © 2013, 2014 by Charisma House
All rights reserved

Cover design by Lisa Rae Cox
Design Director: Bill Johnson

Library of Congress Control Number: 2013915707
International Standard Book Number:
978-1-62136-979-0

14 15 16 17 18 — 9 8 7 6 5 4 3 2 1
Printed in the United States of America

"We have ample evidence that the Lord is able to guide. The promises cover every imaginable situation. All we need to do is to take the hand he stretches out."

ELISABETH ELLIOT

Contents

INTRODUCTION

A person who wholly follows the Lord is one who believes
that the promises of God are trustworthy, that He is with
His people, and that they are well able to overcome.
—WATCHMAN NEE

LIVING A LIFE of faith means learning to trust God for where you are being led. Some days you question where your life is going, and you wonder if God is still guiding you. There are times when you might feel that life is just one great, big battlefield—and you question who is really winning. Other times you might even think He's not talking to you at all. God sees that you often get caught up in the concerns and demands of life, and you don't realize that He is always here to take care of you and provide for all your needs. God wants you to know that He has a very special purpose for your life, and He has provided promises in His Word that supply assurance and direction for every day and every need.

Without a doubt there are spiritual forces waging against God's children and His creation. Satan is definitely our enemy—and his goal is to wreak havoc in our lives. Unfortunately our enemy doesn't acknowledge the Lord's victory and remains in the attack mode. But be assured, Jesus has already won the war—and He shares that victory with you! God offers that victory, that assurance, peace, hope and understanding with every promise He has made. Your biggest needs are answered by His unbreakable promises, showered with His love.

God delights in providing for you. It gives Him great pleasure to bless you—and He loves it when you come to Him! God hates to see you struggle when He has all you could ever want or need. He knows how you've always longed to be a strong person. He fully realizes how you desire more power and purpose in your life. God's Word speaks to all issues in our everyday living. It speaks to our requirements, desires, and requests, as well as our hopes and dreams. God's promises are inspiring reminders and assurances. You can have God's personal pledges, and you can rely on them.

SpiritLed Promises for Every Day and Every Need provides you with the opportunity to easily find thousands of God's promises for more than 250 areas of your life, easily arranged alphabetically by topic so you can always find just the right promise when it's important to know what God's Word says. Apply each scripture personally, and you will see the power of God's Word in action. You will discover confidence and celebrate victory when you trust God and His promises to meet your needs.

God always has your best interests in mind—whether you are concerned about love, forgiveness, safety, money, or speaking to the mountains in your life. His Word has a promise that you can lay claim to for every need. Your prayer life will be strengthened. Your ability to minister to others will be sharper and much more effective. Your attitudes and outlook will begin to change. Your mind will become alert and observant. Your confidence and hope will be enhanced.

Embrace each promise, commit it to memory, and allow them to become life changing for you.

The Bible will always hold first place in the life of the spiritual Christian. Reinforce your faith with the confidence of knowing that any work He has begun in you will be completed according to His will and purpose for your life.

> If God brings you to it, He will bring you through it.
>
> —Unknown

"The permanence of God's character guarantees the fulfillment of his promises."

A. W. PINK

ABORTION

Then God said, "Let Us make man in Our image, after Our likeness, and let them have dominion over the fish of the sea, and over the birds of the air, and over the cattle, and over all the earth, and over every creeping thing that creeps on the earth."

—GENESIS 1:26

You shall not murder.

—DEUTERONOMY 5:17

Look, children are a gift of the LORD, and the fruit of the womb is a reward.

—PSALM 127:3

There is a way that seems right to a man, but its end is the way of death.

—PROVERBS 16:25

"Wash yourselves, make yourselves clean. Put away the evil from your deeds, from before My eyes. Cease to do evil. Learn to do good. Seek justice. Relieve the oppressed. Judge the fatherless. Plead for the widow. Come now, and let us reason together," says the LORD. "Though your sins be as scarlet, they shall be as white as snow. Though they be red like crimson, they shall be as wool."

—ISAIAH 1:16–18

Can a woman forget her nursing child, and have no compassion on the son of her womb? Indeed, they may forget, yet I will not forget.

—ISAIAH 49:15

Let the wicked forsake his way, and the unrighteous man his thoughts. And let him return to the LORD, and He will have mercy upon him, and to our God, for He will abundantly pardon.

—Isaiah 55:7

Before I formed you in the womb I knew you. And before you came forth out of the womb I sanctified you, and I ordained you a prophet to the nations.

—Jeremiah 1:5

When Elizabeth heard the greeting of Mary, the baby leaped in her womb. And Elizabeth was filled with the Holy Spirit.

—Luke 1:41

She said, "No one, Lord." Jesus said to her, "Neither do I condemn you. Go and sin no more."

—John 8:11

But when it pleased God, who set me apart since I was in my mother's womb and called me by His grace…

—Galatians 1:15

But if we walk in the light as He is in the light, we have fellowship one with another, and the blood of Jesus Christ His Son cleanses us from all sin.

—1 John 1:7

ABUSE

I sought the LORD, and He answered me, and delivered me from all my fears. They looked to Him and became radiant, and their faces are not ashamed.

—Psalm 34:4–5

Why, my soul, are you cast down? Why do you groan within me? Wait for God; I will yet thank Him, for He is my deliverance and my God.

—Psalm 42:11

Trust in the Lord forever, for in God the Lord we have an everlasting rock. For He brings down those who dwell on high, the lofty city. He lays it low. He lays it low, even to the ground. He brings it even to the dust.

—Isaiah 26:4–5

Come to Me, all you who labor and are heavily burdened, and I will give you rest.

—Matthew 11:28

Do you not know that the unrighteous will not inherit the kingdom of God? Do not be deceived. Neither the sexually immoral, nor idolaters, nor adulterers, nor male prostitutes, nor homosexuals, nor thieves, nor covetous, nor drunkards, nor revilers, nor extortioners will inherit the kingdom of God. Such were some of you. But you were washed, you were sanctified, and you were justified in the name of the Lord Jesus by the Spirit of our God.

—1 Corinthians 6:9–11

But the fruit of the Spirit is love, joy, peace, patience, gentleness, goodness, faith, meekness, and self-control; against such there is no law.

—Galatians 5:22–23

Husbands, love your wives, just as Christ also loved the church and gave Himself for it.

—Ephesians 5:25

In this way, men ought to love their wives as their own bodies. He who loves his wife loves himself. For no one ever hated his own flesh, but nourishes and cherishes it, just as the Lord cares for the church.

—Ephesians 5:28–29

Fathers, do not provoke your children to anger, but bring them up in the discipline and instruction of the Lord.

—Ephesians 6:4

Confess your faults to one another and pray for one another, that you may be healed. The effective, fervent prayer of a righteous man accomplishes much.

—James 5:16

Likewise, you husbands, live considerately with your wives, giving honor to the woman as the weaker vessel, since they too are also heirs of the grace of life, so that your prayers will not be hindered.

—1 Peter 3:7

Cast all your care upon Him, because He cares for you.

—1 Peter 5:7

ACCEPTING OTHERS

Now, Israel, what does the Lord your God require of you, but to fear the Lord your God, to walk in all His ways, and to love Him, and to serve the Lord your God with all your heart and with all your soul, to keep the commandments of the Lord and His statutes which I am commanding you today for your good?

—Deuteronomy 10:12–13

Truly I say to you, whoever gives you a cup of water to drink in My name, because you belong to Christ, will not lose his reward.

—Mark 9:41

To love Him with all the heart, and with all the understanding, and with all the soul, and with all the strength, and to love one's neighbor as oneself, is more than all burnt offerings and sacrifices.

—Mark 12:33

Do unto others as you would have others do unto you.

—Luke 6:31

For I have given you an example, that you should do as I have done to you.

—John 13:15

This is My commandment: that you love one another, as I have loved you. Greater love has no man than this: that a man lay down his life for his friends.

—John 15:12–13

Then Peter began to speak, saying, "Truthfully, I perceive that God is no respecter of persons. But in every nation he who fears Him and works righteousness is accepted by Him."

—Acts 10:34–35

For He is our peace, who has made both groups one and has broken down the barrier of the dividing wall.

—Ephesians 2:14

And may the Lord make you increase and abound in love for one another and for all men, even as we do for you.

—1 Thessalonians 3:12

And let us consider how to spur one another to love and to good works.

—Hebrews 10:24

If you fulfill the royal law according to the Scripture, "You shall love your neighbor as yourself," you are doing well.

—James 2:8

Above all things, have unfailing love for one another, because love covers a multitude of sins.

—1 Peter 4:8

ACCOUNTABILITY

When I say to the wicked, "O wicked man, you shall surely die," and you do not speak to warn the wicked from his way, that wicked man shall die in his iniquity. But his blood I will require from your hand. Nevertheless, if you on your part warn the wicked to turn from his way and he does not turn from his way, he shall die in his iniquity. But you have delivered your soul.

—Ezekiel 33:8–9

But I say to you that for every idle word that men speak, they will give an account on the Day of Judgment. For by your words you will be justified, and by your words you will be condemned.

—Matthew 12:36–37

He told His disciples: "There was a rich man who had a steward, who was accused to the rich man of wasting his resources. So he called him and said to him, 'How is it that I hear this about you? Give an account of your stewardship, for you may no longer be steward.'"

—Luke 16:1–2

For we must all appear before the judgment seat of Christ, that each one may receive his recompense in the body, according to what he has done, whether it was good or bad.

—2 Corinthians 5:10

Providing for honest things, not only in the sight of the Lord, but also in the sight of men.

—2 Corinthians 8:21

Obey your leaders and submit to them, for they watch over your souls as those who must give an account. Let them do this with joy and not complaining, for that would not be profitable to you.

—Hebrews 13:17

ACTIVATING YOUR FAITH

"…by creating the fruit of the lips. Peace, peace to him who is far off and to him who is near," says the Lord, "and I will heal him."

—Isaiah 57:19

"For I will restore health to you, and I will heal you of your wounds," says the Lord, "because they called you an outcast, saying, 'This is Zion whom no man cares for.'"

—Jeremiah 30:17

When she had heard of Jesus, she came in the crowd behind Him and touched His garment. For she said, "If I may touch His garments, I shall be healed."

—MARK 5:27–28

The apostles said to the Lord, "Increase our faith." The Lord said, "If you had faith as a grain of mustard seed, you could say to this mulberry tree, 'Be uprooted and be planted in the sea,' and it would obey you."

—LUKE 17:5–6

So faith by itself, if it has no works, is dead.

—JAMES 2:17

For you have been born again, not from perishable seed, but imperishable, through the living and eternal word of God.

—1 PETER 1:23

ADULTERY

You shall not commit adultery.

—EXODUS 20:14

If a man commits adultery with another man's wife, the adulterer and the adulteress shall surely be put to death.

—LEVITICUS 20:10

But whoever commits adultery with a woman lacks understanding; he who does it destroys his own soul.

—PROVERBS 6:32

He who covers his sins will not prosper, but whoever confesses and forsakes them will have mercy.

—PROVERBS 28:13

You have heard that it was said by the ancients, "You shall not commit adultery." But I say to you that whoever looks on a woman to lust after her has committed adultery with her already in his heart.

—Matthew 5:27–28

For out of the heart proceed evil thoughts, murders, adulteries, sexual immorality, thefts, false witness, and blasphemies.

—Matthew 15:19

And if a woman divorces her husband and marries another, she commits adultery.

—Mark 10:12

Whoever divorces his wife and marries another commits adultery, and whoever marries her who is divorced by her husband commits adultery.

—Luke 16:18

She said, "No one, Lord." Jesus said to her, "Neither do I condemn you. Go and sin no more."

—John 8:11

Do you not know that the unrighteous will not inherit the kingdom of God? Do not be deceived. Neither the sexually immoral, nor idolaters, nor adulterers, nor male prostitutes, nor homosexuals, nor thieves, nor covetous, nor drunkards, nor revilers, nor extortioners will inherit the kingdom of God.

—1 Corinthians 6:9–10

Marriage is to be honored among everyone, and the bed undefiled. But God will judge the sexually immoral and adulterers.

—Hebrews 13:4

If we confess our sins, He is faithful and just to forgive us our sins and cleanse us from all unrighteousness.

—1 John 1:9

ALCOHOL

Wine is a mocker, strong drink is raging, and whoever is deceived by it is not wise.

—Proverbs 20:1

He who loves pleasure will be a poor man; he who loves wine and oil will not be rich.

—Proverbs 21:17

Do not be among winebibbers, among riotous eaters of meat; for the drunkard and the glutton will come to poverty, and drowsiness will clothe a man with rags.

—Proverbs 23:20–21

Who has woe? Who has sorrow? Who has contentions? Who has babbling? Who has wounds without cause? Who has redness of eyes? Those who tarry long at the wine, those who go to seek mixed wine.

—Proverbs 23:29–30

Woe to those who rise up early in the morning that they may pursue strong drink, who continue late in the evening until wine inflames them!

—Isaiah 5:11

Take heed to yourselves, lest your hearts become burdened by excessiveness and drunkenness and anxieties of life, and that Day comes on you unexpectedly.

—Luke 21:34

Therefore if the Son sets you free, you shall be free indeed.

—John 8:36

I urge you therefore, brothers, by the mercies of God, that you present your bodies as a living sacrifice, holy, and acceptable to God, which is your reasonable service of worship. Do not be conformed to this world, but be transformed by the renewing of your mind, that you may prove what is the good and acceptable and perfect will of God.

—Romans 12:1–2

Let us behave properly, as in the day, not in carousing and drunkenness, not in immorality and wickedness, not in strife and envy.

—Romans 13:13

Do you not know that the unrighteous will not inherit the kingdom of God? Do not be deceived. Neither the sexually immoral, nor idolaters, nor adulterers, nor male prostitutes, nor homosexuals, nor thieves, nor covetous, nor drunkards, nor revilers, nor extortioners will inherit the kingdom of God.

—1 Corinthians 6:9–10

Envy, murders, drunkenness, carousing, and the like. I warn you, as I previously warned you, that those who do such things shall not inherit the kingdom of God.

—Galatians 5:21

Do not be drunk with wine, for that is reckless living. But be filled with the Spirit.

—Ephesians 5:18

AMBITION

But seek first the kingdom of God and His righteousness, and all these things shall be given to you.

—MATTHEW 6:33

For what will it profit a man if he gains the whole world and loses his own soul? Or what shall a man give in exchange for his soul?

—MATTHEW 16:26

For what does it profit a man if he gains the whole world, yet loses or forfeits himself?

—LUKE 9:25

Let nothing be done out of strife or conceit, but in humility let each esteem the other better than himself.

—PHILIPPIANS 2:3

Learn to be calm, and to conduct your own business, and to work with your own hands, as we commanded you, So that you may walk honestly toward those who are outsiders and that you may lack nothing.

—1 THESSALONIANS 4:11–12

For where there is envying and strife, there is confusion and every evil work.

—JAMES 3:16

ANGELS

The angel of the LORD camps around those who fear Him, and delivers them.

—PSALM 34:7

The chariots of God are twice ten thousand, even thousands of thousands; the Lord is among them, as in Sinai, in the holy place.

—Psalm 68:17

And He will send His angels with a great sound of a trumpet, and they shall gather His elect from the four winds, from one end of the heavens to the other.

—Matthew 24:31

Are they not all ministering spirits sent out to minister to those who will inherit salvation?

—Hebrews 1:14

But you have come to Mount Zion and to the city of the living God, the heavenly Jerusalem, and to an innumerable company of angels.

—Hebrews 12:22

Do not forget to entertain strangers, for thereby some have entertained angels unknowingly.

—Hebrews 13:2

ANGER

They refused to obey and were not mindful of Your wonders that You performed among them. But they hardened their necks and in their rebellion appointed a leader to return to their bondage. But, You are a God ready to pardon, gracious and merciful, slow to anger and abounding in kindness, and did not forsake them.

—Nehemiah 9:17

He who is quick tempered deals foolishly, and a man of wicked devices is hated.

—Proverbs 14:17

He who is slow to wrath is of great understanding, but he who is hasty of spirit exalts folly.

—Proverbs 14:29

A wrathful man stirs up strife, but he who is slow to anger appeases strife.

—Proverbs 15:18

He who is slow to anger is better than the mighty, and he who rules his spirit than he who takes a city.

—Proverbs 16:32

Do not be quick in your spirit to be angry for irritation settles in the bosom of fools.

—Ecclesiastes 7:9

But I say to you that whoever is angry with his brother without a cause shall be in danger of the judgment. And whoever says to his brother, "Raca," shall be in danger of the Sanhedrin. But whoever says, "You fool," shall be in danger of fire of hell.

—Matthew 5:22

Love suffers long and is kind; love envies not; love flaunts not itself and is not puffed up, does not behave itself improperly, seeks not its own, is not easily provoked, thinks no evil.

—1 Corinthians 13:4–5

Be angry but do not sin. Do not let the sun go down on your anger.

—Ephesians 4:26

Let all bitterness, wrath, anger, outbursts, and blasphemies, with all malice, be taken away from you. And be kind one to another, tender-hearted, forgiving one another, just as God in Christ also forgave you.

—Ephesians 4:31–32

But now you must also put away all these: anger, wrath, malice, blasphemy, and filthy language out of your mouth.

—Colossians 3:8

Therefore, my beloved brothers, let every man be swift to hear, slow to speak, and slow to anger, for the anger of man does not work the righteousness of God.

—James 1:19–20

ANOINTING

The holy garments belonging to Aaron are to belong to his sons after him, so that they may be anointed in them and be consecrated in them.

—Exodus 29:29

And I will raise up for Myself a faithful priest, what is in My heart and in My soul he will do it. And I will build him a sure house, and it will walk before My anointed forever.

—1 Samuel 2:35

For he was a good man, full of the Holy Spirit and of faith. And many people were added to the Lord.

—Acts 11:24

But the fruit of the Spirit is love, joy, peace, patience, gentleness, goodness, faith, meekness, and self-control; against such there is no law.

—Galatians 5:22–23

I thank Christ Jesus our Lord who has enabled me, because He counted me faithful and appointed me to the ministry.

—1 Timothy 1:12

But you have an anointing from the Holy One, and you know all things. I have written to you, not because you do not know the truth, but because you know it, and because no lie is of the truth. Who is a liar but the one who denies that Jesus is the Christ? Whoever denies the Father and the Son is the antichrist.

—1 John 2:20–22

ANXIETY

And He said, "My presence will go with you, and I will give you rest."

—Exodus 33:14

The Lord, He goes before you. He will be with you. He will not fail you nor forsake you. Do not fear, nor be dismayed.

—Deuteronomy 31:8

Have not I commanded you? Be strong and courageous. Do not be afraid or dismayed, for the Lord your God is with you wherever you go.

—Joshua 1:9

And he went out to meet Asa and said to him, "Listen to me, Asa, and all Judah and Benjamin: The Lord is with you while you are with Him. If you all seek Him, He will be found with you. But if you forsake Him, He will forsake you."

—2 Chronicles 15:2

Watch, stand fast in the faith, be bold like men, and be strong.

—1 Corinthians 16:13

God is able to make all grace abound toward you, so that you, always having enough of everything, may abound to every good work.

—2 Corinthians 9:8

From whom the whole body is joined together and connected by every joint and ligament, as every part effectively does its work and grows, building itself up in love. Therefore this I say and testify in the Lord, that from now on you walk not as other Gentiles walk, in the vanity of their minds, having their understanding darkened, excluded from the life of God through the ignorance that is within them, due to the hardness of their hearts. Being calloused, they have given themselves over to sensuality for the practice of every kind of impurity with greediness.

—Ephesians 3:16–19

Desiring to be teachers of the law, and understanding neither what they say nor what they affirm.

—1 Timothy 1:7

For God has not given us the spirit of fear, but of power, and love, and self-control.

—2 Timothy 1:7

Let us then come with confidence to the throne of grace, that we may obtain mercy and find grace to help in time of need.

—Hebrews 4:16

Let your lives be without love of money, and be content with the things you have. For He has said, "I will never leave you, nor forsake you."

—Hebrews 13:5

So we may boldly say, "The Lord is my helper, I will not fear. What can man do to me?"

—Hebrews 13:6

APPEARANCE

But the Lord said to Samuel, "Do not look on his appearance or on the height of his stature, because I have rejected him. For the Lord sees not as man sees. For man looks on the outward appearance, but the Lord looks on the heart."

—1 Samuel 16:7

Do not judge according to appearance, but practice righteous judgment.

—John 7:24

For we are not commending ourselves again to you. Instead, we give you occasion to boast on our behalf, that you may have something to answer those who boast in appearance and not in heart.

—2 Corinthians 5:12

But of these who seemed to be something—whatever they were, it makes no difference to me; God shows no partiality to anyone—for those who seemed to be something added nothing to me.

—GALATIANS 2:6

Abstain from all appearances of evil.

—1 THESSALONIANS 5:22

Do not let your adorning be the outward adorning of braiding the hair, wearing gold, or putting on fine clothing. But let it be the hidden nature of the heart, that which is not corruptible, even the ornament of a gentle and quiet spirit, which is very precious in the sight of God.

—1 PETER 3:3–4

ASSURANCE

He who believes in the Son has eternal life. He who does not believe the Son shall not see life, but the wrath of God remains on him.

—JOHN 3:36

All that the Father has are Mine. Therefore I said that He will take what is Mine and will declare it to you.

—JOHN 16:15

But standing by the cross of Jesus were His mother, and His mother's sister, Mary the wife of Clopas, and Mary Magdalene. When Jesus saw His mother and the disciple whom He loved standing nearby, He said to His mother, "Woman, here is your son." Then He said to the disciple, "Here is your mother." From that time, this disciple took her to his own home.

—JOHN 19:25–27

The Spirit Himself bears witness with our spirits that we are the children of God.

—Romans 8:16

For I am persuaded that neither death nor life, neither angels nor principalities nor powers, neither things present nor things to come, neither height nor depth, nor any other created thing, shall be able to separate us from the love of God, which is in Christ Jesus our Lord.

—Romans 8:38–39

God is able to make all grace abound toward you, so that you, always having enough of everything, may abound to every good work.

—2 Corinthians 9:8

According to the eternal purpose which He completed in Christ Jesus our Lord, in whom we have boldness and confident access through faith in Him.

—Ephesians 3:11–12

For these things I suffer, but I am not ashamed, for I know whom I have believed, and am persuaded that He is able to keep that which was committed to me until that Day.

—2 Timothy 1:12

Let us draw near with a true heart in full assurance of faith, having our hearts sprinkled to cleanse them from an evil conscience, and our bodies washed with pure water.

—Hebrews 10:22

We know that we have passed from death to life, because we love the brothers. Whoever does not love his brother remains in death.

—1 John 3:14

By this we know that we are of the truth, and shall reassure our hearts before Him. For if our heart condemns us, God is greater than our heart and knows everything. Beloved, if our heart does not condemn us, then we have confidence before God.

—1 John 3:19–21

Whoever has the Son has life, and whoever does not have the Son of God does not have life. I have written these things to you who believe in the name of the Son of God, that you may know that you have eternal life, and that you may continue to believe in the name of the Son of God.

—1 John 5:12–13

ASTROLOGY

And beware, lest you lift up your eyes to heaven and see the sun, and the moon, and the stars, even all the host of heaven, you should not be driven to worship them, and serve them, that which the LORD your God has allotted to all nations under the whole heaven.

—Deuteronomy 4:19

If there be found among you, within any of your gates which the LORD your God gives you, man or woman, who has acted wickedly in the sight of the LORD your God, by transgressing His covenant, and has gone and served other gods and worshipped them, either the sun, or moon, or any of the host of heaven, which I have not commanded...then you must bring forth that man or that woman who has committed that wicked thing to your gates, that very man or woman, and stone them with stones until they die.

—Deuteronomy 17:2–3, 5

There must not be found among you anyone who makes his son or his daughter pass through the fire, or who uses divination, or uses witchcraft, or an interpreter of omens, or a sorcerer, or one who casts spells, or a spiritualist, or an occultist, or a necromancer. For all that do these things are an abomination to the Lord, and because of these abominations the Lord your God will drive them out from before you.

—Deuteronomy 18:10–12

Thus says the Lord, "Do not learn the way of the nations; do not be terrified at the signs of heaven, although the nations are terrified at them. For the customs of the people are vain; for with the axe one cuts a tree out of the forest, the work of the hands of the workman."

—Jeremiah 10:2–3

Therefore do not listen to your prophets, or to your diviners, or to your dreamers, or to your enchanters, or to your sorcerers who speak to you, saying, "You shall not serve the king of Babylon."

—Jeremiah 27:9

Daniel answered in the presence of the king and said, "The secret which the king has demanded, the wise men, the astrologers, the magicians, and the soothsayers cannot tell the king."

—Daniel 2:27

ATTITUDE

That you put off the former way of life in the old nature, which is corrupt according to the deceitful lusts. And be renewed in the spirit of your mind; and that you put on the new nature, which was created according to God in righteousness and true holiness.

—Ephesians 4:22–24

Do not lie one to another, since you have put off the old nature with its deeds, and have embraced the new nature, which is renewed in knowledge after the image of Him who created it.

—Colossians 3:9–10

Let the peace of God, to which also you are called in one body, rule in your hearts. And be thankful.

—Colossians 3:15

And whatever you do in word or deed, do all in the name of the Lord Jesus, giving thanks to God the Father through Him.

—Colossians 3:17

For the word of God is alive, and active, and sharper than any two-edged sword, piercing even to the division of soul and spirit, of joints and marrow, and able to judge the thoughts and intents of the heart.

—Hebrews 4:12

Therefore, since Christ has suffered for us in the flesh, arm yourselves likewise with the same mind, for he who has suffered in the flesh has ceased from sin, so that he no longer should live the rest of his time in the flesh serving human desires, but the will of God.

—1 Peter 4:1–2

AUTHORITY

God gave Solomon wisdom and great depth of understanding as well as compassion, as vast as the sand on the seashore. Solomon's wisdom excelled the wisdom of all the people of the East country and all the wisdom of Egypt.

—1 Kings 4:29–30

My mouth will speak wisdom, and the meditation of my heart will be understanding.

—Psalm 49:3

My son, let them not depart from your eyes—keep sound wisdom and discretion; so they will be life to your soul and grace to your neck. Then you will walk safely in your way, and your foot will not stumble.

—Proverbs 3:21–23

But when the Spirit of truth comes, He will guide you into all truth. For He will not speak on His own authority. But He will speak whatever He hears, and He will tell you things that are to come.

—John 16:13

But He said to me, "My grace is sufficient for you, for My strength is made perfect in weakness." Therefore most gladly I will boast in my weaknesses, that the power of Christ may rest upon me.

—2 Corinthians 12:9

That He would give you, according to the riches of His glory, power to be strengthened by His Spirit in the inner man, and that Christ may dwell in your hearts through faith; that you, being rooted and grounded in love, may be able to comprehend with all saints what is the breadth and length and depth and height.

—Ephesians 3:16–18

BACKSLIDING

Yes, they tested God over and over, and provoked the Holy One of Israel.

—Psalm 78:41

The backslider in heart will be filled with his own ways, but a good man will be satisfied with his.

—Proverbs 14:14

Therefore I said, "Surely these are the poor. They are foolish. For they know not the way of the Lord or the judgment of their God. I will go to the great men and will speak to them. For they have known the way of the Lord and the judgment of their God." But these have altogether broken the yoke and burst the bonds. Therefore a lion out of the forest will slay them, and a wolf from the deserts will destroy them, a leopard will watch over their cities. Everyone who goes out from there will be torn in pieces. Because their transgressions are many and their backslidings have increased.

—Jeremiah 5:4–6

"You who have forsaken Me," says the Lord, "you keep going backward. Therefore I will stretch out My hand against you and destroy you. I am weary of relenting! I will winnow them with a winnowing fork in the gates of the land. I will bereave them of children. I will destroy My people, since they did not repent from their ways."

—Jeremiah 15:6–7

Nor shall they defile themselves anymore with their idols, nor with their detestable things, nor with any of their transgressions. But I will save them out of all their dwelling places in which they have sinned and will cleanse them. So they shall be My people, and I will be their God.

—Ezekiel 37:23

But I have something against you, that you have abandoned the love you had at first. Remember therefore from where you have fallen. Repent, and do the works you did at first, or else I will come to you quickly and remove your candlestick from its place, unless you repent.

—Revelation 2:4–5

BAD HABITS

The truthful lip will be established forever, but a lying tongue is but for a moment. Deceit is in the heart of those who imagine evil, but to the counselors of peace is joy.

—Proverbs 12:19–20

Lying lips are abomination to the Lord, but those who deal truly are His delight.

—Proverbs 12:22

Now the works of the flesh are revealed, which are these: adultery, sexual immorality, impurity, lewdness, idolatry, sorcery, hatred, strife, jealousy, rage, selfishness, dissensions, heresies, envy, murders, drunkenness, carousing, and the like.

I warn you, as I previously warned you, that those who do such things shall not inherit the kingdom of God.

—GALATIANS 5:19–21

But avoid profane foolish babblings, for they will increase to more ungodliness.

—2 TIMOTHY 2:16

Therefore submit yourselves to God. Resist the devil, and he will flee from you.

—JAMES 4:7

Live your lives honorably among the Gentiles, so that though they speak against you as evildoers, they shall see your good works and thereby glorify God in the day of visitation.

—1 PETER 2:12

BAPTISM

In those days John the Baptist came, preaching in the wilderness of Judea, and saying, "Repent, for the kingdom of heaven is at hand."

—MATTHEW 3:1–2

I indeed baptize you with water to repentance, but He who is coming after me is mightier than I, whose shoes I am not worthy to carry. He will baptize you with the Holy Spirit and with fire.

—MATTHEW 3:11

Now when the Lord learned that the Pharisees had heard that Jesus was making and baptizing more disciples than John, (though Jesus Himself did not baptize, but His disciples).

—JOHN 4:1–2

Then Ananias went his way and entered the house. Putting his hands on him, he said, "Brother Saul, the Lord Jesus, who appeared to you on the way as you came, has sent me so that you may see again and be filled with the Holy Spirit." Immediately, something like scales fell from his eyes, and he could see again. And he rose up and was baptized.

—ACTS 9:17–18

"Can anyone forbid water for baptizing these, who have received the Holy Spirit as we have?" So he commanded them to be baptized in the name of the Lord. Then they asked him to stay a few days.

—ACTS 10:47–48

In that hour of the night he took them and washed their wounds. And immediately he and his entire household were baptized.

—ACTS 16:33

And now why do you wait? Rise, be baptized and wash away your sins, and call on the name of the Lord.

—ACTS 22:16

Do you not know that we who were baptized into Jesus Christ were baptized into His death? Therefore we were buried with Him by baptism into death, that just as Christ was raised up from the dead by the glory of the Father, even so, we also should walk in newness of life.

—ROMANS 6:3–4

For by one Spirit we are all baptized into one body, whether we are Jews or Gentiles, whether we are slaves or free, and we have all been made to drink of one Spirit.

—1 Corinthians 12:13

You are all sons of God by faith in Christ Jesus. For as many of you as have been baptized into Christ have put on Christ.

—Galatians 3:26–27

There is one body and one Spirit, even as you were called in one hope of your calling, one Lord, one faith, one baptism, one God and Father of all, who is above all, and through all, and in you all.

—Ephesians 4:4–6

Figuratively, this is like baptism, which also saves us now. It is not washing off the dirt from the body, but a response to God from a good conscience through the resurrection of Jesus Christ.

—1 Peter 3:21

BATTLE FOR YOUR MIND

You will keep him in perfect peace, whose mind is stayed on You, because he trusts in You.

—Isaiah 26:3

The Spirit of the Lord is upon Me, because He has anointed Me to preach the gospel to the poor. He has sent Me to heal the brokenhearted, to preach deliverance to the captives and recovery of sight to the blind, to set at liberty those who are oppressed.

—Luke 4:18

Then Jesus said to those Jews who believed Him, "If you remain in My word, then you are truly My disciples. You shall know the truth, and the truth shall set you free."

—John 8:31–32

You are of your father the devil, and you want to do the desires of your father. He was a murderer from the beginning, and does not stand in the truth, because there is no truth in him. When he lies, he speaks from his own nature, for he is a liar and the father of lies.

—John 8:44

For the weapons of our warfare are not carnal, but mighty through God to the pulling down of strongholds, casting down imaginations and every high thing that exalts itself against the knowledge of God, bringing every thought into captivity to the obedience of Christ.

—2 Corinthians 10:4–5

Therefore this I say and testify in the Lord, that from now on you walk not as other Gentiles walk, in the vanity of their minds.

—Ephesians 4:17

He has delivered us from the power of darkness and has transferred us into the kingdom of His dear Son.

—Colossians 1:13

Do not let anyone cheat you of your reward by delighting in false humility and the worship of angels, dwelling on those things which he has not seen, vainly arrogant due to his unspiritual mind.

—Colossians 2:18

Do not let anyone deceive you in any way. For that Day will not come unless a falling away comes first, and the man of sin is revealed, the son of destruction.

—2 Thessalonians 2:3

Who are protected by the power of God through faith for a salvation ready to be revealed in the last time.

—1 Peter 1:5

But there were also false prophets among the people, just as there will be false teachers among you, who will secretly bring in destructive heresies, even denying the Lord who bought them, bringing swift destruction upon themselves.

—2 Peter 2:1

Little children, let no one deceive you. The one who does righteousness is righteous, just as Christ is righteous.

—1 John 3:7

BEAUTY

Leah's eyes were tender, but Rachel was beautiful in form and appearance.

—Genesis 29:17

The man's name was Nabal and the name of his wife, Abigail. She was a woman of good understanding and beautiful, but the man was harsh and evil in his actions and he was a Calebite.

—1 Samuel 25:3

As a jewel of gold in a swine's snout, so is a fair woman who is without discretion.

—Proverbs 11:22

The glory of young men is their strength, and the beauty of old men is the gray head.

—Proverbs 20:29

Who can find a virtuous woman? For her worth is far above rubies.

—Proverbs 31:10

Strength and honor are her clothing; and she will rejoice in time to come. She opens her mouth with wisdom, and in her tongue is the teaching of kindness.

—Proverbs 31:25–26

Charm is deceitful, and beauty is vain, but a woman who fears the Lord, she shall be praised.

—Proverbs 31:30

He has made everything beautiful in its appropriate time. He has also put obscurity in their hearts so that people do not come to know the work that God has done from the beginning to the end.

—Ecclesiastes 3:11

You are fully beautiful, my beloved, and there is not a blemish on you.

—Song of Solomon 4:7

How beautiful upon the mountains are the feet of him who brings good news, who proclaims peace, who brings good news of happiness, who proclaims salvation, who says to Zion, "Your God reigns!"

—Isaiah 52:7

Woe to you, scribes and Pharisees, hypocrites! You are like whitewashed tombs, which indeed appear beautiful outwardly, but inside are full of dead men's bones and of all uncleanness.

—MATTHEW 23:27

Finally, brothers, whatever things are true, whatever things are honest, whatever things are just, whatever things are pure, whatever things are lovely, whatever things are of good report, if there is any virtue, and if there is any praise, think on these things.

—PHILIPPIANS 4:8

BELIEF

Jesus said, "If you can believe! All things are possible to him who believes."

—MARK 9:23

Yet to all who received Him, He gave the power to become sons of God, to those who believed in His name.

—JOHN 1:12

He who believes in Him is not condemned. But he who does not believe is condemned already, because he has not believed in the name of the only begotten Son of God.

—JOHN 3:18

Jesus said to them, "I am the bread of life. Whoever comes to Me shall never hunger, and whoever believes in Me shall never thirst."

—JOHN 6:35

I have come as a light into the world, that whoever believes in Me should not remain in darkness.

—John 12:46

Truly, truly I say to you, he who believes in Me will do the works that I do also. And he will do greater works than these, because I am going to My Father. I will do whatever you ask in My name, that the Father may be glorified in the Son. If you ask anything in My name, I will do it.

—John 14:12–14

Jesus said to him, "Thomas, because you have seen Me, you have believed. Blessed are those who have not seen, and have yet believed."

—John 20:29

To Him all the prophets bear witness that whoever believes in Him will receive remission of sins through His name.

—Acts 10:43

They said, "Believe in the Lord Jesus Christ, and you and your household will be saved."

—Acts 16:31

As it is written, "Look! I lay in Zion a stumbling stone and rock of offense, and whoever believes in Him will not be ashamed."

—Romans 9:33

How then shall they call on Him in whom they have not believed? And how shall they believe in Him of whom they have not heard? And how shall they hear without a preacher?

—Romans 10:14

For also it is contained in the Scripture, "Look! I lay in Zion a chief cornerstone, elect, precious, and he who believes in Him shall never be put to shame."

—1 PETER 2:6

BINDING THE ENEMY

Your right hand, O LORD, is glorious in power. Your right hand, O LORD, shatters the enemy. In the greatness of Your excellence, You overthrow those who rise up against You. You send out Your wrath; it consumes them like stubble.

—EXODUS 15:6–7

Can you draw out Leviathan with a hook, or snare his tongue with a line which you let down? Can you put a cord into his nose, or pierce his jaw with a hook?

—JOB 41:1–2

No one is so fierce that he dares to stir him up; who then is able to stand before Me?

—JOB 41:10

You crushed the heads of Leviathan in pieces, and gave him for food to the people inhabiting the wilderness.

—PSALM 74:14

The LORD on high is mightier than the noise of many waters; yes, than the mighty waves of the sea.

—PSALM 93:4

Then they cried out to the LORD in their trouble, and He saved them out of their distress. He made the storm calm, and the sea waves were still.

—PSALM 107:28–29

In that day the LORD with His fierce and great and strong sword shall punish Leviathan the fleeing serpent, even Leviathan the twisted serpent. And He shall slay the dragon that is in the sea.

—Isaiah 27:1

Thus says the LORD, who makes a way in the sea and a path in the mighty waters.

—Isaiah 43:16

It is I who says to the deep, "Be dried up!" And I will dry up your rivers.

—Isaiah 44:27

Speak, and say, "Thus says the Lord GOD, 'I am against you, Pharaoh king of Egypt, the great dragon that lies in the midst of his rivers, which has said, "My Nile is my own, and I myself have made it." But I will put hooks in your jaws and will cause the fish of your rivers to stick to your scales and will bring you up out of the midst of your rivers, and all the fish of your rivers shall stick to your scales. I will abandon you to the wilderness, you and all the fish of your rivers. You shall fall upon the open field. You shall not be brought together or gathered. I have given you for food to the beasts of the field and to the fowl of the heavens.'"

—Ezekiel 29:3–5

The ram which you saw having two horns represent the kings of Media and Persia.

—Daniel 8:20

To open their eyes and to turn them from darkness to light, and from the power of Satan to God, that they may receive forgiveness of sins and an inheritance among those who are sanctified by faith in Me.

—Acts 26:18

BITTERNESS

Therefore, if you bring your gift to the altar and there remember that your brother has something against you...

—Matthew 5:23

Bless those who persecute you; bless, and do not curse.

—Romans 12:14

Repay no one evil for evil. Commend what is honest in the sight of all men.

—Romans 12:17

Pursue peace with all men, and the holiness without which no one will see the Lord, watching diligently so that no one falls short of the grace of God, lest any root of bitterness spring up to cause trouble, and many become defiled by it.

—Hebrews 12:14–15

Out of the same mouth proceed blessing and cursing. My brothers, these things ought not to be so.

—James 3:10

For to this you were called, because Christ suffered for us, leaving us an example, that you should follow His steps. "He committed no sin, and no deceit was found in His mouth."

—1 Peter 2:21–22

BLESSING

Then Jabez called on the God of Israel, saying, "Oh that You would indeed bless me and enlarge my territory, that Your hand might be with me, and that You would keep me from evil, that it may not bring me hardship!" So God granted what he asked.

—1 Chronicles 4:10

I called on You, for You will answer me, O God. Incline Your ear to me, and hear my speech. Show marvelously Your lovingkindness, O Deliverer of those who seek refuge by Your right hand from those who arise in opposition. Keep me as the apple of your eye, hide me under the shadow of Your wings, from the wicked who bring ruin to me, from my deadly enemies who surround me.

—Psalm 17:6–9

Arise, O Lord, confront him, make him bow down; deliver my soul from the wicked by Your sword. From men by Your hand, O Lord, from men of the world, whose portion is in this life, and whose belly You fill with Your treasure; they are full of children, and leave their affluence to their babes.

—Psalm 17:13–14

I will sing of the mercies of the Lord forever; with my mouth I will make known Your faithfulness to all generations. For I have said, "Mercy shall be built up forever; Your faithfulness shall be established in the heavens."

—Psalm 89:1–2

The Lord has been mindful of us; He will bless us; He will bless the house of Israel; He will bless the house of Aaron.

He will bless those who fear the Lord, both the small and great ones. The Lord shall increase you more and more, you and your children.

—Psalm 115:12–14

It is an abomination to kings to commit wickedness, for the throne is established by righteousness. Righteous lips are the delight of kings, and they love him who speaks right. The wrath of a king is as messengers of death, but a wise man will pacify it. In the light of the king's countenance is life, and his favor is as a cloud of the latter rain. How much better is it to get wisdom than gold! And to get understanding is to be chosen rather than silver!

—Proverbs 16:12–16

He who walks righteously and speaks uprightly. He who rejects unjust gain and shakes his hands from holding bribes, who stops his ears from hearing of bloodshed, and shuts his eyes from seeing evil. He shall dwell on high. His place of defense shall be the impregnable rock. His bread shall be given him. His waters shall be sure.

—Isaiah 33:15–16

For I the Lord your God will hold your right hand, saying to you, "Do not fear. I will help you."

—Isaiah 41:13

Pursue peace with all men, and the holiness without which no one will see the Lord.

—Hebrews 12:14

But the wisdom that is from above is first pure, then peaceable, gentle, open to reason, full of mercy and good fruits, without partiality, and without hypocrisy.

—James 3:17

For "He who wants to love life, and to see good days, let him keep his tongue from evil, and his lips from speaking deceit. Let him turn away from evil and do good. Let him seek peace and pursue it."

—1 Peter 3:10–11

For the eyes of the Lord are on the righteous, and His ears are open to their prayers, but the face of the Lord is against those who do evil.

—1 Peter 3:12

Boldness in Christ

Look, I am sending you out as sheep in the midst of wolves. Therefore be wise as serpents and harmless as doves.

—Matthew 10:16

The Spirit Himself bears witness with our spirits that we are the children of God, and if children, then heirs: heirs of God and joint-heirs with Christ, if indeed we suffer with Him, that we may also be glorified with Him.

—Romans 8:16–17

Now thanks be to God who always causes us to triumph in Christ and through us reveals the fragrance of His knowledge in every place.

—2 Corinthians 2:14

We have such trust through Christ toward God, not that we are sufficient in ourselves to take credit for anything of ourselves, but our sufficiency is from God.

—2 Corinthians 3:4–5

For God, who commanded the light to shine out of darkness, has shone in our hearts to give the light of the knowledge of the glory of God in the face of Jesus Christ.

—2 Corinthians 4:6

Blessed be the God and Father of our Lord Jesus Christ, who has blessed us with every spiritual blessing in the heavenly places in Christ, just as He chose us in Him before the foundation of the world, to be holy and blameless before Him in love.

—Ephesians 1:3–4

BONDAGE

Therefore say to the children of Israel, I am the Lord, and I will bring you out from under the burdens of the Egyptians, and I will rid you out of their bondage, and I will redeem you with a stretched out arm and with great judgments.

—Exodus 6:6

Have you an arm like God? Or can you thunder with a voice like Him?

—Job 40:9

For they did not take possession of the land by their own sword, nor did their own arm save them; but it was Your right hand, and Your arm, and the light of Your countenance, because You had favor on them.

—Psalm 44:3

O sing to the Lord a new song, for He has done marvelous deeds! His right hand and His holy arm have accomplished deliverance.

—Psalm 98:1

Awake, awake, put on strength, O arm of the Lord. Awake as in the ancient days, in the generations of old. Was it not You who cut Rahab to pieces and wounded the dragon?

—Isaiah 51:9

His brightness was like the light; rays flashed from His hand, and there His power was hidden.

—Habakkuk 3:4

Born Again (How to Be)

Yet to all who received Him, He gave the power to become sons of God, to those who believed in His name.

—John 1:12

Jesus answered him, "Truly, truly I say to you, unless a man is born again, he cannot see the kingdom of God."

—John 3:3

That which is born of the flesh is flesh, and that which is born of the Spirit is spirit.

—John 3:6

For God did not send His Son into the world to condemn the world, but that the world through Him might be saved. He who believes in Him is not condemned. But he who does not believe is condemned already, because he has not believed in the name of the only begotten Son of God.

—John 3:17–18

He then led them out and asked, "Sirs, what must I do to be saved?" They said, "Believe in the Lord Jesus Christ, and you and your household will be saved."

—Acts 16:30–31

For the Scripture says, "Whoever believes in Him will not be ashamed."

—Romans 10:11

Now, brothers, I declare to you the gospel which I preached to you, which you have received, and in which you stand. Through it you are saved, if you keep in memory what I preached to you, unless you have believed in vain.

—1 Corinthians 15:1–2

For I delivered to you first of all that which I also received: how Christ died for our sins according to the Scriptures, was buried, rose again the third day according to the Scriptures.

—1 Corinthians 15:3–4

I have been crucified with Christ. It is no longer I who live, but Christ who lives in me. And the life I now live in the flesh, I live by faith in the Son of God, who loved me and gave Himself for me.

—Galatians 2:20

But God, being rich in mercy, because of His great love with which He loved us, even when we were dead in sins, made us alive together with Christ (by grace you have been saved)....For by grace you have been saved through faith, and this is not of yourselves. It is the gift of God, not of works, so that no one should boast.

—Ephesians 2:4–5, 8–9

He Himself bore our sins in His own body on the tree, that we, being dead to sins, should live unto righteousness. "By His wounds you were healed."

—1 Peter 2:24

Listen! I stand at the door and knock. If anyone hears My voice and opens the door, I will come in and dine with him, and he with Me.

—Revelation 3:20

BREAKTHROUGHS

Let the heavens praise Your wonders, O Lord, and Your faithfulness in the assembly of the divine holy ones.

—Psalm 89:5

Surely He shall deliver you from the snare of the hunter and from the deadly pestilence. He shall cover you with his feathers, and under His wings you shall find protection; His faithfulness shall be your shield and wall. You shall not be afraid of the terror by night, nor of the arrow that flies by day.

—Psalm 91:3–5

"No weapon that is formed against you shall prosper. And every tongue that shall rise against you in judgment, you shall condemn. This is the heritage of the servants of the Lord, and their vindication is from Me," says the Lord.

—Isaiah 54:17

Call to Me, and I will answer you, and show you great and mighty things which you do not know.

—Jeremiah 33:3

It is of the Lord's mercies that we are not consumed, because His compassions do not fail. They are new every morning. Great is Your faithfulness.

—Lamentations 3:22–23

"The Lord your God is in your midst, a Mighty One, who will save. He will rejoice over you with gladness; He will quiet you with His love; He will rejoice over you with singing. 'I will gather those who grieve for the appointed festival, which is a reproach and burden on you. At that time I will deal with all who oppresses you; I will save the lame and gather the outcast; I will give them praise and fame in every land where they have been put to shame. At that time I will bring you in, at the time when I gather you; for I will make you renowned and praised among all peoples of the earth, when I restore your fortunes before your eyes,'" says the Lord.

—Zephaniah 3:17–20

For thus says the Lord of Hosts, "Once more, in a little while, I will shake the heavens and earth, the sea and dry land. And I will shake all the nations, and they will come with the wealth of all nations, and I will fill this house with glory," says the Lord of Hosts.

—Haggai 2:6–7

Or else how can one enter a strong man's house and plunder his goods unless he first binds the strong man? And then he will plunder his house.

—Matthew 12:29

So that now the manifold wisdom of God might be made known by the church to the principalities and powers in the heavenly places.

—Ephesians 3:10

Finally, my brothers, be strong in the Lord and in the power of His might.

—Ephesians 6:10

He has delivered us from the power of darkness and has transferred us into the kingdom of His dear Son.

—Colossians 1:13

You are of God, little children, and have overcome them, because He who is in you is greater than he who is in the world.

—1 John 4:4

BROKENHEARTEDNESS

The Lord is near to the brokenhearted, and saves the contrite of spirit.

—Psalm 34:18

He has put a new song in my mouth, even praise to our God; many will see it, and fear, and will trust in the Lord.

—Psalm 40:3

I will praise the name of God with a song, and will magnify Him with thanksgiving.

—Psalm 69:30

He heals the broken in heart, and binds up their wounds.

—Psalm 147:3

Moreover the light of the moon shall be as the light of the sun, and the light of the sun shall be sevenfold, as the light of seven days, in the day that the LORD binds up the breach of His people and heals the wound from His blow.

—ISAIAH 30:26

Those from among you shall rebuild the old waste places. You shall raise up the foundations of many generations. And you shall be called, "the Repairer of the Breach, the Restorer of Paths in which to Dwell."

—ISAIAH 58:12

BURNING IDOLS

You shall have no other gods before Me.

—EXODUS 20:3

He walked in all the ways that his father walked, served the idols that his father served, and worshipped them.

—2 KINGS 21:21

If My people, who are called by My name, will humble themselves and pray, and seek My face and turn from their wicked ways, then I will hear from heaven, and will forgive their sin and will heal their land.

—2 CHRONICLES 7:14

For the day of the LORD of Hosts shall be upon everything that is proud and lofty, and upon everything that is lifted up, and it shall be brought low. And it will be upon all the cedars of Lebanon that are high and lifted up, and upon all the oaks of Bashan, and upon all the high mountains, and upon all the hills that are lifted up, and upon all the high towers, and upon every fenced wall, and upon all the ships of Tarshish, and upon all pleasant sloops. The loftiness of man shall be bowed down, and the haughtiness of men shall brought low. The Lord alone will be exalted in that day. The idols He shall utterly abolish.

—Isaiah 2:12–18

For in that day every man shall cast away his idols of silver and his idols of gold which your own hands have made for you as a sin.

—Isaiah 31:7

On her forehead a name was written: Mystery, Babylon the Great, the Mother of Prostitutes and of the Abominations of the Earth.

—Revelation 17:5

Calling, My

You are the salt of the earth. But if the salt loses its saltiness, how shall it be made salty? It is from then on good for nothing but to be thrown out and to be trampled underfoot by men.

—Matthew 5:13

You are the light of the world. A city that is set on a hill cannot be hidden.

—Matthew 5:14

"Teaching them to observe all things I have commanded you. And remember, I am with you always, even to the end of the age." Amen.

—Matthew 28:20

Look, I give you authority to trample on serpents and scorpions, and over all the power of the enemy. And nothing shall by any means hurt you.

—LUKE 10:19

So, the Jews persecuted Jesus and sought to kill Him, because He had done these things on the Sabbath day.

—JOHN 5:16

Truly, truly I say to you, he who believes in Me will do the works that I do also. And he will do greater works than these, because I am going to My Father.

—JOHN 14:12

When I was a child, I spoke as a child, I understood as a child, and I thought as a child. But when I became a man, I put away childish things.

—1 CORINTHIANS 13:11

Therefore, my beloved brothers, be steadfast, unmovable, always abounding in the work of the Lord, knowing that your labor in the Lord is not in vain.

—1 CORINTHIANS 15:58

All this is from God, who has reconciled us to Himself through Jesus Christ and has given to us the ministry of reconciliation, that is, that God was in Christ reconciling the world to Himself, not counting their sins against them, and has entrusted to us the message of reconciliation.

—2 CORINTHIANS 5:18–19

For by grace you have been saved through faith, and this is not of yourselves. It is the gift of God, not of works, so that no one should boast. For we are His workmanship, created in Christ Jesus for good works, which God prepared beforehand, so that we should walk in them.

—Ephesians 2:8–10

When Christ who is our life shall appear, then you also shall appear with Him in glory.

—Colossians 3:4

Therefore, holy brothers, partakers in a heavenly calling, consider the Apostle and High Priest of our profession, Jesus Christ.

—Hebrews 3:1

CHALLENGES

No man will be able to stand against you all the days of your life. As I was with Moses, I will be with you. I will not abandon you. I will not leave you.

—Joshua 1:5

Seeing his days are determined, the number of his months are with You; You have appointed his bounds that he cannot pass.

—Job 14:5

As for man, his days are as grass; as a flower of the field he flourishes.

—Psalm 103:15

My son, do not forget my teaching, but let your heart keep my commandments; for length of days and long life and peace will they add to you.

—Proverbs 3:1–2

The fear of the LORD prolongs days, but the years of the wicked will be shortened.

—PROVERBS 10:27

The gray-haired head is a crown of glory, if it is found in the way of righteousness.

—PROVERBS 16:31

There is nothing better than a person who eats and drinks and makes his life see the good in his labor. So this I have seen is from the hand of God. For who can even eat or have enjoyment more so than I?

—ECCLESIASTES 2:24–25

And in the days of your youth remember your Creator, before the difficult days come and the years arrive when you say, "There is no pleasure for me in these days and years."

—ECCLESIASTES 12:1

And even to your old age I am He. And even to your greying years I will carry you. I have done it, and I will bear you. Even I will carry, and will deliver you.

—ISAIAH 46:4

Truly, truly I say to you, the hour is coming, and is now here, when the dead will hear the voice of the Son of God, and those who hear will live. For as the Father has life in Himself, so He has given to the Son to have life in Himself.

—JOHN 5:25–26

When I was a child, I spoke as a child, I understood as a child, and I thought as a child. But when I became a man, I put away childish things.

—1 CORINTHIANS 13:11

My brothers, count it all joy when you fall into diverse temptations, knowing that the trying of your faith develops patience. But let patience perfect its work, that you may be perfect and complete, lacking nothing.

—James 1:2–4

CHANGE

The eternal God is your refuge, and underneath you are the everlasting arms. He will drive out the enemy before you, and will say, "Destroy them."

—Deuteronomy 33:27

I said, "Age should speak, and multitude of years should teach wisdom." But there is a spirit in man, and the breath of the Almighty gives them understanding.

—Job 32:7–8

God will hear and afflict them, even He who sits enthroned from of old. Selah. Because they do not change, and they do not fear God.

—Psalm 55:19

With long life I will satisfy him and show him My salvation.

—Psalm 91:16

To show that the Lord is upright; He is my rock, and there is no unrighteousness in Him.

—Psalm 92:15

My son, do not forget my teaching, but let your heart keep my commandments; for length of days and long life and peace will they add to you.

—Proverbs 3:1–2

For by me your days will be multiplied, and the years of your life will be increased.

—Proverbs 9:11

The fear of the Lord prolongs days, but the years of the wicked will be shortened.

—Proverbs 10:27

The gray-haired head is a crown of glory, if it is found in the way of righteousness.

—Proverbs 16:31

He has made everything beautiful in its appropriate time. He has also put obscurity in their hearts so that people do not come to know the work that God has done from the beginning to the end. I experienced that there is nothing better for people than to be glad and do good in their life. And also that everyone should eat and drink and experience good in all their labor. This is a gift of God.

—Ecclesiastes 3:11–13

And in the days of your youth remember your Creator, before the difficult days come and the years arrive when you say, "There is no pleasure for me in these days and years."

—Ecclesiastes 12:1

Listen, I tell you a mystery: We shall not all sleep, but we shall all be changed.

—1 Corinthians 15:51

CHARACTER

And you shall love the LORD your God, with all your heart and with all your soul and with all your might. These words, which I am commanding you today, shall be in your heart.

—DEUTERONOMY 6:5–6

Beware that you do not forget the LORD your God by not keeping His commandments, and His judgments, and His statutes, which I am commanding you today.

—DEUTERONOMY 8:11

For to the person who is pleasing before Him, God gives wisdom, knowledge, and joy, but to the one who sins, He gives the task to gather and collect in order to give to the other person who is pleasing before God. Also this is vanity and chasing the wind.

—ECCLESIASTES 2:26

But the noble devises noble things, and by noble things he stands.

—ISAIAH 32:8

Thus says the LORD, "Stand in the ways and see, and ask for the old paths where the good way is and walk in it, and you shall find rest for your souls." But they said, "We will not walk in it."

—JEREMIAH 6:16

Therefore, everything you would like men to do to you, do also to them, for this is the Law and the Prophets.

—MATTHEW 7:12

Jesus said to him, "'You shall love the Lord your God with all your heart, and with all your soul, and with all your mind.' This is the first and great commandment. And the second is like it: 'You shall love your neighbor as yourself.' On these two commandments hang all the Law and the Prophets."

—MATTHEW 22:37–40

Therefore, my beloved, as you have always obeyed, not only in my presence, but so much more in my absence, work out your own salvation with fear and trembling. For God is the One working in you, both to will and to do His good pleasure. Do all things without murmuring and disputing, that you may be blameless and harmless.

—PHILIPPIANS 2:12–15

Remembering without ceasing your work of faith, labor of love, and patient hope in our Lord Jesus Christ in the sight of God and our Father.

—1 THESSALONIANS 1:3

Watching diligently so that no one falls short of the grace of God, lest any root of bitterness spring up to cause trouble, and many become defiled by it.

—HEBREWS 12:15

Dearly beloved, I implore you as aliens and refugees, abstain from fleshly lusts, which wage war against the soul.

—1 PETER 2:11

Likewise you younger ones, submit yourselves to the elders. Yes, all of you be submissive one to another and clothe yourselves with humility, because "God resists the proud, and gives grace to the humble."

—1 Peter 5:5

CHARITY

Then the Levite (because he has no portion or inheritance with you), the foreigner, the fatherless, and the widow, who are within your gates, shall come and shall eat and be satisfied, so that the Lord your God may bless you in all the work of your hand which you do.

—Deuteronomy 14:29

Send out your grain on the waters by ships, for after a number of days you will find financial return.

—Ecclesiastes 11:1

Is it not to divide your bread with the hungry and bring the poor who are outcasts into your house? When you see the naked, to cover him and not hide yourself from your own flesh? Then your light shall break forth as the morning, and your recovery shall spring forth speedily, and your righteousness shall go before you. The glory of the Lord shall be your reward.

—Isaiah 58:7–8

And if you give yourself to the hungry and satisfy the afflicted soul, then your light shall rise in obscurity, and your darkness shall become as the noon day.

—Isaiah 58:10

Be sure that you not do your charitable deeds before men to be seen by them. Otherwise you have no reward from your Father who is in heaven. Therefore, when you do your charitable deeds, do not sound a trumpet before you as the hypocrites do in the synagogues and in the streets, that they may be honored by men. Truly I say to you, they have their reward. But when you do your charitable deeds, do not let your left hand know what your right hand is doing, that your charitable deeds may be in secret. And your Father who sees in secret will Himself reward you openly.

—MATTHEW 6:1–4

The King will answer, "Truly I say to you, as you have done it for one of the least of these brothers of Mine, you have done it for Me."

—MATTHEW 25:40

Then Jesus, looking upon him, loved him and said to him, "You lack one thing: Go your way, sell whatever you have and give to the poor, and you will have treasure in heaven. And come, take up the cross and follow Me."

—MARK 10:21

Give, and it will be given to you: Good measure, pressed down, shaken together, and running over, will men give unto you. For with the measure you use, it will be measured unto you.

—LUKE 6:38

Sell your possessions and give alms. Provide yourselves purses that do not grow old, an unfailing treasure in the heavens, where no thief comes near and no moth destroys.

—LUKE 12:33

But when you prepare a banquet, call the poor, the maimed, the lame, the blind, and you will be blessed, for they cannot repay you. You shall be repaid at the resurrection of the just.

—Luke 14:13–14

So now abide faith, hope, and love, these three. But the greatest of these is love.

—1 Corinthians 13:13

Let every man give according to the purposes in his heart, not grudgingly or out of necessity, for God loves a cheerful giver.

—2 Corinthians 9:7

CHILDREN

They send forth their little ones like a flock, and their children dance.

—Job 21:11

Blessed be the Lord, who daily loads us with benefits, even the God who is our salvation. Selah.

—Psalm 68:19

Yet He raises up the poor from affliction and cares for their families like flocks of sheep.

—Psalm 107:41

Look, children are a gift of the Lord, and the fruit of the womb is a reward. As arrows in the hand of a mighty warrior, so are the children of one's youth. Happy is the man who has his quiver full of them; he shall not be ashamed when he speaks with the enemies at the gate.

—Psalm 127:3–5

Your wife shall be as a fruitful vine in your house; your children like olive shoots around your table.

—Psalm 128:3

In the fear of the Lord is strong confidence, and His children will have a place of refuge. The fear of the Lord is a fountain of life, to depart from the snares of death.

—Proverbs 14:26–27

Grandchildren are the crown of old men, and the glory of children are their fathers.

—Proverbs 17:6

Train up a child in the way he should go, and when he is old he will not depart from it.

—Proverbs 22:6

For I will pour water on him who is thirsty, and floods on the dry ground. I will pour out My Spirit on your descendants, and My blessing on your offspring.

—Isaiah 44:3

All your sons shall be taught of the Lord. And great shall be the peace of your sons.

—Isaiah 54:13

But when Jesus saw it, He was very displeased and said to them, "Allow the little children to come to Me, and do not forbid them, for of such is the kingdom of God. Truly I say to you, whoever does not receive the kingdom of God as a little child shall not enter it." And He took them up in His arms, put His hands on them, and blessed them.

—Mark 10:14–16

For the promise is to you, and to your children, and to all who are far away, as many as the Lord our God will call.

—Acts 2:39

Children's Duties

Every person among you shall revere his mother and his father, and you will keep My Sabbaths: I am the your God.

—Leviticus 19:3

Honor your father and your mother, just as the Lord your God has commanded you, that your days may be prolonged, and that it may go well with you in the land which the Lord your God is giving you.

—Deuteronomy 5:16

"Cursed is he who disrespects his father or his mother." And all the people shall say, "Amen."

—Deuteronomy 27:16

My son, if sinners entice you, do not consent.

—Proverbs 1:10.

The proverbs of Solomon. A wise son makes a glad father, but a foolish son is the grief of his mother.

—Proverbs 10:1

A wise son heeds his father's instruction, but a scoffer does not listen to rebuke.

—Proverbs 13:1

A fool despises his father's instruction, but he who regards reproof is prudent.

—Proverbs 15:5

Even a child is known by his doings, whether his work is pure and whether it is right.

—Proverbs 20:11

My son, if your heart is wise, my heart will rejoice—even mine. Yes, my inmost being will rejoice when your lips speak right things. Do not let your heart envy sinners, but continue in the fear of the Lord all day long.

—Proverbs 23:15–17

You know the commandments: "Do not commit adultery," "Do not kill," "Do not steal," "Do not bear false witness," "Honor your father and your mother."

—Luke 18:20

Children, obey your parents in the Lord, for this is right. "Honor your father and mother," which is the first commandment with a promise: "So that it may be well with you and you may live long on the earth."

—Ephesians 6:1–3

Children, obey your parents in all things, for this is well pleasing to the Lord.

—Colossians 3:20

CHURCH

They continued steadfastly in the apostles' teaching and fellowship, in the breaking of bread and in the prayers.

—Acts 2:42

For as the body is one and has many parts, and all the many parts of that one body are one body, so also is Christ. For by one Spirit we are all baptized into one body, whether we are

Jews or Gentiles, whether we are slaves or free, and we have all been made to drink of one Spirit. The body is not one part, but many.

—1 Corinthians 12:12–14

He is the head of the body, the church. He is the beginning, the firstborn from the dead, so that in all things He may have the pre-eminence.

—Colossians 1:18

But the firm foundation of God stands, having this seal, "The Lord knows those who are His," and, "Let every one who calls on the name of Christ depart from iniquity."

—2 Timothy 2:19

You also, as living stones, are being built up into a spiritual house as a holy priesthood to offer up spiritual sacrifices that are acceptable to God through Jesus Christ.

—1 Peter 2:5

But you are a chosen people, a royal priesthood, a holy nation, a people for God's own possession, so that you may declare the goodness of Him who has called you out of darkness into His marvelous light.

—1 Peter 2:9

COMFORT

The Lord also will be a refuge for the oppressed, a refuge in times of trouble.

—Psalm 9:9

For He has not despised nor abhorred the affliction of the afflicted; nor has He hid His face from that one; but when that one cried to Him, He heard.

—Psalm 22:24

Wait on the Lord; be strong, and may your heart be stout; Wait on the Lord.

—Psalm 27:14

Delight yourself in the Lord, and He will give you the desires of your heart.

—Psalm 37:4

But the salvation of the righteous is from the Lord; He is their refuge in the time of distress.

—Psalm 37:39

God is our refuge and strength, a well-proven help in trouble. Therefore we will not fear, though the earth be removed, and though the mountains be carried into the midst of the sea; though its waters roar and foam, though the mountains shake with its swelling. Selah.

—Psalm 46:1–3

Cast your care on the Lord, and He will sustain you; He will not allow the righteous to totter forever.

—Psalm 55:22

Though I walk in the midst of trouble, You will preserve me; You stretch forth Your hand against the wrath of my enemies, and Your right hand saves me.

—Psalm 138:7

For the Lord will not cast off forever. But though He causes grief, yet He will have compassion according to the multitude of His mercies. For He does not afflict willingly nor grieve the sons of men.

—Lamentations 3:31–33

The Lord is good, a stronghold in the day of distress; and He knows those who take refuge in Him.

—Nahum 1:7

I have told you these things so that in Me you may have peace. In the world you will have tribulation. But be of good cheer. I have overcome the world.

—John 16:33

As the sufferings of Christ abound in us, so our consolation also abounds through Christ.

—2 Corinthians 1:5

COMMITMENT

See, I am setting before you today a blessing and a curse: The blessing if you obey the commandments of the Lord your God, which I am commanding you today, and the curse, if you will not obey the commandments of the Lord your God, but turn from the way which I am commanding you today, to go after other gods which you have not known.

—Deuteronomy 11:26–28

And I will give them one heart and one way, that they may fear Me forever, for their good and for their children after them. And I will make an everlasting covenant with them that I will not turn away from them, to do them good. But I will put My fear in their hearts so that they shall not depart from Me.

—Jeremiah 32:39–40

But let your "Yes" mean "Yes," and "No" mean "No." For whatever is more than these comes from the evil one.

—Matthew 5:37

Whoever will confess Me before men, him will I confess also before My Father who is in heaven. But whoever will deny Me before men, him will I also deny before My Father who is in heaven.

—Matthew 10:32–33

If a man does not remain in Me, he is thrown out as a branch and withers. And they gather them and throw them into the fire, and they are burned. If you remain in Me, and My words remain in you, you will ask whatever you desire, and it shall be done for you.

—John 15:6–7

Do not be conformed to this world, but be transformed by the renewing of your mind, that you may prove what is the good and acceptable and perfect will of God.

—Romans 12:2

COMPASSION

Nothing of the cursed thing there must cling to your hand, so that the Lord may turn from the fierceness of His anger and show you mercy, have compassion on you, and multiply you, just as He swore to your fathers.

—Deuteronomy 13:17

A good man shows generous favor, and lends; he will guide his affairs with justice.

—Psalm 112:5

He who has pity on the poor lends to the Lord, and He will repay what he has given.

—Proverbs 19:17

Thus says the Lord of Hosts: "Execute true justice, show mercy and compassion, every man to his brother. Do not oppress the widow, orphan, sojourner, or poor. And let none of you contemplate evil deeds in your hearts against his brother."

—Zechariah 7:9–10

So embrace, as the elect of God, holy and beloved, a spirit of mercy, kindness, humbleness of mind, meekness, and longsuffering.

—Colossians 3:12

Religion that is pure and undefiled before God, the Father, is this: to visit the fatherless and widows in their affliction and to keep oneself unstained by the world.

—James 1:27

CONCEIT

For wisdom is better than rubies, and all the things that may be desired are not to be compared to it. I, wisdom, dwell with prudence, and find out knowledge and discretion.

—Proverbs 8:11–12

Pride goes before destruction, and a haughty spirit before a fall. Better it is to be of a humble spirit with the lowly than to divide the spoil with the proud.

—Proverbs 16:18–19

Do you see a man wise in his own conceit? There is more hope for a fool than for him.

—Proverbs 26:12

See, the Lord, the Lord of Hosts, shall lop the bough with terror and the tall ones of stature shall be hewn down, and the haughty shall be humbled.

—Isaiah 10:33

Be of the same mind toward one another. Do not be haughty, but associate with the lowly. Do not pretend to be wiser than you are.

—Romans 12:16

Let nothing be done out of strife or conceit, but in humility let each esteem the other better than himself.

—Philippians 2:3

CONDEMNATION

And He said, "What comes out of a man is what defiles a man. For from within, out of the heart of men, proceed evil thoughts, adultery, fornication, murder, theft, covetousness, wickedness, deceit, licentiousness, an evil eye, blasphemy, pride and foolishness. All these evil things come from within and defile a man."

—Mark 7:20–23

For all have sinned and come short of the glory of God.

—ROMANS 3:23

Who is he who condemns? It is Christ who died, yes, who is risen, who is also at the right hand of God, who also intercedes for us.

—ROMANS 8:34

If I speak with the tongues of men and of angels, and have not love, I have become as sounding brass or a clanging cymbal.

—1 CORINTHIANS 13:1

Now this is the main point of the things that we are saying: We have such a High Priest, who is seated at the right hand of the throne of the Majesty in the heavens, a minister in the sanctuary and the true tabernacle, which the Lord, not man, set up.

—HEBREWS 8:1–2

There shall be no more curse. The throne of God and of the Lamb shall be in it, and His servants shall serve Him. They shall see His face, and His name shall be on their foreheads.

—REVELATION 22:3–4

CONFESSION

I acknowledged my sin to You, and my iniquity I did not conceal. I said, "I will confess my transgressions to the LORD," and You forgave the iniquity of my sin. Selah.

—PSALM 32:5

He who covers his sins will not prosper, but whoever confesses and forsakes them will have mercy.

—PROVERBS 28:13

Whoever will confess Me before men, him will I confess also before My Father who is in heaven. But whoever will deny Me before men, him will I also deny before My Father who is in heaven.

—Matthew 10:32–33

I say to you, whoever confesses Me before men, him will the Son of Man also confess before the angels of God.

—Luke 12:8

That if you confess with your mouth Jesus is Lord, and believe in your heart that God has raised Him from the dead, you will be saved, for with the heart one believes unto righteousness, and with the mouth confession is made unto salvation.

—Romans 10:9–10

Therefore God highly exalted Him and gave Him the name which is above every name, that at the name of Jesus every knee should bow, of those in heaven and on earth and under the earth, and every tongue should confess that Jesus Christ is Lord, to the glory of God the Father.

—Philippians 2:9–11

But the firm foundation of God stands, having this seal, "The Lord knows those who are His," and, "Let every one who calls on the name of Christ depart from iniquity."

—2 Timothy 2:19

Confess your faults to one another and pray for one another, that you may be healed. The effective, fervent prayer of a righteous man accomplishes much.

—James 5:16

And every spirit that does not confess that Jesus Christ has come in the flesh is not from God. This is the spirit of the antichrist, which you have heard is coming and is already in the world.

—1 John 4:3

Whoever confesses that Jesus is the Son of God, God lives in him, and he in God.

—1 John 4:15

For many deceivers, who do not confess that Jesus Christ has come in the flesh, have gone out into the world. Each one is a deceiver and an antichrist.

—2 John 7

He who overcomes shall be clothed in white garments. I will not blot his name out of the Book of Life, but I will confess his name before My Father and before His angels.

—Revelation 3:5

CONFIDENCE

For You are my hope, O Lord God; You are my confidence from my youth.

—Psalm 71:5

It is better to trust in the Lord than to put confidence in man. It is better to trust in the Lord than to put confidence in princes.

—Psalm 118:8–9

For the Lord will be your confidence, and will keep your foot from being caught.

—Proverbs 3:26

In the fear of the LORD is strong confidence, and His children will have a place of refuge.

—PROVERBS 14:26

He who trusts in his own heart is a fool, but whoever walks wisely will be delivered.

—PROVERBS 28:26

Do not trust in a companion, do not rely on a friend. From her who lies in your embrace, guard the doors of your mouth. For the son dishonors the father, the daughter rises up against her mother, the daughter-in-law against her mother-in-law—the enemies of a man are members of his own household. But as for me, I watch for the LORD, I await the God of my salvation—my God will hear me.

—MICAH 7:5–7

I have confidence in you through the Lord that you will not think otherwise. But he who is troubling you shall bear his judgment, whoever he is.

—GALATIANS 5:10

For we are the circumcision who worship God in the Spirit, and boast in Christ Jesus, and place no trust in the flesh.

—PHILIPPIANS 3:3

Therefore do not throw away your confidence, which will be greatly rewarded.

—HEBREWS 10:35

And now, little children, remain in Him, so that when He appears, we may have confidence and not be ashamed before Him when He comes.

—1 JOHN 2:28

Beloved, if our heart does not condemn us, then we have confidence before God.

—1 John 3:21

This is the confidence that we have in Him, that if we ask anything according to His will, He hears us. So if we know that He hears whatever we ask, we know that we have whatever we asked of Him.

—1 John 5:14–15

Conflict

Hatred stirs up strife, but love covers all sins.

—Proverbs 10:12

A fool's wrath is presently known, but a prudent man covers shame.

—Proverbs 12:16

Blessed are the peacemakers, for they shall be called the sons of God.

—Matthew 5:9

But I say to you, love your enemies, bless those who curse you, do good to those who hate you, and pray for those who spitefully use you and persecute you.

—Matthew 5:44

Now I ask you, brothers, by the name of our Lord Jesus Christ, that you all speak in agreement and that there be no divisions among you. But be perfectly joined together in the same mind and in the same judgment.

—1 Corinthians 1:10

Love suffers long and is kind; love envies not; love flaunts not itself and is not puffed up, does not behave itself improperly, seeks not its own, is not easily provoked, thinks no evil.

—1 Corinthians 13:4–5

I, therefore, the prisoner of the Lord, exhort you to walk in a manner worthy of the calling with which you were called. With all humility, meekness, and patience, bearing with one another in love, be eager to keep the unity of the Spirit in the bond of peace.

—Ephesians 4:1–3

Be angry but do not sin. Do not let the sun go down on your anger. Do not give place to the devil.

—Ephesians 4:26–27

Only let your conduct be worthy of the gospel of Christ, that whether or not I come and see you, I may hear of your activities, that you are standing fast in one spirit, with one mind, striving together for the faith of the gospel.

—Philippians 1:27

Then fulfill my joy and be like-minded, having the same love, being in unity with one mind. Let nothing be done out of strife or conceit, but in humility let each esteem the other better than himself. Let each of you look not only to your own interests, but also to the interests of others.

—Philippians 2:2–4

Let everyone come to know your gentleness. The Lord is at hand.

—Philippians 4:5

Finally, be all of one mind, be loving toward one another, be gracious, and be kind. Do not repay evil for evil, or curse for curse, but on the contrary, bless, knowing that to this you are called, so that you may receive a blessing.

—1 Peter 3:8–9

CONFORMITY

Thus you shall know that I am the Lord. For you have not walked in My statutes, or executed My judgments, but have done after the customs of the nations round about you.

—Ezekiel 11:12

Whoever therefore is ashamed of Me and of My words in this adulterous and sinful generation, of him will the Son of Man also be ashamed when He comes in the glory of His Father with the holy angels.

—Mark 8:38

Do not be unequally yoked together with unbelievers. For what fellowship has righteousness with unrighteousness? What communion has light with darkness?

—2 Corinthians 6:14

"So come out from among them and be separate," says the Lord. "Do not touch what is unclean, and I will receive you. I will be a Father to you, and you shall be My sons and daughters," says the Lord Almighty.

—2 Corinthians 6:17–18

As obedient children do not conduct yourselves according to the former lusts in your ignorance. But as He who has called you is holy, so be holy in all your conduct.

—1 Peter 1:14–15

Do not love the world or the things in the world. If anyone loves the world, the love of the Father is not in him. For all that is in the world—the lust of the flesh, the lust of the eyes, and the pride of life—is not of the Father, but is of the world. The world and its desires are passing away, but the one who does the will of God lives forever.

—1 JOHN 2:15–17

CONFUSION

But when the Spirit of truth comes, He will guide you into all truth. For He will not speak on His own authority. But He will speak whatever He hears, and He will tell you things that are to come.

—JOHN 16:13

For God is not the author of confusion, but of peace, as in all churches of the saints.

—1 CORINTHIANS 14:33

Finally, brothers, whatever things are true, whatever things are honest, whatever things are just, whatever things are pure, whatever things are lovely, whatever things are of good report, if there is any virtue, and if there is any praise, think on these things. Do those things which you have both learned and received, and heard and seen in me, and the God of peace will be with you.

—PHILIPPIANS 4:8–9

For this I was appointed a preacher and an apostle (I speak the truth in Christ and do not lie), a teacher of the Gentiles in faith and truth.

—1 TIMOTHY 2:7

Be sober and watchful, because your adversary the devil walks around as a roaring lion, seeking whom he may devour.

—1 Peter 5:8

Beloved, do not believe every spirit, but test the spirits to see whether they are from God, because many false prophets have gone out into the world.

—1 John 4:1

CONTENTMENT

A sound heart is the life of the flesh, but envy the rottenness of the bones.

—Proverbs 14:30

A merry heart makes a cheerful countenance, but by sorrow of the heart the spirit is broken.

—Proverbs 15:13

All the days of the afflicted are evil, but he who is of a merry heart has a continual feast.

—Proverbs 15:15

The light of the eyes rejoices the heart, and a good report makes the bones healthy.

—Proverbs 15:30

Better is a little with righteousness than great revenues with injustice.

—Proverbs 16:8

Better is a dry morsel with quietness than a house full of sacrifices with strife.

—Proverbs 17:1

A merry heart does good like a medicine, but a broken spirit dries the bones.

—Proverbs 17:22

I experienced that there is nothing better for people than to be glad and do good in their life. And also that everyone should eat and drink and experience good in all their labor. This is a gift of God.

—Ecclesiastes 3:12–13

Better is a full hand of quietness than handfuls of toil and chasing the wind.

—Ecclesiastes 4:6

And I praise gladness, because there is no good for people under the sun except to eat, and drink, and enjoy life. And this enjoyment will accompany a person in his labor all the days of his life that God has granted to him under the sun.

—Ecclesiastes 8:15

I do not speak because I have need, for I have learned in whatever state I am to be content. I know both how to face humble circumstances and how to have abundance. Everywhere and in all things I have learned the secret, both to be full and to be hungry, both to abound and to suffer need. I can do all things because of Christ who strengthens me.

—Philippians 4:11–13

But, godliness with contentment is great gain.

—1 Timothy 6:6

CORRECTION, GOD'S

You must also consider in your heart that, as a man disciplines his son, so the LORD your God disciplines you. Therefore you must keep the commandments of the LORD your God, to walk in His ways and to fear Him.

—DEUTERONOMY 8:5–6

Blessed is the man whom you chasten, O LORD, and teach from Your law; that You may give him rest from the days of adversity, until a pit is dug for the wicked.

—PSALM 94:12–13

For whom the LORD loves He corrects, even as a father the son in whom he delights.

—PROVERBS 3:12

But when we are judged, we are disciplined by the Lord, so that we would not be condemned with the world.

—1 CORINTHIANS 11:32

For this reason we do not lose heart: Even though our outward man is perishing, yet our inward man is being renewed day by day. Our light affliction, which lasts but for a moment, works for us a far more exceeding and eternal weight of glory.

—2 CORINTHIANS 4:16–17

"For whom the Lord loves He disciplines, and He scourges every son whom He receives." Endure for discipline; God is dealing with you as with sons. For what son is there whom a father does not discipline?

—HEBREWS 12:6–7

COURAGE

Be strong and of a good courage. Fear not, nor be afraid of them, for the Lord your God, it is He who goes with you. He will not fail you, nor forsake you.

—Deuteronomy 31:6

Be strong and let us fight with resolve for the sake of our people and the cities of our God. May the Lord do what seems good to Him.

—2 Samuel 10:12

I am going the way of all the earth. Be strong, and show yourself to be a man. And keep the charge of the Lord your God, walking in His ways, keeping His statutes, His commandments, His judgments, and His testimonies, as it is written in the law of Moses, that you may prosper in all that you do and wherever you turn.

—1 Kings 2:2–3

And he said, "Do not be afraid, for there are more with us than with them."

—2 Kings 6:16

Then you will prosper if you carefully observe the statutes and the judgments which the Lord commanded Moses for Israel.

—1 Chronicles 22:13

Note that Amariah the chief priest is over you all matters of the Lord; and Zebadiah the son of Ishmael, the ruler of the house of Judah, for all the king's matters; also, the Levites will be officials before you. Deal courageously, and the LORD will be with the good.

—2 CHRONICLES 19:11

"Be strong and brave. Do not fear or have terror before the king of Assyria or before all this army that is with him because there are more who are with us than with him. With this king is a strong arm of flesh, but with us is the LORD our God who will help us and fight our battles." So the people leaned on the words of Hezekiah king of Judah.

—2 CHRONICLES 32:7–8

He gives power to the faint, and to those who have no might He increases strength.

—ISAIAH 40:29

Do not fear, for I am with you. Do not be dismayed, for I am your God. I will strengthen you. Indeed, I will help you. Indeed, I will uphold you with My righteous right hand.

—ISAIAH 41:10

When they saw the boldness of Peter and John and perceived that they were illiterate and uneducated men, they marveled. And they recognized that they had been with Jesus.

—ACTS 4:13

But Christ is faithful over God's house as a Son, whose house we are if we firmly hold our confidence and the rejoicing of our hope to the end.

—HEBREWS 3:6

Beloved, do not be surprised at the fiery ordeal that is taking place among you to test you, as though some strange thing happened to you. But rejoice in so far as you share in Christ's sufferings, so that you may rejoice and be glad also in the revelation of His glory.

—1 Peter 4:12–13

COVENANT PLAN

If you listen to these judgments, keep them, and do them, then the Lord your God shall keep with you the covenant and the mercy which He swore to your fathers. He will love you and bless you and multiply you. He will also bless the fruit of your womb and the fruit of your land, your corn, and your wine, and your oil, the increase of your herd and the young of your flock, in the land which He swore to your fathers to give you.

—Deuteronomy 7:12–13

Let the peoples praise You, O God; let all the peoples praise You. Oh, let the nations be glad and sing for joy; for You will judge the people uprightly, and lead the nations on earth. Selah.

—Psalm 67:3–4

They shall speak of the glory of Your kingdom and talk of Your power, to make known to people His mighty acts, and the glorious majesty of His kingdom. Your kingdom is an everlasting kingdom, and Your dominion endures throughout all generations.

—Psalm 145:11–13

The wilderness and the solitary place shall be glad. And the desert shall rejoice and blossom as the rose. It shall blossom abundantly and rejoice even with joy and singing. The glory of Lebanon shall be given to it, the excellency of Carmel and

Sharon. They shall see the glory of the LORD and the excellency of our God.

—Isaiah 35:1–2

"For the mountains may be removed, and the hills may shake, but My kindness shall not depart from you, nor shall My covenant of peace be removed," says the LORD who has mercy on you.

—Isaiah 54:10

The Spirit of the Lord GOD is upon Me because the LORD has anointed Me to preach good news to the poor.

—Isaiah 61:1

When He was asked by the Pharisees when the kingdom of God would come, He answered them, "The kingdom of God does not come with observation. Nor will they say, 'Here it is!' or 'There it is!' For remember, the kingdom of God is within you."

—Luke 17:20–21

"After this I will return, and I will rebuild the tabernacle of David, which has fallen. I will rebuild its ruins, and I will set it up, that the rest of men may seek the Lord, and all the Gentiles who are called by My name," says the Lord who does all these things.

—Acts 15:16–17

When Paul had laid his hands on them, the Holy Spirit came on them, and they spoke in other tongues and prophesied. There were about twelve men in all. He went into the synagogue and spoke boldly for three months, lecturing and persuading concerning the kingdom of God.

—Acts 19:6–8

And that you put on the new nature, which was created according to God in righteousness and true holiness.

—Ephesians 4:24

For this reason He is the Mediator of a new covenant, since a death has occurred for the redemption of the sins that were committed under the first covenant, so that those who are called might receive the promise of eternal inheritance.

—Hebrews 9:15

But you have come to Mount Zion and to the city of the living God, the heavenly Jerusalem, and to an innumerable company of angels.

—Hebrews 12:22

CREATIVITY

And He has filled him with the Spirit of God, in wisdom, in understanding, and in knowledge, and in all manner of craftsmanship, to design artistic works, to work in gold, in silver, and in bronze, and in the cutting of stones for settings and in the carving of wood in order to make every manner of artistic work.

—Exodus 35:31–33

For the Lord God is a sun and shield; the Lord will give favor and glory, for no good thing will He withhold from the one who walks uprightly.

—Psalm 84:11

O God, my heart is determined; I will sing and give praise with my whole heart.

—Psalm 108:1

She makes herself coverings of tapestry; her clothing is silk and purple. Her husband is known in the gates, when he sits among the elders of the land. She makes fine linen and sells it, and delivers sashes to the merchant.

—Proverbs 31:22–24

It is He who changes the times and the seasons. He removes kings and sets up kings. He gives wisdom to the wise and knowledge to those who know understanding.

—Daniel 2:21

We have diverse gifts according to the grace that is given to us: if prophecy, according to the proportion of faith; if service, in serving; he who teaches, in teaching; he who exhorts, in exhortation; he who gives, with generosity; he who rules, with diligence; he who shows mercy, with cheerfulness.

—Romans 12:6–8

By Him you are enriched in everything, in all speech and in all knowledge.

—1 Corinthians 1:5

For I would that all men were even as I myself. But every man has his proper gift from God, one after this manner and another after that.

—1 Corinthians 7:7

There are various gifts, but the same Spirit. There are differences of administrations, but the same Lord. There are various operations, but it is the same God who operates them all in all people.

—1 Corinthians 12:4–6

For if there is a willing mind first, the gift is accepted according to what a man possesses and not according to what he does not possess.

—2 Corinthians 8:12

Every good gift and every perfect gift is from above and comes down from the Father of lights, with whom is no change or shadow of turning.

—James 1:17

As every one has received a gift, even so serve one another with it, as good stewards of the manifold grace of God. If anyone speaks, let him speak as the oracles of God. If anyone serves, let him serve with the strength that God supplies, so that God in all things may be glorified through Jesus Christ, to whom be praise and dominion forever and ever.

—1 Peter 4:10–11

CRITICISM

O Lord my God, in You I put my trust. Save me from all those who persecute me, and deliver me.

—Psalm 7:1

When pride comes, then comes shame; but with the humble is wisdom.

—Proverbs 11:2

Blessed are you when men revile you, and persecute you, and say all kinds of evil against you falsely for My sake.

—Matthew 5:11

You have heard that it was said, "You shall love your neighbor and hate your enemy." But I say to you, love your enemies, bless those who curse you, do good to those who hate you, and pray for those who spitefully use you and persecute you.

—Matthew 5:43–44

Remember the word that I said to you: "A servant is not greater than his master." If they persecuted Me, they will also persecute you. If they kept My words, they will keep yours also.

—John 15:20

To prevent any man from blaming us in administering this abundant gift.

—2 Corinthians 8:20

CULTS

Then if anyone says to you, "Look, here is the Christ," or "There He is," do not believe it. For false christs and false prophets will arise and show great signs and wonders to deceive, if possible, even the elect. Listen, I have told you beforehand. So, if they say to you, "Look, He is in the desert," do not go there; or, "Look, He is in the private chambers," do not believe it.

—Matthew 24:23–26

Many will come in My name, saying, "I am He," and will deceive many.

—Mark 13:6

There is no salvation in any other, for there is no other name under heaven given among men by which we must be saved.

—Acts 4:12

For no one can lay another foundation than that which was laid, which is Jesus Christ.

—1 Corinthians 3:11

For such are false apostles and deceitful workers, disguising themselves as apostles of Christ. And no wonder! For even Satan disguises himself as an angel of light.

—2 Corinthians 11:13–14

As we said before, so I say now again: If anyone preaches any other gospel to you than the one you have received, let him be accursed.

—Galatians 1:9

Beware, lest anyone captivate you through philosophy and vain deceit, in the tradition of men and the elementary principles of the world, and not after Christ.

—Colossians 2:8

But evil men and seducers will grow worse and worse, deceiving and being deceived. But continue in the things that you have learned and have been assured of, knowing those from whom you have learned them.

—2 Timothy 3:13–14

For the time will come when people will not endure sound doctrine, but they will gather to themselves teachers in accordance with their own desires, having itching ears, and they will turn their ears away from the truth and turn to myths.

—2 Timothy 4:3–4

Who is a liar but the one who denies that Jesus is the Christ? Whoever denies the Father and the Son is the antichrist.

—1 John 2:22

Whoever practices sin is of the devil, for the devil has been sinning from the beginning. For this purpose the Son of God was revealed, that He might destroy the works of the devil.

—1 John 3:8

I testify to everyone who hears the words of the prophecy of this book: If anyone adds to these things, God shall add to him the plagues that are written in this book. And if anyone takes away from the words of the book of this prophecy, God shall take away his part out of the Book of Life and out of the Holy City and out of the things which are written in this book.

—Revelation 22:18–19

Curses

And to Adam He said, "Because you have listened to the voice of your wife and have eaten from the tree about which I commanded you, saying, 'You shall not eat of it,' cursed is the ground on account of you. In hard labor you will eat of it all the days of your life."

—Genesis 3:17

For you shall eat the fruit of the labor of your hands; you will be happy, and it shall be well with you.

—Psalm 128:2

A righteous man falling down before the wicked is as a troubled fountain and a corrupt spring.

—Proverbs 25:26

Your covenant with death shall be annulled, and your agreement with hell shall not stand. When the overflowing scourge passes through, then you shall be trodden down by it.

—Isaiah 28:18

For he is the servant of God for your good. But if you do what is evil, be afraid, for he does not bear the sword in vain, for he is the servant of God, an avenger to execute wrath upon him who practices evil.

—Romans 13:4

So that the blessing of Abraham might come on the Gentiles through Jesus Christ, that we might receive the promise of the Spirit through faith.

—Galatians 3:14

Dancing

Miriam the prophetess, the sister of Aaron, took a timbrel in her hand, and all the women went out after her with timbrels and with dancing.

—Exodus 15:20

For You have turned my mourning into dancing; You have put off my sackcloth and girded me with gladness, so that my glory may sing praise to You and not be silent. O Lord my God, I will give thanks to You forever.

—Psalm 30:11–12

Let them praise His name with dancing; let them sing praises unto Him with the tambourine and harp.

—Psalm 149:3

Praise Him with the tambourine and dancing; praise Him with stringed instruments and flute.

—Psalm 150:4

To everything there is a season, a time for every purpose under heaven…a time to weep, and a time to laugh; a time to mourn, and a time to dance.

—Ecclesiastes 3:1, 4

Then the virgin shall rejoice in the dance, both young men and old together. For I will turn their mourning into joy, and will comfort them, and make them rejoice from their sorrow.

—Jeremiah 31:13

Dating

Honor your father and your mother, that your days may be prolonged in the land which the Lord your God is giving you.

—Exodus 20:12

How shall a young man keep his way pure? By keeping it according to Your word.

—Psalm 119:9

Your word I have hidden in my heart, that I might not sin against You.

—Psalm 119:11

The integrity of the upright will guide them, but the perverseness of transgressors will destroy them.

—Proverbs 11:3

Even a child is known by his doings, whether his work is pure and whether it is right.

—PROVERBS 20:11

Blessed are the pure in heart, for they shall see God.

—MATTHEW 5:8

But take heed, lest by any means this liberty of yours becomes a stumbling block to those who are weak.

—1 CORINTHIANS 8:9

And by your knowledge shall the weak brother perish, for whom Christ died? When you thus sin against the brothers, wounding their weak conscience, you sin against Christ.

—1 CORINTHIANS 8:11–12

Do not be deceived: "Bad company corrupts good morals."

—1 CORINTHIANS 15:33

Do not be unequally yoked together with unbelievers. For what fellowship has righteousness with unrighteousness? What communion has light with darkness?

—2 CORINTHIANS 6:14

Walk in love, as Christ loved us and gave Himself for us as a fragrant offering and a sacrifice to God. And do not let sexual immorality, or any impurity, or greed, be named among you, as these are not proper among saints.

—EPHESIANS 5:2–3

So flee youthful desires and pursue righteousness, faith, love, and peace, with those who call on the Lord out of a pure heart.

—2 TIMOTHY 2:22

DEATH

In a moment will they die, and the people will be troubled at midnight and pass away, and the mighty will be taken away without a hand.

—Job 34:20

He will swallow up death for all time, and the Lord God will wipe away tears from all faces. And the reproach of His people He shall take away from all the earth, for the Lord has spoken it.

—Isaiah 25:8

I will ransom them from the power of Sheol. I will redeem them from Death. O Death, where are your plagues! O Sheol, where is your sting! Compassion is hidden from My eyes.

—Hosea 13:14

Truly, truly I say to you, if anyone keeps My word, he shall never see death.

—John 8:51

For since death came by man, by man came also the resurrection of the dead. For as in Adam all die, even so in Christ shall all be made alive.

—1 Corinthians 15:21–22

The last enemy that will be destroyed is death.

—1 Corinthians 15:26

"O death, where is your sting? O grave, where is your victory?" The sting of death is sin, and the strength of sin is the law.

But thanks be to God, who gives us the victory through our Lord Jesus Christ!

—1 Corinthians 15:55–57

For this reason we do not lose heart: Even though our outward man is perishing, yet our inward man is being renewed day by day.

—2 Corinthians 4:16

For if we believe that Jesus died and arose again, so God will bring with Him those who sleep in Jesus.

—1 Thessalonians 4:14

So then, as the children share in flesh and blood, He likewise took part in these, so that through death He might destroy him who has the power of death, that is, the devil, and deliver those who through fear of death were throughout their lives subject to bondage.

—Hebrews 2:14–15

As it is appointed for men to die once, but after this comes the judgment, so Christ was offered once to bear the sins of many, and He will appear a second time, not to bear sin but to save those who eagerly wait for Him.

—Hebrews 9:27–28

Beloved, now are we children of God, and it has not yet been revealed what we shall be. But we know that when He appears, we shall be like Him, for we shall see Him as He is.

—1 John 3:2

DECEIT

You shall not steal, nor deal falsely, nor lie to one another.

—LEVITICUS 19:11

He who practices deceit shall not dwell within my house; he who tells lies shall not remain in my sight.

—PSALM 101:7

His grave was assigned with the wicked, yet with the rich in His death because He had done no violence, nor was any deceit in His mouth.

—ISAIAH 53:9

The heart is more deceitful than all things and desperately wicked. Who can understand it? I, the LORD, search the heart, I test the mind, even to give to every man according to his ways, and according to the fruit of his deeds.

—JEREMIAH 17:9–10

But exhort one another daily, while it is called "Today," lest any of you be hardened through the deceitfulness of sin.

—HEBREWS 3:13

For "He who wants to love life, and to see good days, let him keep his tongue from evil, and his lips from speaking deceit."

—1 PETER 3:10

DEFEAT

He also brought me up out of a horrible pit, out of the miry clay, and set my feet on a rock, and established my steps. He has put a new song in my mouth, even praise to our God; many will see it, and fear, and will trust in the LORD.

—PSALM 40:2–3

For a just man falls seven times and rises up again, but the wicked will fall into mischief.

—Proverbs 24:16

Beloved, do not avenge yourselves, but rather give place to God's wrath, for it is written: "Vengeance is Mine. I will repay," says the Lord.

—Romans 12:19

Now therefore it is already an utter failure for you that you go to law against one another. Why not rather be wronged? Why not rather be defrauded? But you yourselves do wrong and defraud, and do this to your brothers.

—1 Corinthians 6:7–8

For this reason we do not lose heart: Even though our outward man is perishing, yet our inward man is being renewed day by day.

—2 Corinthians 4:16

But He said to me, "My grace is sufficient for you, for My strength is made perfect in weakness." Therefore most gladly I will boast in my weaknesses, that the power of Christ may rest upon me.

—2 Corinthians 12:9

DELIVERANCE

The Lord is my rock and my fortress and my deliverer.

—2 Samuel 22:2

But the worthless individual is like a thorn tossed away, all of them, for they cannot be taken with the hand; but the one who touches them must have an iron implement and the shaft of a spear, and they must be burned with fire on the spot.

—2 Samuel 23:6–7

With the kind You will show Yourself kind; with an upright person You will show Yourself upright.

—Psalm 18:25

For You will cause my lamp to shine; the Lord my God will enlighten my darkness. For by You I can run through a troop, and by my God I can leap a wall.

—Psalm 18:28–29

I will bless the Lord at all times; His praise will continually be in my mouth. My soul will make its boast in the Lord; the humble will hear of it and be glad. O magnify the Lord with me, and let us exalt His name together. I sought the Lord, and He answered me, and delivered me from all my fears. They looked to Him and became radiant, and their faces are not ashamed. This poor man cried, and the Lord heard, and saved him out of all his troubles.

—Psalm 34:1–6

Many are the afflictions of the righteous, but the Lord delivers him out of them all. A righteous one keeps all his bones; not one of them is broken. Evil will slay the wicked, and those who hate a righteous person will be punished. The Lord redeems the life of His servants, and all who take refuge in Him will not be punished.

—Psalm 34:19–22

The LORD is merciful and gracious, slow to anger, and abounding in mercy.

—PSALM 103:8

But the mercy of the LORD is from everlasting to everlasting upon those who fear Him, and His righteousness to children's children, to those who keep His covenant, and to those who remember to do His commandments.

—PSALM 103:17–18

An ungodly man digs up evil, and in his lips there is as a burning fire.

—PROVERBS 16:27

Awake, awake! Put on your strength, O Zion. Put on your beautiful garments, O Jerusalem, the holy city. For the uncircumcised and the unclean will no longer enter you. Shake yourself from the dust. Arise, O captive Jerusalem. Loose yourself from the bonds of your neck, O captive daughter of Zion.

—ISAIAH 52:1–2

Then Paul and Barnabas boldly said, "It was necessary that the word of God should be spoken to you first. But seeing you reject it, and judge yourselves unworthy of eternal life, we are turning to the Gentiles. For thus has the Lord commanded us, 'I have established you to be a light of the Gentiles, that you may bring salvation to the ends of the earth.'"

—ACTS 13:46–47

And a great many of the brothers in the Lord, having become confident because of my incarcerations, have dared to speak the word without fear.

—Philippians 1:14

Demons

When the evening came, they brought to Him many who were possessed with demons. And He cast out the spirits with His word, and healed all who were sick.

—Matthew 8:16

So the demons begged Him, saying, "If You cast us out, permit us to go away into the herd of swine." He said to them, "Go!" And when they came out, they went into the herd of swine. And suddenly, the whole herd of swine ran violently down a steep place into the sea, and perished in the waters.

—Matthew 8:31–32

Jesus rebuked the demon, and he came out of him. And the child was healed instantly.

—Matthew 17:18

Then He called His twelve disciples together and gave them power and authority over all demons and to cure diseases.

—Luke 9:1

But I say that the things which the Gentiles sacrifice, they sacrifice to demons, and not to God. I do not want you to have fellowship with demons.

—1 Corinthians 10:20

Do not give place to the devil.

—Ephesians 4:27

Put on the whole armor of God that you may be able to stand against the schemes of the devil.

—Ephesians 6:11

For our fight is not against flesh and blood, but against principalities, against powers, against the rulers of the darkness of this world, and against spiritual forces of evil in the heavenly places. Therefore take up the whole armor of God that you may be able to resist in the evil day, and having done all, to stand.

—Ephesians 6:12–13

Now the Spirit clearly says that in the last times some will depart from the faith and pay attention to seducing spirits and doctrines of devils.

—1 Timothy 4:11

You believe that there is one God; you do well. The demons also believe and tremble.

—James 2:19

For if God did not spare the angels that sinned, but cast them down to hell and delivered them into chains of darkness to be kept for judgment.

—2 Peter 2:4

Beloved, do not believe every spirit, but test the spirits to see whether they are from God, because many false prophets have gone out into the world. This is how you know the Spirit of God: Every spirit that confesses that Jesus Christ has come in the flesh is from God, and every spirit that does not confess that Jesus Christ has come in the flesh is not from God. This is the spirit of the antichrist, which you have heard is coming and is already in the world.

—1 John 4:1–3

DEPRESSION

For You are my lamp, O Lord; the Lord illuminates my darkness.

—2 Samuel 22:29

If you yourself would seek God earnestly, and seek favor from the Almighty, if you were pure and upright, surely now He would rouse Himself on your behalf, and He would prosper your righteous dwelling.

—Job 8:5–6

For I the Lord your God will hold your right hand, saying to you, "Do not fear. I will help you."

—Isaiah 41:13

Surely He has borne our grief and carried our sorrows. Yet we esteemed Him stricken, smitten of God, and afflicted. But He was wounded for our transgressions. He was bruised for our iniquities. The chastisement of our peace was upon Him, and by His stripes we are healed.

—Isaiah 53:4–5

For I will set My eyes upon them for good and I will bring them again to this land. And I will build them and not pull them down. And I will plant them and not pluck them up. I will give them a heart to know Me, that I am the Lord; and they will be My people, and I will be their God, for they will return to Me with their whole heart.

—Jeremiah 24:6–7

For I satiate the weary souls and I replenish every languishing soul.

—JEREMIAH 31:25

For the Lord will not cast off forever. But though He causes grief, yet He will have compassion according to the multitude of His mercies.

—LAMENTATIONS 3:31–32

He said: "I called to the LORD out of my distress, and He answered me. Out of the belly of Sheol I cried, and You heard my voice."

—JONAH 2:2

Then Jesus came and spoke to them saying, "All authority has been given to Me in heaven and on earth."

—MATTHEW 28:18

Peace I leave with you. My peace I give to you. Not as the world gives do I give to you. Let not your heart be troubled, neither let it be afraid.

—JOHN 14:27

Nevertheless when anyone turns to the Lord, the veil is removed. Now the Lord is the Spirit. And where the Spirit of the Lord is, there is liberty.

—2 CORINTHIANS 3:16–17

You are of God, little children, and have overcome them, because He who is in you is greater than he who is in the world.

—1 JOHN 4:4

DESERT PLACES

Yet You in Your great mercy did not forsake them in the wilderness: The pillar of the cloud did not depart from them by day, to lead them in the way, nor the pillar of fire by night, to light for them the way they should go. You gave Your good Spirit to instruct them, did not withhold Your manna from their mouth, and gave them water for their thirst. Forty years You sustained them in the wilderness, so that they lacked nothing—their clothing did not wear out nor did their feet swell.

—Nehemiah 9:19–21

He split rocks in the wilderness and gave them abundance to drink as out of the great depths. He brought streams out of the rock and caused waters to run down like rivers.

—Psalm 78:15–16

He chose David His servant and took him from the sheepfolds. From following the nursing ewes He brought him to shepherd Jacob His people, and Israel His inheritance. So he shepherded them according to the integrity of his heart and guided them by the skillfulness of his hands.

—Psalm 78:70–72

He turns a wilderness into pools of water, a parched ground into springs of water. There He makes the hungry dwell, and they prepare a city to live; and sow fields and plant vineyards, and yield a fruitful harvest. He blesses them, so that they are greatly multiplied, and He does not let their livestock decrease.

—Psalm 107:35–38

But there the glorious LORD will be to us a place of broad rivers and streams on which no boat with oars shall go and on which no gallant ship shall pass.

—ISAIAH 33:21

I will open rivers in high places, and fountains in the midst of the valleys. I will make the wilderness a pool of water, and the dry land springs of water.

—ISAIAH 41:18

You shall no more be termed, Forsaken, nor shall your land any more be termed, Desolate. But you shall be called, My Delight Is In Her, and your land, Married. For the LORD delights in you, and your land shall be married. For as a young man marries a virgin, so your sons shall marry you. And as the bridegroom rejoices over the bride, so your God shall rejoice over you.

—ISAIAH 62:4–5

They will come with weeping, and with supplications I will lead them. I will cause them to walk by the rivers of waters, in a straight way in which they shall not stumble. For I am a father to Israel, and Ephraim is My firstborn.

—JEREMIAH 31:9

Therefore they will come and sing in the height of Zion, and will be joyful over the goodness of the LORD, for wheat and for wine and for oil and for the young of the flock and of the herd; and their souls will be as a watered garden. And they will not sorrow any more at all.

—JEREMIAH 31:12

Jesus said to her, "Everyone who drinks of this water will thirst again, but whoever drinks of the water that I shall give him will never thirst. Indeed, the water that I shall give him will become in him a well of water springing up into eternal life."

—John 4:13–14

He who believes in Me, as the Scripture has said, out of his heart shall flow rivers of living water.

—John 7:38

DESTROYING STRONGHOLDS

You have broken down all his walls; You have brought his strongholds to ruin.

—Psalm 89:40

You have also turned back the edge of his sword and have not made him stand in battle. You have made his glory cease and cast his throne down to the ground.

—Psalm 89:43–44

For though we walk in the flesh, we do not war according to the flesh. For the weapons of our warfare are not carnal, but mighty through God to the pulling down of strongholds, casting down imaginations and every high thing that exalts itself against the knowledge of God, bringing every thought into captivity to the obedience of Christ.

—2 Corinthians 10:3–5

Take the helmet of salvation and the sword of the Spirit, which is the word of God.

—Ephesians 6:17

For the word of God is alive, and active, and sharper than any two-edged sword, piercing even to the division of soul and spirit, of joints and marrow, and able to judge the thoughts and intents of the heart.

—Hebrews 4:12

Whoever practices sin is of the devil, for the devil has been sinning from the beginning. For this purpose the Son of God was revealed, that He might destroy the works of the devil.

—1 John 3:8

DISAPPOINTMENT

You are my hiding place; You will preserve me from trouble; You will surround me with shouts of deliverance. Selah.

—Psalm 32:7

The eye of the Lord is on those who fear Him, on those who hope in His lovingkindness.

—Psalm 33:18

Trust in Him at all times; you people, pour out your heart before Him; God is a shelter for us. Selah.

—Psalm 62:8

In the day of benefit, be joyful. But in the day of distress, consider: God has made the one as well as the other. For this reason people will not be able to understand anything that comes after them.

—Ecclesiastes 7:14

Blessed are those who mourn, for they shall be comforted.

—Matthew 5:4

Blessed are you who hunger now, for you shall be filled. Blessed are you who weep now, for you shall laugh.

—Luke 6:21

Discipleship

Lord, who will abide in Your tabernacle? Who will dwell in Your holy hill? He who walks uprightly, and does righteousness, and speaks truth in his own heart.

—Psalm 15:1–2

The work of righteousness shall be peace, and the effect of righteousness quietness and assurance forever.

—Isaiah 32:17

"…has walked in My statutes, and has kept My judgments to deal truly, he is righteous and shall surely live," says the Lord God.

—Ezekiel 18:9

Whoever hears these sayings of Mine and does them, I will liken him to a wise man who built his house on a rock. And the rain descended, the floods came, and the winds blew and beat on that house. And it did not fall, for it was founded a rock.

—Matthew 7:24–25

He who loves father or mother more than Me is not worthy of Me. And he who loves son or daughter more than Me is not worthy of Me. And He who does not take his cross and follow after Me is not worthy of Me. He who finds his life will lose it, and he who loses his life for My sake will find it.

—Matthew 10:37–39

But he who does the truth comes to the light, that it may be revealed that his deeds have been done in God.

—JOHN 3:21

When he brings out his own sheep, he goes before them. And the sheep follow him, for they know his voice.

—JOHN 10:4

Jesus answered him, "If a man loves Me, he will keep My word. My Father will love him, and We will come to him, and make Our home with him."

—JOHN 14:23

Remain in Me, as I also remain in you. As the branch cannot bear fruit by itself, unless it remains in the vine, neither can you, unless you remain in Me. I am the vine, you are the branches. He who remains in Me, and I in him, bears much fruit. For without Me you can do nothing.

—JOHN 15:4–5

For those who live according to the flesh set their minds on the things of the flesh, but those who live according to the Spirit, the things of the Spirit.

—ROMANS 8:5

I have been crucified with Christ. It is no longer I who live, but Christ who lives in me. And the life I now live in the flesh, I live by faith in the Son of God, who loved me and gave Himself for me.

—GALATIANS 2:20

For the grace of God that brings salvation has appeared to all men, teaching us that, denying ungodliness and worldly desires, we should live soberly, righteously, and in godliness in this present world.

—TITUS 2:11–12

DISCOURAGEMENT

See, the LORD your God has set the land before you. Go up and possess it, just as the LORD, the God of your fathers, spoke to you. Do not fear or be discouraged.

—DEUTERONOMY 1:21

The sacrifices of God are a broken spirit, a broken and a contrite heart, O God, You will not despise.

—PSALM 51:17

I cried out to God with my voice, even to God with my voice; and He listened to me.

—PSALM 77:1

But those who wait upon the LORD shall renew their strength. They shall mount up with wings as eagles. They shall run, and not be weary. And they shall walk, and not faint.

—ISAIAH 40:31

We are troubled on every side, yet not distressed; we are perplexed, but not in despair.

—2 CORINTHIANS 4:8

Knowing that He who raised the Lord Jesus will also raise us through Jesus and will present us with you.

—2 CORINTHIANS 4:14

DIVINE PROTECTION

Only do not rebel against the LORD, nor fear the people of the land because they are bread for us. Their defense is gone from them, and the LORD is with us. Do not fear them.

—NUMBERS 14:9

Have You not made a hedge around him, around his household, and around all that he has on every side? You have blessed the work of his hands, and his possessions have increased in the land.

—JOB 1:10

You are my hiding place; You will preserve me from trouble; You will surround me with shouts of deliverance. Selah.

—PSALM 32:7

As the mountains are around Jerusalem, so the LORD surrounds His people, from now and forever.

—PSALM 125:2

O GOD my Lord, the strength of my salvation, You have covered my head in the day of battle.

—PSALM 140:7

But the Lord stood with me and strengthened me, so that through me the preaching might be fully known, and that all the Gentiles might hear. And I was delivered out of the mouth of the lion.

—2 TIMOTHY 4:17

DIVORCE

Therefore a man will leave his father and his mother and be joined to his wife, and they will become one flesh. They were both naked, the man and his wife, and were not ashamed.

—GENESIS 2:24–25

"For the LORD, the God of Israel, says that He hates divorce; for it covers one's garment with violence," says the LORD of Hosts. Therefore take heed to your spirit, that you do not deal treacherously.

—MALACHI 2:16

It was said, "Whoever divorces his wife, let him give her a certificate of divorce." But I say to you that whoever divorces his wife, except for marital unfaithfulness, causes her to commit adultery. And whoever marries her who is divorced commits adultery.

—MATTHEW 5:31–32

He said to them, "Moses, for the hardness of your hearts, permitted you to divorce your wives, but from the beginning it was not so. But I say to you, whoever divorces his wife, except for sexual immorality, and marries another, commits adultery. And whoever marries her who is divorced commits adultery."

—MATTHEW 19:8–9

He said to them, "Whoever divorces his wife and marries another commits adultery against her. And if a woman divorces her husband and marries another, she commits adultery."

—MARK 10:11–12

Now to the married I command, not I, but the Lord, do not let the wife depart from her husband. But if she departs, let her remain unmarried or be reconciled to her husband. And do not let the husband divorce his wife.

—1 Corinthians 7:10–11

DOMINION OVER SIN

For their Redeemer is mighty; He will plead their cause with you.

—Proverbs 23:11

I will feed those who oppress you with their own flesh. And they shall be drunk with their own blood as with sweet wine. And all flesh shall know that I the Lord am your Savior and your Redeemer, the Mighty One of Jacob.

—Isaiah 49:26

For sin shall not have dominion over you, for you are not under the law, but under grace.

—Romans 6:14

Christ has redeemed us from the curse of the law by being made a curse for us—as it is written, "Cursed is every one who hangs on a tree."

—Galatians 3:13

To redeem those who were under the law, that we might receive the adoption as sons.

—Galatians 4:5

But if we walk in the light as He is in the light, we have fellowship one with another, and the blood of Jesus Christ His Son cleanses us from all sin.

—1 John 1:7

DOUBT

The fool has said in his heart, "There is no God." They are corrupt, they do abominable deeds, there is none who does good.

—Psalm 14:1

I will instruct you and teach you in the way which you will go; I will counsel you with my eye on you.

—Psalm 32:8

Forever, O Lord, Your word is established in heaven. Your faithfulness is for all generations; You have established the earth, and it is firm.

—Psalm 119:89–90

I hate those who are double-minded, but I love Your law.

—Psalm 119:113

Trust in the Lord with all your heart, and lean not on your own understanding. In all your ways acknowledge Him, and He will direct your paths. Do not be wise in your own eyes; fear the Lord and depart from evil. It will be health to your body, and strength to your bones.

—Proverbs 3:5–8

He replied, "Why are you fearful, O you of little faith?" Then He rose and rebuked the winds and the sea. And there was a great calm.

—Matthew 8:26

Then He said to Thomas, "Put your finger here, and look at My hands. Put your hand here and place it in My side. Do not be faithless, but believing."

—John 20:27

Jesus said to him, "Thomas, because you have seen Me, you have believed. Blessed are those who have not seen, and have yet believed."

—John 20:29

And without faith it is impossible to please God, for he who comes to God must believe that He exists and that He is a rewarder of those who diligently seek Him.

—Hebrews 11:6

Therefore, since we are encompassed with such a great cloud of witnesses, let us also lay aside every weight and the sin that so easily entangles us, and let us run with endurance the race that is set before us. Let us look to Jesus, the author and finisher of our faith, who for the joy that was set before Him endured the cross, despising the shame, and is seated at the right hand of the throne of God.

—Hebrews 12:1–2

A double-minded man is unstable in all his ways.

—James 1:8

On some have compassion, using discernment.

—Jude 22

Draw From the Well

Then he moved away from there and dug another well, and they did not quarrel over it. So he called the name of it Rehoboth, for he said, "For now the Lord has made room for us, and we will be fruitful in the land."

—Genesis 26:22

He turns a wilderness into pools of water, a parched ground into springs of water.

—Psalm 107:35

They shall not hunger nor thirst. Neither shall the heat nor sun strike them. For He who has mercy on them shall lead them, even by the springs of water He shall guide them.

—Isaiah 49:10

Jesus said to her, "Everyone who drinks of this water will thirst again, but whoever drinks of the water that I shall give him will never thirst. Indeed, the water that I shall give him will become in him a well of water springing up into eternal life."

—John 4:13–14

For I know that through your prayer and the support of the Spirit of Jesus Christ, this will result in my deliverance.

—Philippians 1:19

Dreams and Visions

Where there is no vision, the people perish; but happy is he who keeps the teaching.

—Proverbs 29:18

As for these four youths, God gave them knowledge and skill in every branch of learning and wisdom. And Daniel had understanding in all kinds of visions and dreams.

—Daniel 1:17

And it will be that, afterwards, I will pour out My Spirit on all flesh. Then your sons and your daughters will prophesy, your old men will dream dreams, and your young men will see visions.

—Joel 2:28

Surely the Lord God does nothing without revealing His purpose to His servants the prophets.

—Amos 3:7

When they did not find His body, they returned saying that they had even seen a vision of angels, who said that He was alive.

—Luke 24:23

"In the last days," says God, "I will pour out My Spirit on all flesh. Your sons and your daughters shall prophesy, your young men shall see visions, and your old men shall dream dreams. Even on My menservants and maidservants in those days I will pour out My Spirit. And they shall prophesy."

—Acts 2:17–18

Drug Abuse

The Spirit of the Lord is upon Me, because He has anointed Me to preach the gospel to the poor. He has sent Me to heal the brokenhearted, to preach deliverance to the captives and recovery of sight to the blind, to set at liberty those who are oppressed, to preach the acceptable year of the Lord.

—Luke 4:18–19

And He began to say to them, "Today this Scripture is fulfilled in your hearing."

—Luke 4:21

They were all amazed and said among themselves, "What a word this is! For with authority and power He commands the unclean spirits, and they come out."

—Luke 4:36

Therefore if the Son sets you free, you shall be free indeed.

—John 8:36

No temptation has taken you except what is common to man. God is faithful, and He will not permit you to be tempted above what you can endure, but will with the temptation also make a way to escape, that you may be able to bear it.

—1 Corinthians 10:13

For in earlier times of our lives, it may have sufficed us to do what the Gentiles like to do, when we walked in immorality: lusts, drunkenness, carousing, debauchery, and abominable idolatries.

—1 Peter 4:3

EGO

And everything that my eyes wanted I did not refuse them. And I did not withhold my heart from any selfish pleasure for my heart was glad from all my efforts. And this was my reward for all my efforts. Then I turned to all the work that my hands had designed and all the labor that I had toiled to make, and notice, all of it was vanity and chasing the wind. And there was no benefit under the sun.

—Ecclesiastes 2:10–11

Even the youths shall faint and be weary, and the young men shall utterly fall. But those who wait upon the Lord shall renew their strength. They shall mount up with wings as eagles. They shall run, and not be weary. And they shall walk, and not faint.

—Isaiah 40:30–31

Now, therefore, thus says the Lord of Hosts: "Consider your ways."

—Haggai 1:5

And said to them, "Whoever receives this child in My name receives Me, and whoever receives Me receives Him who sent Me. For he who is least among you all will be great."

—Luke 9:48

A certain ruler asked Him, "Good Teacher, what must I do to inherit eternal life?" Jesus said to him, "Why do you call Me good? No one is good, except God alone."

—Luke 18:18–19

I can do nothing of Myself. As I hear, I judge. My judgment is just, because I seek not My own will, but the will of the Father who sent Me.

—John 5:30

Who is he who condemns? It is Christ who died, yes, who is risen, who is also at the right hand of God, who also intercedes for us.

—Romans 8:34

We who are strong ought to bear the weaknesses of the weak and not please ourselves. Let each of us please his neighbor for his good, leading to edification.

—Romans 15:1–2

Love suffers long and is kind; love envies not; love flaunts not itself and is not puffed up, does not behave itself improperly, seeks not its own, is not easily provoked, thinks no evil.

—1 Corinthians 13:4–5

Let each of you look not only to your own interests, but also to the interests of others. Let this mind be in you all, which was also in Christ Jesus.

—Philippians 2:4–5

If you fulfill the royal law according to the Scripture, "You shall love your neighbor as yourself," you are doing well.

—James 2:8

Whoever has the world's goods and sees his brother in need, but closes his heart of compassion from him, how can the love of God remain in him? My little children, let us love not in word and speech, but in action and truth.

—1 John 3:17–18

EMOTIONAL NEEDS

Indeed, may he deliver the needy when he cries; the poor also, and him who has no helper.

—Psalm 72:12

I will pray the Father, and He will give you another Counselor, that He may be with you forever: The Spirit of truth, whom the world cannot receive, for it does not see Him, neither does it know Him. But you know Him, for He lives with you, and will be in you. I will not leave you fatherless. I will come to you.

—John 14:16–18

But the Counselor, the Holy Spirit, whom the Father will send in My name, will teach you everything and remind you of all that I told you.

—John 14:26

For whatever was previously written was written for our instruction, so that through perseverance and encouragement of the Scriptures we might have hope.

—Romans 15:4

Nevertheless God, who comforts the downcast, comforted us through the coming of Titus, and not only by his coming, but also by the comfort with which he was comforted in you, when he told us about your sincere desire, your mourning, and your zeal toward me, so that I rejoiced even more.

—2 Corinthians 7:6–7

Let your lives be without love of money, and be content with the things you have. For He has said, "I will never leave you, nor forsake you."

—Hebrews 13:5

ENCOURAGEMENT

Heaviness in the heart of man makes it droop, but a good word makes it glad.

—Proverbs 12:25

This I recall to my mind, therefore I have hope. It is of the Lord's mercies that we are not consumed, because His compassions do not fail. They are new every morning. Great is Your faithfulness.

—Lamentations 3:21–23

The Lord is good to those who wait for Him, to the soul that seeks Him.

—Lamentations 3:25

God is faithful, and by Him you were called to the fellowship of His Son, Jesus Christ our Lord.

—1 Corinthians 1:9

Now may our Lord Jesus Christ Himself, and God our Father, who has loved us and has given us eternal consolation and good hope through grace, comfort your hearts and establish you in every good word and work.

—2 Thessalonians 2:16–17

And let us consider how to spur one another to love and to good works.

—Hebrews 10:24

ENEMIES

Your right hand, O Lord, is glorious in power. Your right hand, O Lord, shatters the enemy.

—Exodus 15:6

The Lord will help them and deliver them; He will deliver them from the wicked, and save them, because they take refuge in Him.

—Psalm 37:40

Through God we will do valiantly, for He will tread down our enemies.

—Psalm 60:12

You who love the Lord, hate evil! He preserves the lives of His devoted ones; He delivers them from the hand of the wicked.

—Psalm 97:10

When a man's ways please the Lord, He makes even his enemies to be at peace with him.

—Proverbs 16:7

"But I will deliver you in that day," says the Lord, "and you shall not be given into the hand of the men of whom you are afraid. For I will surely deliver you, and you will not fall by the sword; but your life will be as plunder to you, because you have put your trust in Me," says the Lord.

—Jeremiah 39:17–18

Then Peter came to Him and said, "Lord, how often shall I forgive my brother who sins against me? Up to seven times?"

Jesus said to him, "I do not say to you up to seven times, but up to seventy times seven."

—MATTHEW 18:21–22

That we should be saved from our enemies and from the hand of all who hate us.

—LUKE 1:71

That He would grant to us that we, being delivered out of the hand of our enemies, might serve Him without fear.

—LUKE 1:74

Judge not, and you shall not be judged. Condemn not, and you will not be condemned. Forgive, and you shall be forgiven.

—LUKE 6:37

For I am with you, and no one shall attack you and hurt you, for I have many people in this city.

—ACTS 18:10

Repay no one evil for evil. Commend what is honest in the sight of all men. If it is possible, as much as it depends on you, live peaceably with all men. Beloved, do not avenge yourselves, but rather give place to God's wrath, for it is written: "Vengeance is Mine. I will repay," says the Lord.

—ROMANS 12:17–19

ENVY

Do not envy the oppressor, and choose none of his ways.

—PROVERBS 3:31

When you walk, your steps will not be hindered, and when you run, you will not stumble. Take firm hold of instruction, do not let her go; keep her, for she is your life.

—Proverbs 4:12–13

Do not let your heart envy sinners, but continue in the fear of the Lord all day long.

—Proverbs 23:17

Wrath is cruel, and anger is outrageous, but who is able to stand before envy?

—Proverbs 27:4

Then He said to them, "Take heed and beware of covetousness. For a man's life does not consist in the abundance of his possessions."

—Luke 12:15

And do not let sexual immorality, or any impurity, or greed, be named among you, as these are not proper among saints.

—Ephesians 5:3

ETERNAL LIFE

Many of those who sleep in the dust of the earth shall awake, some to everlasting life, but others to shame and everlasting contempt.

—Daniel 12:2

Be it known to you all, and to all the people of Israel, that by the name of Jesus Christ of Nazareth, whom you crucified, whom God raised from the dead, by Him this man stands before you whole. He is "the stone you builders rejected, which has become the cornerstone." There is no salvation in any other, for there is no other name under heaven given among men by which we must be saved.

—Acts 4:10–12

Therefore, brothers, let it be known to you that through this Man forgiveness of sins is proclaimed to you. And by Him everyone who believes is justified from everything from which you could not be justified by the law of Moses.

—Acts 13:38–39

So also is the resurrection of the dead. It is sown in corruption, it is raised in incorruption. It is sown in dishonor, it is raised in glory. It is sown in weakness, it is raised in power. It is sown a natural body, it is raised a spiritual body. There is a natural body, and there is a spiritual body.

—1 Corinthians 15:42–44

We know that if our earthly house, this tent, were to be destroyed, we have an eternal building of God in the heavens, a house not made with hands.

—2 Corinthians 5:1

For the Lord Himself will descend from heaven with a shout, with the voice of the archangel, and with the trumpet call of God. And the dead in Christ will rise first.

—1 Thessalonians 4:16

But is now revealed by the appearing of our Savior, Jesus Christ, who has abolished death and has brought life and immortality to light through the gospel.

—2 Timothy 1:10

Blessed be the God and Father of our Lord Jesus Christ, who according to His abundant mercy has given us a new birth into a living hope through the resurrection of Jesus Christ from the dead.

—1 Peter 1:3

And this is the promise that He has promised us—eternal life.

—1 John 2:25

And this is the testimony: that God has given us eternal life, and this life is in His Son.

—1 John 5:11

I have written these things to you who believe in the name of the Son of God, that you may know that you have eternal life, and that you may continue to believe in the name of the Son of God.

—1 John 5:13

And we know that the Son of God has come and has given us understanding, so that we may know Him who is true, and we are in Him who is true—His Son Jesus Christ. He is the true God and eternal life.

—1 John 5:20

EVERLASTING KINGDOM

The Lord has established His throne in the heavens, and His kingdom rules over all.

—Psalm 103:19

They shall speak of the glory of Your kingdom and talk of Your power.

—Psalm 145:11

Your kingdom is an everlasting kingdom, and Your dominion endures throughout all generations.

—Psalm 145:13

Seventy weeks have been determined for your people and upon your holy city, to finish the transgression, and to make an end of sins, and to make atonement for iniquity, and to bring in everlasting righteousness, and to seal up the vision and prophecy, and to anoint the most holy place.

—Daniel 9:24

Jesus answered, "Truly, truly I say to you, unless a man is born of water and the Spirit, he cannot enter the kingdom of God."

—John 3:5

For the kingdom of God does not mean eating and drinking, but righteousness and peace and joy in the Holy Spirit.

—Romans 14:17

EVIL

And call on Me in the day of trouble; I will deliver you, and you will glorify Me.

—Psalm 50:15

Indeed, may he deliver the needy when he cries; the poor also, and him who has no helper. May he have compassion on the poor and needy, and save the lives of the needy. May he redeem their life from deceit and violence; and may their blood be precious in his sight.

—Psalm 72:12–14

Surely the righteous man shall not be moved; the righteous shall be in everlasting remembrance. He shall not be afraid of evil tidings; his heart is fixed, trusting in the LORD. His heart is established; he shall not be afraid, until he sees triumph upon his enemies.

—PSALM 112:6–8

The LORD shall protect you from all evil; He shall preserve your soul. The LORD shall preserve your going out and your coming in from now and for evermore.

—PSALM 121:7–8

The LORD said, "Truly I will set you free for good purposes. Truly I will cause the enemy to entreat you in the time of evil and in the time of affliction."

—JEREMIAH 15:11

You went forth to deliver Your people, to deliver Your anointed one. You wounded the head of the house of the wicked, laying him bare from head to foot.

—HABAKKUK 3:13

I do not pray that You should take them out of the world, but that You should keep them from the evil one.

—JOHN 17:15

Now we have received not the spirit of the world, but the Spirit which is of God, so that we might know the things that are freely given to us by God.

—1 CORINTHIANS 2:12

Lest Satan should take advantage of us. For we are not ignorant of his devices.

—2 CORINTHIANS 2:11

And you were dead in your trespasses and sins, in which you formerly walked according to the age of this world and according to the prince of the power of the air, the spirit who now works in the sons of disobedience.... Even when we were dead in sins, made us alive together with Christ (by grace you have been saved).

—Ephesians 2:1–2, 5

Remind them of these things, commanding them before the Lord that they not argue about words, which leads to nothing of value and to the destruction of those who hear them.

—2 Timothy 2:14

Therefore guard your minds, be sober, and hope to the end for the grace that is to be brought to you at the revelation of Jesus Christ. As obedient children do not conduct yourselves according to the former lusts in your ignorance. But as He who has called you is holy, so be holy in all your conduct.

—1 Peter 1:13–15

FAILURE

Then David said to Solomon his son, "Be strong and courageous, and take action. Do not be afraid nor be dismayed for the Lord God, my God, is with you. He will not leave you nor forsake you, until you have finished all the work of the service of the house of the Lord."

—1 Chronicles 28:20

I will lift up my eyes to the hills, from where comes my help? My help comes from the Lord, who made heaven and earth.

—Psalm 121:1–2

Though I walk in the midst of trouble, You will preserve me; You stretch forth Your hand against the wrath of my enemies, and Your right hand saves me.

—Psalm 138:7

When you pass through the waters, I will be with you. And through the rivers, they shall not overflow you. When you walk through the fire, you shall not be burned. Neither shall the flame kindle on you.

—Isaiah 43:2

It is of the Lord's mercies that we are not consumed, because His compassions do not fail. They are new every morning. Great is Your faithfulness.

—Lamentations 3:22–23

The Lord is good, a stronghold in the day of distress; and He knows those who take refuge in Him.

—Nahum 1:7

We know that all things work together for good to those who love God, to those who are called according to His purpose.

—Romans 8:28

For whatever was previously written was written for our instruction, so that through perseverance and encouragement of the Scriptures we might have hope.

—Romans 15:4

Blessed be God, the Father of our Lord Jesus Christ, the Father of mercies, and the God of all comfort, who comforts us in all our tribulation, that we may be able to comfort those who are in any trouble by the comfort with which we ourselves are comforted by God.

—2 Corinthians 1:3–4

All these things are for your sakes, so that the abundant grace through the thanksgiving of many might overflow to the glory of God. For this reason we do not lose heart: Even though our outward man is perishing, yet our inward man is being renewed day by day.

—2 Corinthians 4:15–16

But He said to me, "My grace is sufficient for you, for My strength is made perfect in weakness." Therefore most gladly I will boast in my weaknesses, that the power of Christ may rest upon me.

—2 Corinthians 12:9

I can do all things because of Christ who strengthens me.

—Philippians 4:13

FAITH

Abram believed the Lord, and He credited it to him as righteousness.

—Genesis 15:6

For we walk by faith, not by sight.

—2 Corinthians 5:7

You are all sons of God by faith in Christ Jesus.

—Galatians 3:26

For by grace you have been saved through faith, and this is not of yourselves. It is the gift of God.

—Ephesians 2:8

And that Christ may dwell in your hearts through faith; that you, being rooted and grounded in love, may be able to comprehend with all saints what is the breadth and length and depth and height, and to know the love of Christ which surpasses knowledge; that you may be filled with all the fullness of God.

—EPHESIANS 3:17–19

We give thanks to God and the Father of our Lord Jesus Christ, praying always for you. For we heard of your faith in Christ Jesus and your love for all the saints, because of the hope which is laid up for you in heaven, of which you have already heard in the word of the truth of the gospel.

—COLOSSIANS 1:3–5

As you have received Christ Jesus the Lord, so walk in Him, rooted and built up in Him and established in the faith, as you have been taught, and abounding with thanksgiving.

—COLOSSIANS 2:6–7

But continue in the things that you have learned and have been assured of, knowing those from whom you have learned them, and that since childhood you have known the Holy Scriptures, which are able to make you wise unto salvation through the faith that is in Christ Jesus.

—2 TIMOTHY 3:14–15

Now faith is the substance of things hoped for, the evidence of things not seen.

—HEBREWS 11:1

If any of you lacks wisdom, let him ask of God, who gives to all men liberally and without criticism, and it will be given to him. But let him ask in faith, without wavering. For he who wavers is like a wave of the sea, driven and tossed with the wind.

—James 1:5–6

In this you greatly rejoice, even though now, if for a little while, you have had to suffer various trials, in order that the genuineness of your faith, which is more precious than gold that perishes, though it is tried by fire, may be found to result in praise, glory, and honor at the revelation of Jesus Christ, whom, having not seen, you love; and in whom, though you do not see Him now, you believe and you rejoice with joy unspeakable and full of glory, receiving as the result of your faith the salvation of your souls.

—1 Peter 1:6–9

For this reason, make every effort to add virtue to your faith; and to your virtue, knowledge; and to your knowledge, self-control; and to your self-control, patient endurance; and to your patient endurance, godliness; and to your godliness, brotherly kindness; and to your brotherly kindness, love. For if these things reside in you and abound, they ensure that you will neither be useless nor unfruitful in the knowledge of our Lord Jesus Christ.

—2 Peter 1:5–8

Faithfulness, God's

Also the Strength of Israel will not lie nor repent. For He is not a man, that He should repent.

—1 Samuel 15:29

The Lord has recompensed me according to my righteousness, according to my cleanness in His sight. With the faithful You prove Yourself faithful, with the blameless You prove Yourself blameless.

—2 Samuel 22:25–26

Blessed be the Lord who has given rest to His people Israel according to all that He promised. Not one word of His promises which He gave by the hand of Moses His servant has failed.

—1 Kings 8:56

For the Lord is good; His mercy endures forever, and His faithfulness to all generations.

—Psalm 100:5

Do not let mercy and truth forsake you; bind them around your neck, write them on the tablet of your heart. So will you find favor and good understanding in the sight of God and man.

—Proverbs 3:3–4

Who then is a faithful and wise servant, whom his master has made ruler over his household to give them food at the appointed time? Blessed is that servant whom his master will find so doing when he comes. Truly, I say to you that he will make him ruler over all his goods.

—Matthew 24:45–47

His master said to him, "Well done, you good and faithful servant. You have been faithful over a few things. I will make you ruler over many things. Enter the joy of your master."

—Matthew 25:21

Moreover it is required in stewards that a man be found faithful.

—1 Corinthians 4:2

For all the promises of God in Him are "Yes," and in Him "Amen," to the glory of God through us.

—2 Corinthians 1:20

If we are faithless, He remains faithful; He cannot deny Himself.

—2 Timothy 2:13

Let us firmly hold the profession of our faith without wavering, for He who promised is faithful.

—Hebrews 10:23

The Lord is not slow concerning His promise, as some count slowness. But He is patient with us, because He does not want any to perish, but all to come to repentance.

—2 Peter 3:9

FAME

The lips of the wise disperse knowledge, but the heart of the foolish does not do so.

—Proverbs 15:7

Better is the poor who walks in his integrity, than he who is perverse in his lips and is a fool.

—Proverbs 19:1

Better is the poor who walks in his uprightness, than he who is perverse in his ways, though he be rich.

—Proverbs 28:6

I urge you therefore, brothers, by the mercies of God, that you present your bodies as a living sacrifice, holy, and acceptable to God, which is your reasonable service of worship.

—Romans 12:1

In all things presenting yourself as an example of good works: in doctrine, showing integrity, seriousness, sincerity...

—Titus 2:7

For "All flesh is as grass, and all the glory of man as the flower of grass: The grass withers, and its flower falls away."

—1 Peter 1:24

Family Needs

I will establish My covenant between Me and you and your descendants after you throughout their generations for an everlasting covenant, to be God to you and your descendants after you.

—Genesis 17:7

Bless the Lord, you His angels, who are mighty, and do His commands, and obey the voice of His word.

—Psalm 103:20

Look, children are a gift of the Lord, and the fruit of the womb is a reward.

—Psalm 127:3

In the fear of the Lord is strong confidence, and His children will have a place of refuge. The fear of the Lord is a fountain of life, to depart from the snares of death.

—Proverbs 14:26–27

And I will compensate you for the years the locusts have eaten—the larval locust, hopper locust and fledging locust—My great army which I sent among you.

—Joel 2:25

They brought young children to Him, that He might touch them. But the disciples rebuked those who brought them. But when Jesus saw it, He was very displeased and said to them, "Allow the little children to come to Me, and do not forbid them, for of such is the kingdom of God. Truly I say to you, whoever does not receive the kingdom of God as a little child shall not enter it." And He took them up in His arms, put His hands on them, and blessed them.

—Mark 10:13–16

FATHERHOOD

In distress You make room for me. Have mercy on me, and hear my prayer. O people, how long will you turn my glory into shame? How long will you love vanity, and seek after lies? Selah.

—Psalm 4:1–2

Like a father shows compassion to his children, so the Lord gives compassion to those who fear Him.

—Psalm 103:13

He who spares his rod hates his son, but he who loves him disciplines him early.

—Proverbs 13:24

Chasten your son while there is hope, and let not your soul spare for his crying.

—Proverbs 19:18

The just man walks in his integrity; his children are blessed after him.

—Proverbs 20:7

Have we not all one Father? Has not one God created us? Why do we deal treacherously with one another, by profaning the covenant of our fathers?

—Malachi 2:10

FAVOR, GOD'S

By this I know that You favor me, because my enemy does not triumph over me.

—Psalm 41:11

May God be gracious to us, and bless us, and cause His face to shine on us.... God will bless us, and all the ends of the earth will fear Him.

—Psalm 67:1, 7

Remember me, O Lord, when You give favor to Your people; visit me with Your deliverance.

—Psalm 106:4

In righteousness you shall be established. You shall be far from oppression, for you shall not fear, and from terror, for it shall not come near you.

—Isaiah 54:14

"No weapon that is formed against you shall prosper. And every tongue that shall rise against you in judgment, you shall condemn. This is the heritage of the servants of the Lord, and their vindication is from Me," says the Lord.

—Isaiah 54:17

To proclaim the acceptable year of the LORD and the day of vengeance of our God; to comfort all who mourn.

—ISAIAH 61:2

For the weapons of our warfare are not carnal, but mighty through God to the pulling down of strongholds.

—2 CORINTHIANS 10:4

Christ has redeemed us from the curse of the law by being made a curse for us—as it is written, "Cursed is every one who hangs on a tree."

—GALATIANS 3:13

Blessed be the God and Father of our Lord Jesus Christ, who has blessed us with every spiritual blessing in the heavenly places in Christ.

—EPHESIANS 1:3

And above all, taking the shield of faith, with which you will be able to extinguish all the fiery arrows of the evil one.

—EPHESIANS 6:16

Take the helmet of salvation and the sword of the Spirit, which is the word of God.

—EPHESIANS 6:17

You are of God, little children, and have overcome them, because He who is in you is greater than he who is in the world.

—1 JOHN 4:4

FEAR

God is our refuge and strength, a well-proven help in trouble.

—PSALM 46:1

He shall cover you with his feathers, and under His wings you shall find protection; His faithfulness shall be your shield and wall. You shall not be afraid of the terror by night, nor of the arrow that flies by day; nor of the pestilence that pursues in darkness, nor of the destruction that strikes at noonday.

—PSALM 91:4–6

But whoever listens to me will dwell safely, and will be secure from fear of evil.

—PROVERBS 1:33

When you lie down, you will not be afraid; yes, you will lie down and your sleep will be sweet.

—PROVERBS 3:24

The fear of man brings a snare, but whoever puts his trust in the LORD will be safe.

—PROVERBS 29:25

It shall come to pass in the day that the LORD shall give you rest from your sorrow, and from your fear, and from the hard bondage in which you were made to serve.

—ISAIAH 14:3

I, even I, am He who comforts you. Who are you that you should be afraid of a man who shall die, and of the son of man who shall be made as grass…?

—ISAIAH 51:12

Do not fear those who kill the body, but are not able to kill the soul. But rather fear Him who is able to destroy both soul and body in hell.

—MATTHEW 10:28

He said to them, "Why are you so fearful? How is that you have no faith?"

—MARK 4:40

For you have not received the spirit of slavery again to fear. But you have received the Spirit of adoption, by whom we cry, "Abba, Father."

—ROMANS 8:15

For God has not given us the spirit of fear, but of power, and love, and self-control.

—2 TIMOTHY 1:7

"For the eyes of the Lord are on the righteous, and His ears are open to their prayers, but the face of the Lord is against those who do evil." Who is he who will harm you if you follow that which is good? But even if you suffer for the sake of righteousness, you are blessed. "Do not be afraid of their terror, do not be troubled."

—1 PETER 3:12–14

FELLOWSHIP

Iron sharpens iron, so a man sharpens the countenance of his friend.

—PROVERBS 27:17

For where two or three are assembled in My name, there I am in their midst.

—MATTHEW 18:20

For we are members of His body.

—EPHESIANS 5:30

Concerning the times and the seasons, brothers, you have no need that I write to you.

—1 Thessalonians 5:1

So comfort yourselves together, and edify one another, just as you are doing.

—1 Thessalonians 5:11

We declare to you that which we have seen and heard, that you also may have fellowship with us. And our fellowship is with the Father and with His Son Jesus Christ.

—1 John 1:3

FINDING GOD IN THE VALLEYS

Even though I walk through the valley of the shadow of death, I will fear no evil for You are with me; Your rod and Your staff they comfort me.

—Psalm 23:4

Say to those who are of a fearful heart, "Be strong, fear not. Your God will come with vengeance, even God with a recompense. He will come and save you."

—Isaiah 35:4

Therefore, I will allure her, and bring her into the wilderness, and speak tenderly to her. From there, I will give her vineyards to her, and the valley of Achor as a door of hope. She will respond there, as in the days of her youth, and as in the day when she came up out of the land of Egypt.

—Hosea 2:14–15

And it will be that in that day the mountains will drip sweet wine, and the hills will flow with milk, and all the streambeds of Judah will flow with water. A spring will proceed from the house of the LORD and will water the valley of Shittim.

—JOEL 3:18

Every valley shall be filled, and every mountain and hill shall be brought low. And the crooked shall be made straight, and the rough ways shall be made smooth.

—LUKE 3:5

The invisible things about Him—His eternal power and deity—have been clearly seen since the creation of the world and are understood by the things that are made, so that they are without excuse.

—ROMANS 1:20

FLATTERY

The LORD will cut off all flattering lips, and the tongue that speaks proud things.

—PSALM 12:3

He who goes about as a talebearer reveals secrets; therefore do not meddle with him who flatters with his lips.

—PROVERBS 20:19

A lying tongue hates those who are afflicted by it, and a flattering mouth works ruin.

—PROVERBS 26:28

For there shall be no more any vain vision or flattering divination within the house of Israel.

—EZEKIEL 12:24

For such people do not serve our Lord Jesus Christ, but their own appetites, and through smooth talk and flattery they deceive the hearts of the unsuspecting.

—ROMANS 16:18

These men are grumblers, complainers, who walk after their own lusts. Their mouths speak arrogant words, and they flatter others to gain profit.

—JUDE 16

FORGIVENESS

If My people, who are called by My name, will humble themselves and pray, and seek My face and turn from their wicked ways, then I will hear from heaven, and will forgive their sin and will heal their land.

—2 CHRONICLES 7:14

"Come now, and let us reason together," says the LORD. "Though your sins be as scarlet, they shall be as white as snow. Though they be red like crimson, they shall be as wool."

—ISAIAH 1:18

I, even I, am He who blots out your transgressions for My own sake, and will not remember your sins.

—ISAIAH 43:25

Peter said to them, "Repent and be baptized, every one of you, in the name of Jesus Christ for the forgiveness of sins, and you shall receive the gift of the Holy Spirit. For the promise is to you, and to your children, and to all who are far away, as many as the Lord our God will call."

—ACTS 2:38–39

In Him we have redemption through His blood and the forgiveness of sins according to the riches of His grace.

—Ephesians 1:7

And be kind one to another, tender-hearted, forgiving one another, just as God in Christ also forgave you.

—Ephesians 4:32

And you, who were formerly alienated and enemies in your mind by wicked works, yet now He has reconciled in the body of His flesh through death, to present you holy and blameless and above reproach in His sight.

—Colossians 1:21–22

And you, being dead in your sins and the uncircumcision of your flesh, He has resurrected together with Him, having forgiven you all sins.

—Colossians 2:13

Bear with one another and forgive one another. If anyone has a quarrel against anyone, even as Christ forgave you, so you must do.

—Colossians 3:13

For I will be merciful toward their unrighteousness, and their sins and their iniquities I will remember no more.

—Hebrews 8:12

If we say that we have no sin, we deceive ourselves, and the truth is not in us. If we confess our sins, He is faithful and just to forgive us our sins and cleanse us from all unrighteousness.

—1 John 1:8–9

My little children, I am writing these things to you, so that you do not sin. But if anyone does sin, we have an Advocate with the Father, Jesus Christ the Righteous One.

—1 John 2:1

FRIENDSHIP

The Lord spoke to Moses face to face, just as a man speaks to his friend. When he returned to the camp, his servant Joshua, the son of Nun, a young man, did not depart from the tent.

—Exodus 33:11

Jonathan made David swear again, because he loved him. For he loved him as he loved his own soul.

—1 Samuel 20:17

A despairing man should be shown kindness from his friend, or he forsakes the fear of the Almighty.

—Job 6:14

The righteous is a guide to his neighbors, but the way of the wicked leads them astray.

—Proverbs 12:26

He who walks with wise men will be wise, but a companion of fools will be destroyed.

—Proverbs 13:20

Two are better than one because there is a good reward for their labor together. For if they fall, then one will help up his companion. But how tragic to the one who falls, and there is no one else to help him up.

—Ecclesiastes 4:9–10

Also if two people lie together, then they will keep warm. But how can one keep warm by himself? And if someone might overpower another by himself, two people together can withstand him.

—Ecclesiastes 4:11–12

Do two people walk together, if they have not agreed?

—Amos 3:3

A new commandment I give to you, that you love one another, even as I have loved you, that you also love one another.

—John 13:34

I no longer call you servants, for a servant does not know what his master does. But I have called you friends, for everything that I have heard from My Father have I made known to you.

—John 15:15

Bear one another's burdens, and so fulfill the law of Christ.

—Galatians 6:2

You adulterers and adulteresses, do you not know that the friendship with the world is enmity with God? Whoever therefore will be a friend of the world is the enemy of God.

—James 4:4

FRUITFULNESS

He will be like a tree planted by the rivers of water, that brings forth its fruit in its season. Its leaf will not wither; and whatever he does will prosper.

—Psalm 1:3

They shall still bring forth fruit in old age; they shall be filled with vitality and foliage.

—Psalm 92:14

Therefore they will come and sing in the height of Zion, and will be joyful over the goodness of the Lord, for wheat and for wine and for oil and for the young of the flock and of the herd; and their souls will be as a watered garden. And they will not sorrow any more at all.

—Jeremiah 31:12

I will be like the dew to Israel; he shall grow like the lily and shall strike his roots like Lebanon.

—Hosea 14:5

I am the true vine, and My Father is the vinedresser. Every branch in Me that bears no fruit, He takes away. And every branch that bears fruit, He prunes, that it may bear more fruit. You are already clean through the word which I have spoken to you. Remain in Me, as I also remain in you. As a branch cannot bear fruit by itself, unless it remains in the vine, neither can you, unless you remain in Me.

—John 15:1–4

For if these things reside in you and abound, they ensure that you will neither be useless nor unfruitful in the knowledge of our Lord Jesus Christ.

—2 Peter 1:8

FRUSTRATION

In all your ways acknowledge Him, and He will direct your paths.

—Proverbs 3:6

Every way of a man is right in his own eyes, but the LORD weighs the hearts. To do justice and judgment is more acceptable to the LORD than sacrifice.

—PROVERBS 21:2–3

And I will make an everlasting covenant with them that I will not turn away from them, to do them good. But I will put My fear in their hearts so that they shall not depart from Me.

—JEREMIAH 32:40

Call to Me, and I will answer you, and show you great and mighty things which you do not know.

—JEREMIAH 33:3

Let us know, let us press on to know the LORD. His appearance is as sure as the dawn. He will come to us like the rain, like the spring rains, He will water the earth.

—HOSEA 6:3

Come to Me, all you who labor and are heavily burdened, and I will give you rest. Take My yoke upon you, and learn from Me. For I am meek and lowly in heart, and you will find rest for your souls.

—MATTHEW 11:28–29

We know that all things work together for good to those who love God, to those who are called according to His purpose.

—ROMANS 8:28

What then shall we say to these things? If God is for us, who can be against us? He who did not spare His own Son, but delivered Him up for us all, how shall He not with Him also freely give us all things?

—ROMANS 8:31–32

No temptation has taken you except what is common to man. God is faithful, and He will not permit you to be tempted above what you can endure, but will with the temptation also make a way to escape, that you may be able to bear it.

—1 Corinthians 10:13

Let us firmly hold the profession of our faith without wavering, for He who promised is faithful.

—Hebrews 10:23

Indeed we count them happy who endure. You have heard of the patience of Job and have seen the purpose of the Lord, that the Lord is very gracious and merciful.

—James 5:11

Cast all your care upon Him, because He cares for you.

—1 Peter 5:7

FULFILLMENT

Peter said to them, "Repent and be baptized, every one of you, in the name of Jesus Christ for the forgiveness of sins, and you shall receive the gift of the Holy Spirit."

—Acts 2:38

That if you confess with your mouth Jesus is Lord, and believe in your heart that God has raised Him from the dead, you will be saved.

—Romans 10:9

For by grace you have been saved through faith, and this is not of yourselves. It is the gift of God, not of works, so that no one should boast.

—Ephesians 2:8–9

Study to show yourself approved by God, a workman who need not be ashamed, rightly dividing the word of truth.

—2 Timothy 2:15

Then He said, "See, I have come to do Your will, O God." He takes away the first that He may establish the second.

—Hebrews 10:9

But you are a chosen people, a royal priesthood, a holy nation, a people for God's own possession, so that you may declare the goodness of Him who has called you out of darkness into His marvelous light.

—1 Peter 2:9

FUTURE

Hear this, all you people; give ear, all you inhabitants of the world, both low and high, rich and poor, together. My mouth will speak wisdom, and the meditation of my heart will be understanding. I will incline my ear to a parable; I will expound my riddle with a harp.

—Psalm 49:1–4

My son, do not forget my teaching, but let your heart keep my commandments; for length of days and long life and peace will they add to you.

—Proverbs 3:1–2

Without counsel, purposes are disappointed, but in the multitude of counselors they are established.

—Proverbs 15:22

A man's heart devises his way, but the Lord directs his steps.

—Proverbs 16:9

Do not let your heart envy sinners, but continue in the fear of the LORD all day long. For surely there is an end, and your expectation will not be cut off.

—PROVERBS 23:17–18

Do not fear, for I am with you. Do not be dismayed, for I am your God. I will strengthen you. Indeed, I will help you. Indeed, I will uphold you with My righteous right hand....I will open rivers in high places, and fountains in the midst of the valleys. I will make the wilderness a pool of water, and the dry land springs of water.

—ISAIAH 41:10, 18

"For I know the plans that I have for you," says the LORD, "plans for peace and not for evil, to give you a future and a hope."

—JEREMIAH 29:11

"There is hope for your future," says the LORD, "that your children will come back to their own border."

—JEREMIAH 31:17

Jesus said, "If you can believe! All things are possible to him who believes."

—MARK 9:23

In My Father's house are many dwelling places. If it were not so, I would have told you. I am going to prepare a place for you. And if I go and prepare a place for you, I will come again and receive you to Myself, that where I am, you may be also.

—JOHN 14:2–3

I have told you these things so that in Me you may have peace. In the world you will have tribulation. But be of good cheer. I have overcome the world.

—John 16:33

Come now, you who say, "Today or tomorrow we will go into this city, spend a year there, buy and sell, and make a profit," whereas you do not know what will happen tomorrow. What is your life? It is just a vapor that appears for a little while and then vanishes away. Instead you ought to say, "If the Lord wills, we shall live and do this or that."

—James 4:13–15

GAMBLING

You shall not steal....You shall not covet your neighbor's house; you shall not covet your neighbor's wife, or his man-servant, or his maidservant, or his ox, or his donkey, or anything that is your neighbor's.

—Exodus 20:15, 17

I will not be brought under the power of anything.

—1 Corinthians 6:12

Therefore, whether you eat, or drink, or whatever you do, do it all to the glory of God.

—1 Corinthians 10:31

I am ready to come to you this third time. And I will not be burdensome to you, for I do not seek what is yours, but you. For the children ought not to lay up for the parents, but the parents for the children.

—2 Corinthians 12:14

Therefore put to death the parts of your earthly nature: sexual immorality, uncleanness, inordinate affection, evil desire, and covetousness, which is idolatry. Because of these things, the wrath of God comes on the sons of disobedience.

—Colossians 3:5–6

For when we were with you, we commanded you that if any will not work, neither shall he eat.

—2 Thessalonians 3:10

Garment of Righteousness

For You have turned my mourning into dancing; You have put off my sackcloth and girded me with gladness, so that my glory may sing praise to You and not be silent. O Lord my God, I will give thanks to You forever.

—Psalm 30:11–12

I will greatly rejoice in the Lord, my soul shall be joyful in my God. For He has clothed me with the garments of salvation. He has covered me with the robe of righteousness, as a bridegroom decks himself with ornaments, and as a bride adorns herself with her jewels.

—Isaiah 61:10

"Now when I passed by you and looked upon you, you were old enough for love. So I spread My garment over you and covered your nakedness. Indeed, I swore to you, and entered into a covenant with you," says the Lord God, "and you became Mine."

—Ezekiel 16:8

But the father said to his servants, "Bring out the best robe and put it on him. And put a ring on his hand and shoes on his feet."

—Luke 15:22

For as many of you as have been baptized into Christ have put on Christ.

—Galatians 3:27

Stand therefore, having your waist girded with truth, having put on the breastplate of righteousness.

—Ephesians 6:14

Generational Curses

Then God said, "This is the sign of the covenant which I am making between Me and you and every living creature that is with you, for all future generations."

—Genesis 9:12

I will set your boundaries from the Red Sea to the sea of the Philistines, and from the desert to the River; for I will deliver the inhabitants of the land into your hand, and you will drive them out before you. You must not make a covenant with them or with their gods. They shall not live in your land, lest they cause you to sin against Me, for if you serve their gods, it will surely be a snare to you.

—Exodus 23:31–33

Thus says the Lord, I am bringing disaster on this place and all who dwell in it, even all the curses that are written in the book that they read before the king of Judah.

—2 Chronicles 34:24

I the LORD have called You in righteousness, and will hold Your hand, and will keep You, and appoint You for a covenant of the people, for a light of the Gentiles.

—ISAIAH 42:6

The Spirit of the Lord GOD is upon Me because the LORD has anointed Me to preach good news to the poor. He has sent Me to heal the brokenhearted, to proclaim liberty to the captives, and the opening of the prison to those who are bound; to proclaim the acceptable year of the LORD and the day of vengeance of our God; to comfort all who mourn.

—ISAIAH 61:1–2

But they rebelled and grieved His Holy Spirit. Therefore, He turned Himself to be their enemy, and He fought against them.

—ISAIAH 63:10

Jesus went throughout all Galilee teaching in their synagogues, preaching the gospel of the kingdom, and healing all kinds of sickness and all sorts of diseases among the people.

—MATTHEW 4:23

Again, you have heard that it was said by the ancients, "You shall not swear falsely, but shall fulfill your oaths to the Lord."

—MATTHEW 5:33

He called His twelve disciples to Him and gave them authority over unclean spirits, to cast them out, and to heal all kinds of sickness and all kinds of disease.

—MATTHEW 10:1

Therefore if the Son sets you free, you shall be free indeed.

—JOHN 8:36

You stiff-necked people, uncircumcised in heart and ears! You always resist the Holy Spirit. As your fathers did, so do you.
—Acts 7:51

Follow the pattern of sound teaching which you have heard from me in the faith and love that is in Christ Jesus.
—2 Timothy 1:13

GIFTS FROM GOD

If you then, being evil, know how to give good gifts to your children, how much more will your heavenly Father give the Holy Spirit to those who ask Him?
—Luke 11:13

Jesus answered her, "If you knew the gift of God, and who it is who is saying to you, 'Give Me a drink,' you would have asked Him, and He would have given you living water."
—John 4:10

Being assembled with them, He commanded them, "Do not depart from Jerusalem, but wait for the promise of the Father, of which you have heard from Me."
—Acts 1:4

We have diverse gifts according to the grace that is given to us: if prophecy, according to the proportion of faith.
—Romans 12:6

There are various gifts, but the same Spirit. There are differences of administrations, but the same Lord. There are various operations, but it is the same God who operates them all in all people. But the manifestation of the Spirit is given to everyone for the common good.

—1 Corinthians 12:4–7

God has put these in the church: first apostles, second prophets, third teachers, after that miracles, then gifts of healings, helps, governments, and various tongues. Are all apostles? Are all prophets? Are all teachers? Are all workers of miracles? Do all have the gifts of healings? Do all speak with tongues? Do all interpret? But earnestly covet the greater gifts.

—1 Corinthians 12:28–31

So, seeing that you are zealous of spiritual gifts, seek that you may excel to the edifying of the church.

—1 Corinthians 14:12

For by grace you have been saved through faith, and this is not of yourselves. It is the gift of God.

—Ephesians 2:8

Do not neglect the gift that is in you, which was given to you by prophecy, with the laying on of hands by the elders.

—1 Timothy 4:14

Therefore I remind you to stir up the gift of God, which is in you by the laying on of my hands.

—2 Timothy 1:6

Every good gift and every perfect gift is from above and comes down from the Father of lights, with whom is no change or shadow of turning.

—James 1:17

As every one has received a gift, even so serve one another with it, as good stewards of the manifold grace of God.

—1 PETER 4:10

GIFTS OF THE SPIRIT

We have diverse gifts according to the grace that is given to us: if prophecy, according to the proportion of faith; if service, in serving; he who teaches, in teaching; he who exhorts, in exhortation; he who gives, with generosity; he who rules, with diligence; he who shows mercy, with cheerfulness.

—ROMANS 12:6–8

But the manifestation of the Spirit is given to everyone for the common good.

—1 CORINTHIANS 12:7

To one is given by the Spirit the word of wisdom, to another the word of knowledge by the same Spirit, to another faith by the same Spirit, to another gifts of healings by the same Spirit, to another the working of miracles, to another prophecy, to another discerning of spirits, to another various kinds of tongues, and to another the interpretation of tongues.

—1 CORINTHIANS 12:8–10

He gave some to be apostles, prophets, evangelists, pastors and teachers, for the equipping of the saints, for the work of service, and for the building up of the body of Christ.

—EPHESIANS 4:11–12

Do not neglect the gift that is in you, which was given to you by prophecy, with the laying on of hands by the elders. Meditate on these things. Give yourself completely to them, that your progress may be known to everyone. Take heed to

163

yourself and to the doctrine. Continue in them, for in doing this you will save both yourself and those who hear you.

—1 Timothy 4:14–16

As every one has received a gift, even so serve one another with it, as good stewards of the manifold grace of God.

—1 Peter 4:10

GIVING

Honor the Lord with your substance, and with the first-fruits of all your increase; so your barns will be filled with plenty, and your presses will burst out with new wine.

—Proverbs 3:9–10

Do not withhold good from those to whom it is due, when it is in the power of your hand to do it.

—Proverbs 3:27

There is one who scatters, and yet increases; and there is one who withholds more than is right, but it leads to poverty.

—Proverbs 11:24

The generous soul will be made rich, and he who waters will be watered also himself.

—Proverbs 11:25

He covets greedily all the day long, but the righteous gives and does not spare.

—Proverbs 21:26

Will a man rob God? Yet you have robbed Me. But you say, "How have we robbed You?" In tithes and offerings.

—Malachi 3:8

"Bring all the tithes into the storehouse, that there may be food in My house, and test Me now in this," says the Lord of Hosts, "if I will not open for you the windows of heaven and pour out for you a blessing, that there will not be room enough to receive it. I will rebuke the devourer for your sakes, so that it will not destroy the fruit of your ground, and the vines in your field will not fail to bear fruit," says the Lord of Hosts.

—Malachi 3:10–11

Heal the sick, cleanse the lepers, raise the dead, and cast out demons. Freely you have received, freely give.

—Matthew 10:8

And whoever gives even a cup of cold water to one of these little ones in the name of a disciple, truly I tell you, he shall in no way lose his reward.

—Matthew 10:42

Give, and it will be given to you: Good measure, pressed down, shaken together, and running over, will men give unto you. For with the measure you use, it will be measured unto you.

—Luke 6:38

In all things I have shown you how, working like this, you must help the weak, remembering the words of the Lord Jesus, how He said, "It is more blessed to give than to receive."

—Acts 20:35

Let every man give according to the purposes in his heart, not grudgingly or out of necessity, for God loves a cheerful giver.

—2 Corinthians 9:7

GOALS

But seek first the kingdom of God and His righteousness, and all these things shall be given to you.

—MATTHEW 6:33

Do you not know that all those who run in a race run, but one receives the prize? So run, that you may obtain it. Everyone who strives for the prize exercises self-control in all things. Now they do it to obtain a corruptible crown, but we an incorruptible one.

—1 CORINTHIANS 9:24–25

So whether present or absent, we labor that we may be accepted by Him.

—2 CORINTHIANS 5:9

And let us not grow weary in doing good, for in due season we shall reap, if we do not give up.

—GALATIANS 6:9

Not that I have already attained or have already been perfected, but I follow after it so that I may lay hold of that for which I was seized by Christ Jesus. Brothers, I do not count myself to have attained, but this one thing I do, forgetting those things which are behind and reaching forward to those things which are ahead, I press toward the goal to the prize of the high calling of God in Christ Jesus.

—PHILIPPIANS 3:12–14

Now the goal of this command is love from a pure heart, and from a good conscience, and from sincere faith.

—1 TIMOTHY 1:5

GOD HEARS OUR PRAYERS

I called on You, for You will answer me, O God. Incline Your ear to me, and hear my speech. Show marvelously Your lovingkindness, O Deliverer of those who seek refuge by Your right hand from those who arise in opposition. Keep me as the apple of your eye, hide me under the shadow of Your wings, from the wicked who bring ruin to me, from my deadly enemies who surround me.

—PSALM 17:6–9

Arise, O LORD, confront him, make him bow down; deliver my soul from the wicked by Your sword. From men by Your hand, O LORD, from men of the world, whose portion is in this life, and whose belly You fill with Your treasure; they are full of children, and leave their affluence to their babes.

—PSALM 17:13–14

I will abundantly bless her provisions; I will satisfy her poor with bread.

—PSALM 132:15

But this thing I commanded them, saying, "Obey My voice, and I will be your God, and you shall be My people. And walk in all the ways that I have commanded you, that it may be well with you."

—JEREMIAH 7:23

I will make them and the places round about My hill a blessing. And I will cause the showers to come down in their season. They shall be showers of blessing.

—EZEKIEL 34:26

For the eyes of the Lord are on the righteous, and His ears are open to their prayers, but the face of the Lord is against those who do evil.

—1 Peter 3:12

GOD'S CARE

You must remember that the Lord your God led you all the way these forty years in the wilderness, to humble you, and to prove you, to know what was in your heart, whether you would keep His commandments or not.

—Deuteronomy 8:2

For the eyes of the Lord move about on all the earth to strengthen the heart that is completely toward Him. You have acted foolishly in this, and from this point forward you will have wars.

—2 Chronicles 16:9

Bless the Lord, O my soul, and forget not all His benefits, who forgives all your iniquities, who heals all your diseases, who redeems your life from the pit, who crowns you with lovingkindness and tender mercies, He satisfies your mouth with good things, so that your youth is renewed like the eagle's.

—Psalm 103:2–5

I love the Lord, because He has heard my voice and my supplications.

—Psalm 116:1

O Lord, You have searched me and known me. You know when I sit down and when I get up; You understand my thought from far off. You search my path and my lying down and are aware of all my ways.

—Psalm 139:1–3

You brought my inner parts into being; You wove me in my mother's womb.

—Psalm 139:13

"But this shall be the covenant that I will make with the house of Israel after those days," says the Lord, "I will put My law within them and write it in their hearts. And will be their God, and they shall be My people."

—Jeremiah 31:33

It is of the Lord's mercies that we are not consumed, because His compassions do not fail. They are new every morning. Great is Your faithfulness. "The Lord is my portion," says my soul, "therefore I will hope in Him." The Lord is good to those who wait for Him, to the soul that seeks Him. It is good that a man should both hope and quietly wait for the salvation of the Lord.

—Lamentations 3:22–26

Are not two sparrows sold for a penny? And not one of them will fall to the ground without your Father. But the very hairs of your head are all numbered. Therefore do not fear. You are more valuable than many sparrows.

—Matthew 10:29–31

For I will give you a mouth and wisdom, which all your opponents will neither be able to refute nor resist.

—Luke 21:15

Not that we are sufficient in ourselves to take credit for anything of ourselves, but our sufficiency is from God.

—2 Corinthians 3:5

I can do all things because of Christ who strengthens me.

—Philippians 4:13

God's Name Endures

The heavens declare the glory of God, and the firmament shows His handiwork.

—Psalm 19:1

May his name endure forever; may his name increase as long as the sun; and may people bless themselves by him; may all nations call him blessed.

—Psalm 72:17

The Lord reigns; He is clothed with majesty; the Lord is robed with a belt of strength. Indeed, the world is established; it cannot be moved.

—Psalm 93:1

For I know that the Lord is great, and that our Lord is above all gods. Whatever the Lord pleases, He does in heaven and on earth, in the seas and all the depths. He causes the clouds to ascend from the ends of the earth; He makes lightning for the rain; He brings the wind out from His storehouses.

—Psalm 135:5–7

Your name, O Lord, endures forever; and Your renown, O Lord, throughout all generations. For the Lord will defend His people, and He will have compassion on His servants.

—Psalm 135:13–14

For unto us a child is born, unto us a son is given, and the government shall be upon his shoulder. And his name shall be called Wonderful Counselor, Mighty God, Eternal Father, Prince of Peace. Of the increase of his government and peace there shall be no end, upon the throne of David and over his kingdom, to order it and to establish it with justice and with righteousness, from now until forever. The zeal of the LORD of Hosts will perform this.

—ISAIAH 9:6–7

GOD'S PRESENCE

And He said, "My presence will go with you, and I will give you rest."

—EXODUS 33:14

If my father and my mother forsake me, then the LORD will take me in.

—PSALM 27:10

Be still and know that I am God; I will be exalted among the nations, I will be exalted in the earth.

—PSALM 46:10

He shall call upon Me, and I will answer him; I will be with him in trouble, and I will deliver him and honor him. With long life I will satisfy him and show him My salvation.

—PSALM 91:15–16

See, I have inscribed you on the palms of My hands. Your walls are continually before Me.

—ISAIAH 49:16

"For the mountains may be removed, and the hills may shake, but My kindness shall not depart from you, nor shall My covenant of peace be removed," says the LORD who has mercy on you.

—ISAIAH 54:10

You shall seek Me and find Me, when you shall search for Me with all your heart.

—JEREMIAH 29:13

Remain in Me, as I also remain in you. As the branch cannot bear fruit by itself, unless it remains in the vine, neither can you, unless you remain in Me.

—JOHN 15:4

As the Father loved Me, I also loved you. Remain in My love.

—JOHN 15:9

Who shall separate us from the love of Christ? Shall tribulation, or distress, or persecution, or famine, or nakedness, or peril, or sword?...No, in all these things we are more than conquerors through Him who loved us. For I am persuaded that neither death nor life, neither angels nor principalities nor powers, neither things present nor things to come, neither height nor depth, nor any other created thing, shall be able to separate us from the love of God, which is in Christ Jesus our Lord.

—ROMANS 8:35, 37–39

Jesus Christ is the same yesterday, and today, and forever.

—HEBREWS 13:8

No one has seen God at any time. If we love one another, God dwells in us, and His love is perfected in us.

—1 John 4:12

GOSSIP

You shall not go around as a slanderer among your people, nor shall you stand by while the life of your neighbor is in danger: I am the Lord.

—Leviticus 19:16

Keep your tongue from evil, and your lips from speaking deceit.

—Psalm 34:13

I said, "I will take heed of my ways so that I do not sin with my tongue; I will keep my mouth muzzled while the wicked are before me."

—Psalm 39:1

These six things the Lord hates, yes, seven are an abomination to Him: a proud look, a lying tongue, and hands that shed innocent blood, a heart that devises wicked imaginations, feet that are swift in running to mischief, a false witness who speaks lies, and he who sows discord among brethren.

—Proverbs 6:16–19

A talebearer reveals secrets, but he who is of a faithful spirit conceals the matter.

—Proverbs 11:13

The words of a talebearer are as wounds, and they go down into the innermost parts of the body.

—Proverbs 18:8

He who goes about as a talebearer reveals secrets; therefore do not meddle with him who flatters with his lips.

—Proverbs 20:19

Where there is no wood, the fire goes out; so where there is no talebearer, the strife ceases. As charcoal is to burning coals, and wood to fire, so is a contentious man to kindle strife.

—Proverbs 26:20–21

Let no unwholesome word proceed out of your mouth, but only that which is good for building up, that it may give grace to the listeners.

—Ephesians 4:29

If anyone among you seems to be religious and does not bridle his tongue, but deceives his own heart, this man's religion is vain.

—James 1:26

Even so, the tongue is a little part of the body and boasts great things. See how great a forest a little fire kindles.

—James 3:5

Out of the same mouth proceed blessing and cursing. My brothers, these things ought not to be so.

—James 3:10

GRACE

Because if you return to the Lord, your brothers and children will find compassion before those who have taken them captive, in order to return you to this land. For the Lord your God is gracious and compassionate. He will not turn His face from you if you all return to Him.

—2 Chronicles 30:9

The righteous also will hold to his way, and he who has clean hands will be stronger and stronger.

—Job 17:9

Surely He scorns the scornful, but He gives favor to the humble.

—Proverbs 3:34

But the path of the just is as the shining light, that shines more and more unto the perfect day.

—Proverbs 4:18

We have all received from His fullness grace upon grace. For the law was given through Moses; grace and truth came through Jesus Christ. No one has seen God at any time. The only Son, who is at the Father's side, has made Him known.

—John 1:16–18

Jesus said to him, "Rise, take up your bed and walk."

—John 5:8

Therefore, if any man is in Christ, he is a new creature. Old things have passed away. Look, all things have become new.

—2 Corinthians 5:17

For you know the grace of our Lord Jesus Christ, that though He was rich, yet for your sakes He became poor, that through His poverty you might be rich.

—2 Corinthians 8:9

And this I pray, that your love may abound yet more and more in knowledge and in all discernment.

—Philippians 1:9

Which has come to you, as it has in all the world, and brings forth fruit, as it has also in you, since the day you heard it and knew the grace of God in truth.

—Colossians 1:6

And you, being dead in your sins and the uncircumcision of your flesh, He has resurrected together with Him, having forgiven you all sins. He blotted out the handwriting of ordinances that was against us and contrary to us, and He took it out of the way, nailing it to the cross.

—Colossians 2:13–14

Grace, mercy, and peace will be with us from God the Father and from the Lord Jesus Christ, the Son of the Father, in truth and love.

—2 John 3

GRIEF AND DEATH

The Lord kills and makes alive. He brings down to the grave and brings up.

—1 Samuel 2:6

You will guide me with Your counsel, and afterward receive me to glory. Whom have I in heaven but You? And there is nothing on earth that I desire besides You. My flesh and my heart fails, but God is the strength of my heart and my portion forever.

—Psalm 73:24–26

This is my comfort in my affliction, for Your word revives me.

—Psalm 119:50

He shall enter into peace. They shall rest in their beds, each one walking in his uprightness.

—Isaiah 57:2

And at that time Michael shall stand up, the great prince who stands guard over the sons of your people. And there shall be a time of trouble such as never was since there was a nation even to that time. And at that time your people shall be delivered, everyone who shall be found written in the book. Many of those who sleep in the dust of the earth shall awake, some to everlasting life, but others to shame and everlasting contempt.

—Daniel 12:1–2

Jesus wept. Then the Jews said, "See how He loved him."

—John 11:35–36

If in this life only we have hope in Christ, we are of all men most miserable. But now is Christ risen from the dead and become the firstfruits of those who have fallen asleep. For since death came by man, by man came also the resurrection of the dead. For as in Adam all die, even so in Christ shall all be made alive.

—1 Corinthians 15:19–22

We know that if our earthly house, this tent, were to be destroyed, we have an eternal building of God in the heavens, a house not made with hands.

—2 Corinthians 5:1

Who died for us, so that whether we are awake or asleep, we should live together with Him.

—1 Thessalonians 5:10

From now on a crown of righteousness is laid up for me, which the Lord, the righteous Judge, will give me on that Day, and not only to me but also to all who have loved His appearing.

—2 Timothy 4:8

So that by two immutable things, in which it was impossible for God to lie, we who have fled for refuge might have strong encouragement to hold fast to the hope set before us. We have this hope as a sure and steadfast anchor of the soul, which enters the Inner Place behind the veil.

—Hebrews 6:18–19

Blessed be the God and Father of our Lord Jesus Christ, who according to His abundant mercy has given us a new birth into a living hope through the resurrection of Jesus Christ from the dead, to an incorruptible and undefiled inheritance that does not fade away, kept in heaven for you, who are protected by the power of God through faith for a salvation ready to be revealed in the last time.

—1 Peter 1:3–5

GUIDANCE

This book of the law must not depart from your mouth. Meditate on it day and night so that you may act carefully according to all that is written in it. For then you will make your way successful, and you will be wise.

—Joshua 1:8

For the Lord gives wisdom; out of His mouth come knowledge and understanding.

—Proverbs 2:6

When you go, they will lead you; when you sleep, they will keep you; and when you awake, they will speak with you. For the commandment is a lamp, and the law is light; and reproofs of instruction are the way of life.

—Proverbs 6:22–23

The righteousness of the upright will direct his way, but the wicked will fall by his own wickedness.

—Proverbs 11:5

The way of a fool is right in his own eyes, but he who listens to counsel is wise.

—Proverbs 12:15

Incline your ear and hear the words of the wise, and apply your heart to my knowledge. For it is a pleasant thing if you keep them within you; they will readily be fitted in your lips. That your trust may be in the Lord, I have made known to you this day, even to you.

—Proverbs 22:17–19

Your ears shall hear a word behind you saying, "This is the way, walk in it," whenever you turn to the right hand and when you turn to the left.

—Isaiah 30:21

I will bring the blind by a way that they did not know. I will lead them in paths that they have not known. I will make darkness light before them and crooked things straight. These things I will do for them and not forsake them.

—Isaiah 42:16

Thus says the Lord, your Redeemer, the Holy One of Israel. "I am the Lord your God who teaches you to profit, who leads you by the way that you should go."

—Isaiah 48:17

And the Lord shall guide you continually, and satisfy your soul in drought, and strengthen your bones. And you shall be like a watered garden, and like a spring of water, whose waters do not fail.

—Isaiah 58:11

Jesus answered him, "If a man loves Me, he will keep My word. My Father will love him, and We will come to him, and make Our home with him. He who does not love Me does not keep My words. The word which you hear is not Mine, but the Father's who sent Me."

—John 14:23–24

If any of you lacks wisdom, let him ask of God, who gives to all men liberally and without criticism, and it will be given to him.

—James 1:5

GUILT

When I kept silent about my sin, my bones wasted away through my groaning pain all day long....I acknowledged my sin to You, and my iniquity I did not conceal. I said, "I will confess my transgressions to the LORD," and You forgave the iniquity of my sin. Selah.

—PSALM 32:3, 5

For my iniquities have passed over my head, as a heavy burden they are too heavy for me.

—PSALM 38:4

As far as the east is from the west, so far has He removed our transgressions from us.

—PSALM 103:12

"Come now, and let us reason together," says the LORD. "Though your sins be as scarlet, they shall be as white as snow. Though they be red like crimson, they shall be as wool."

—ISAIAH 1:18

And he laid it on my mouth, and said, "This has touched your lips, and your iniquity is taken away, and your sin purged."

—ISAIAH 6:7

I, even I, am He who blots out your transgressions for My own sake, and will not remember your sins.

—ISAIAH 43:25

"For though you wash yourself with lye, and take much soap, yet your iniquity is marked before Me," says the Lord GOD.

—JEREMIAH 2:22

"They shall teach no more every man his neighbor and every man his brother, saying, 'Know the LORD,' for they all shall know Me, from the least of them to the greatest of them," says the Lord, "for I will forgive their iniquity, and I will remember their sin no more."

—Jeremiah 31:34

I will cleanse them from all their iniquity whereby they have sinned against Me. And I will pardon all their iniquities whereby they have sinned and whereby they have transgressed against Me.

—Jeremiah 33:8

For I will be merciful toward their unrighteousness, and their sins and their iniquities I will remember no more.

—Hebrews 8:12

For whoever shall keep the whole law and yet offend in one point is guilty of breaking the whole law.

—James 2:10

I am writing to you, little children, because your sins are forgiven for His name's sake.

—1 John 2:12

HEALING

The Lord will sustain them on the sickbed; You will restore all his lying down in his illness.

—Psalm 41:3

It will be health to your body, and strength to your bones.

—Proverbs 3:8

I will bring it health and healing, and I will heal them; and I will reveal to them the abundance of peace and truth.

—Jeremiah 33:6

To fulfill what was spoken by Isaiah the prophet, "He Himself took our infirmities and bore our sicknesses."

—Matthew 8:17

Then a woman, who was ill with a flow of blood for twelve years, came behind Him and touched the hem of His garment.

—Matthew 9:20

Jesus answered them, "Have faith in God. For truly I say to you, whoever says to this mountain, 'Be removed and be thrown into the sea,' and does not doubt in his heart, but believes that what he says will come to pass, he will have whatever he says. Therefore I say to you, whatever things you ask when you pray, believe that you will receive them, and you will have them."

—Mark 11:22–24

These signs will accompany those who believe: In My name they will cast out demons; they will speak with new tongues. They will take up serpents; if they drink any deadly thing, it will not hurt them; they will lay hands on the sick, and they will recover.

—Mark 16:17–18

Then He called His twelve disciples together and gave them power and authority over all demons and to cure diseases. And He sent them to preach the kingdom of God and to heal the sick.

—Luke 9:1–2

When you were buried with Him in baptism, in which also you are risen with Him through the faith of the power of God, who has raised Him from the dead. And you, being dead in your sins and the uncircumcision of your flesh, He has resurrected together with Him, having forgiven you all sins.

—Colossians 2:12–13

Is anyone among you suffering? Let him pray. Is anyone merry? Let him sing psalms. Is anyone sick among you? Let him call for the elders of the church, and let them pray over him, anointing him with oil in the name of the Lord. And the prayer of faith will save the sick, and the Lord will raise him up. And if he has committed any sins, he will be forgiven. Confess your faults to one another and pray for one another, that you may be healed. The effective, fervent prayer of a righteous man accomplishes much.

—James 5:13–16

For you know that you were not redeemed from your vain way of life inherited from your fathers with perishable things, like silver or gold, but with the precious blood of Christ, as of a lamb without blemish and without spot. He was foreordained before the creation of the world, but was revealed in these last times for you. Through Him you believe in God who raised Him up from the dead and gave Him glory, so that your faith and hope might be in God.

—1 Peter 1:18–21

And whatever we ask, we will receive from Him, because we keep His commandments and do the things that are pleasing in His sight. And this is His commandment: that we should believe on the name of His Son Jesus Christ and love one another as He commanded us.

—1 John 3:22–23

HEAVEN

And I say to you that many will come from the east and west and will dine with Abraham, Isaac, and Jacob in the kingdom of heaven.

—MATTHEW 8:11

Jesus said to him, "Truly, I tell you, today you will be with Me in Paradise."

—LUKE 23:43

In My Father's house are many dwelling places. If it were not so, I would have told you. I am going to prepare a place for you. And if I go and prepare a place for you, I will come again and receive you to Myself, that where I am, you may be also.

—JOHN 14:2–3

But as it is written, "Eye has not seen, nor ear heard, neither has it entered into the heart of man, the things which God has prepared for those who love Him."

—1 CORINTHIANS 2:9

For Christ did not enter holy places made with hands, which are patterned after the true one, but into heaven itself, now to appear in the presence of God for us.

—HEBREWS 9:24

But they desired a better country, that is, a heavenly one. Therefore God is not ashamed to be called their God, for He has prepared a city for them.

—HEBREWS 11:16

But you have come to Mount Zion and to the city of the living God, the heavenly Jerusalem, and to an innumerable company of angels.

—Hebrews 12:22

Beloved, now are we children of God, and it has not yet been revealed what we shall be. But we know that when He appears, we shall be like Him, for we shall see Him as He is.

—1 John 3:2

Then I looked. And there was a great multitude which no one could count, from all nations and tribes and peoples and tongues, standing before the throne and before the Lamb, clothed with white robes, with palm branches in their hands.

—Revelation 7:9

They sang the song of Moses, the servant of God, and the song of the Lamb, saying, "Great and marvelous are Your works, Lord God Almighty! Just and true are Your ways, O King of saints!"

—Revelation 15:3

"God shall wipe away all tears from their eyes. There shall be no more death." Neither shall there be any more sorrow nor crying nor pain, for the former things have passed away.

—Revelation 21:4

I saw no temple in the city, for the Lord God Almighty and the Lamb are its temple. The city has no need of sun or moon to shine upon it, for the glory of God is its light, and its lamp is the Lamb. In its light shall the nations of the saved walk, and the kings of the earth shall bring into it their glory and honor.

—Revelation 21:22–24

HELL

The wicked will be turned to Sheol, and all the nations that forget God.

—Psalm 9:17

"Stolen waters are sweet, and bread eaten in secret is pleasant." But he does not know that the dead are there, and that her guests are in the depths of the grave.

—Proverbs 9:17–18

You have heard that it was said by the ancients, "You shall not kill," and whoever murders shall be in danger of the judgment. But I say to you that whoever is angry with his brother without a cause shall be in danger of the judgment. And whoever says to his brother, "Raca," shall be in danger of the Sanhedrin. But whoever says, "You fool," shall be in danger of fire of hell.

—Matthew 5:21–22

Enter at the narrow gate, for wide is the gate and broad is the way that leads to destruction, and there are many who are going through it.

—Matthew 7:13

If your hand causes you to sin, cut it off. It is better for you to enter life maimed than with two hands to go into hell, into the fire that shall never be quenched, where "their worm does not die, and the fire is not quenched."

—Mark 9:43–44

I say to you, My friends, do not be afraid of those who kill the body, and after that can do no more. But I will warn you whom you shall fear: Fear Him who, after He has killed, has power to cast into hell. Yes, I say to you, fear Him.

—Luke 12:4–5

And beside all this, between us and you there is a great gulf, so that those who pass from here to you cannot, nor can those who would pass from there to us.

—Luke 16:26

How shall we escape if we neglect such a great salvation, which was first declared by the Lord, and was confirmed to us by those who heard Him?

—Hebrews 2:3

For if God did not spare the angels that sinned, but cast them down to hell and delivered them into chains of darkness to be kept for judgment.

—2 Peter 2:4

But the beast was captured and with him the false prophet who worked signs in his presence, by which he deceived those who received the mark of the beast and those who worshipped his image. These two were thrown alive into the lake of fire that burns with brimstone.

—Revelation 19:20

Then Death and Hades were cast into the lake of fire. This is the second death. Anyone whose name was not found written in the Book of Life was cast into the lake of fire.

—Revelation 20:14–15

He who overcomes shall inherit all things, and I will be his God and he shall be My son. But the cowardly, the unbelieving, the abominable, the murderers, the sexually immoral, the sorcerers, the idolaters, and all liars shall have their portion in the lake which burns with fire and brimstone. This is the second death.

—Revelation 21:7–8

HELP IN TROUBLES

The Lord is my pillar, and my fortress, and my deliverer; my God, my rock, in whom I take refuge; my shield, and the horn of my salvation, my high tower.

—Psalm 18:2

For You will cause my lamp to shine; the Lord my God will enlighten my darkness.

—Psalm 18:28

The Lord is my strength and my shield; my heart trusted in Him, and I was helped; therefore my heart rejoices, and with my song I will thank Him.

—Psalm 28:7

Oh, love the Lord, all you His saints, for the Lord preserves the faithful, but amply repays the one who acts in pride.

—Psalm 31:23

Though he falls, he will not be hurled down, for the Lord supports him with His hand.

—Psalm 37:24

But the salvation of the righteous is from the Lord; He is their refuge in the time of distress.

—Psalm 37:39

Though you sleep between the sheepfolds, yet you will be like the wings of a dove overlaid with silver, and its feathers with yellow gold.

—Psalm 68:13

You who have shown me great distresses and troubles will revive me again, and will bring me up again from the depths of the earth.

—Psalm 71:20

Those who sow in tears shall reap in joy. He who goes forth and weeps, bearing precious seed to sow, shall come home again with rejoicing, bringing his grain sheaves with him.

—Psalm 126:5–6

The Lord opens the eyes of the blind; the Lord raises those who are brought down; the Lord loves the righteous.

—Psalm 146:8

Certainly the Lord God will help Me. Who is he who condemns me? Indeed they all shall grow old as a garment. The moth shall eat them up.

—Isaiah 50:9

For the Lord will not cast off forever. But though He causes grief, yet He will have compassion according to the multitude of His mercies. For He does not afflict willingly nor grieve the sons of men.

—Lamentations 3:31–33

HOLINESS

Now, Israel, what does the LORD your God require of you, but to fear the LORD your God, to walk in all His ways, and to love Him, and to serve the LORD your God with all your heart and with all your soul.

—DEUTERONOMY 10:12

As for you, Solomon my son, know the God of your fathers and serve Him with a whole heart and with a willing spirit, for the LORD searches every heart and understands the intent of every thought. If you seek Him, He will be found by you, but if you abandon Him, He will reject you utterly.

—1 CHRONICLES 28:9

Thus I will magnify Myself, and sanctify Myself, and I will be known in the eyes of many nations. Then they shall know that I am the LORD.

—EZEKIEL 38:23

And has raised up a horn of salvation for us in the house of His servant David.

—LUKE 1:69

But because of Him you are in Christ Jesus, whom God made unto us wisdom, righteousness, sanctification, and redemption.

—1 CORINTHIANS 1:30

Since we have these promises, beloved, let us cleanse ourselves from all filthiness of the flesh and spirit, perfecting holiness in the fear of God.

—2 CORINTHIANS 7:1

Just as He chose us in Him before the foundation of the world, to be holy and blameless before Him in love.

—Ephesians 1:4

That you put off the former way of life in the old nature, which is corrupt according to the deceitful lusts. And be renewed in the spirit of your mind; and that you put on the new nature, which was created according to God in righteousness and true holiness.

—Ephesians 4:22–24

By this will we have been sanctified through the offering of the body of Jesus Christ once for all.

—Hebrews 10:10

For they indeed disciplined us for a short time according to their own judgment, but He does so for our profit, that we may partake of His holiness.

—Hebrews 12:10

But as He who has called you is holy, so be holy in all your conduct, because it is written, "Be holy, for I am holy."

—1 Peter 1:15–16

His divine power has given to us all things that pertain to life and godliness through the knowledge of Him who has called us by His own glory and excellence.

—2 Peter 1:3

HOLY SPIRIT

Turn at my reproof; surely I will pour out my spirit on you; I will make my words known to you.

—Proverbs 1:23

"As for Me, this is My covenant with them," says the Lord, "My Spirit who is upon you, and My words which I have put in your mouth shall not depart out of your mouth, nor out of the mouth of your descendants, nor out of the mouth of your descendants' descendants," says the Lord, "from henceforth and forever."

—Isaiah 59:21

I will put My Spirit within you and cause you to walk in My statutes, and you will keep My judgments and do them.

—Ezekiel 36:27

If you then, being evil, know how to give good gifts to your children, how much more will your heavenly Father give the Holy Spirit to those who ask Him?

—Luke 11:13

I will pray the Father, and He will give you another Counselor, that He may be with you forever: The Spirit of truth, whom the world cannot receive, for it does not see Him, neither does it know Him. But you know Him, for He lives with you, and will be in you.

—John 14:16–17

But the Counselor, the Holy Spirit, whom the Father will send in My name, will teach you everything and remind you of all that I told you.

—John 14:26

But when the Spirit of truth comes, He will guide you into all truth. For He will not speak on His own authority. But

He will speak whatever He hears, and He will tell you things that are to come.

—John 16:13

Peter said to them, "Repent and be baptized, every one of you, in the name of Jesus Christ for the forgiveness of sins, and you shall receive the gift of the Holy Spirit."

—Acts 2:38

For you have not received the spirit of slavery again to fear. But you have received the Spirit of adoption, by whom we cry, "Abba, Father."

—Romans 8:15

Likewise, the Spirit helps us in our weaknesses, for we do not know what to pray for as we ought, but the Spirit Himself intercedes for us with groanings too deep for words. He who searches the hearts knows what the mind of the Spirit is, because He intercedes for the saints according to the will of God.

—Romans 8:26–27

For the kingdom of God does not mean eating and drinking, but righteousness and peace and joy in the Holy Spirit.

—Romans 14:17

But the anointing which you have received from Him remains in you, and you do not need anyone to teach you. For as the same anointing teaches you concerning all things, and is truth, and is no lie, and just as it has taught you, remain in Him.

—1 John 2:27

HOME

I chose him, and he will instruct his children and his household after him to keep the way of the LORD by doing righteousness and justice, so that the LORD may bring to Abraham what He promised him.

—GENESIS 18:19

These words, which I am commanding you today, shall be in your heart. You shall teach them diligently to your children and shall talk of them when you sit in your house, and when you walk by the way and when you lie down and when you rise up.

—DEUTERONOMY 6:6–7

If it is displeasing to you to serve the LORD, then choose today whom you will serve, if it should be the gods your ancestors served on the other side of the Euphrates River or the gods of the Amorites' land where you are now living. Yet as for me and my house, we will serve the LORD.

—JOSHUA 24:15

I will consider the path that is blameless. When will you come unto me? I will walk within my house with a perfect heart.

—PSALM 101:2

Train up a child in the way he should go, and when he is old he will not depart from it.

—PROVERBS 22:6

But if any widow has children or grandchildren, let them learn first to show piety at home and to repay their parents. For this is good and acceptable before God.

—1 Timothy 5:4

HOMOSEXUALITY

You shall not lie with a man as one does with a woman. It is an abomination.

—Leviticus 18:22

If a man lies with another man as with a woman, both of them have committed an abomination. They shall surely be put to death. Their blood guilt shall be upon them.

—Leviticus 20:13

Therefore God gave them up to uncleanness through the lusts of their hearts, to dishonor their own bodies among themselves. They turned the truth of God into a lie and worshipped and served the creature rather than the Creator, who is blessed forever. Amen. For this reason God gave them up to dishonorable passions. Their women exchanged the natural function for what is against nature. Likewise the men, leaving the natural function of the woman, burned in their lust toward one another, men with men doing that which is shameful, and receiving in themselves the due penalty of their error.

—Romans 1:24–27

Who know the righteous requirement of God, that those who commit such things are worthy of death. They not only do them, but also give hearty approval to those who practice them.

—Romans 1:32

Do you not know that the unrighteous will not inherit the kingdom of God? Do not be deceived. Neither the sexually immoral, nor idolaters, nor adulterers, nor male prostitutes, nor homosexuals, nor thieves, nor covetous, nor drunkards, nor revilers, nor extortioners will inherit the kingdom of God.

—1 Corinthians 6:9–10

Such were some of you. But you were washed, you were sanctified, and you were justified in the name of the Lord Jesus by the Spirit of our God.

—1 Corinthians 6:11

HONESTY

The Lord will judge the peoples. Grant me justice, O Lord, according to my righteousness, and according to my integrity within me.

—Psalm 7:8

The wicked borrows and does not repay, but the righteous is gracious and gives.

—Psalm 37:21

Do not withhold Your compassion from me, O Lord; may Your lovingkindness and Your truth always guard me.

—Psalm 40:11

He who speaks truth shows forth righteousness, but a false witness deceit.

—Proverbs 12:17

Righteous lips are the delight of kings, and they love him who speaks right.

—Proverbs 16:13

Are there still in the house of the wicked treasures of wickedness? And the short ephah which is accursed? Should I acquit the scales of wickedness and the sack of dishonest weights? Her wealthy men are full of violence, and her inhabitants speak deception, and their tongue in their mouth is treachery.

—Micah 6:10–12

You know the commandments, "Do not commit adultery," "Do not kill," "Do not steal," "Do not bear false witness," "Do not defraud," "Honor your father and mother."

—Mark 10:19

Now the parable means this: The seed is the word of God....But the seed on the good ground are those who, having heard the word, keep it in an honest and good heart and bear fruit with patience.

—Luke 8:11, 15

Servants, obey your masters in all things according to the flesh, serving not only when they are watching, as the servants of men, but in singleness of heart, fearing God. And whatever you do, do it heartily, as to the Lord, and not for people.

—Colossians 3:22–23

And that no man take advantage of and defraud his brother in any matter, because the Lord is the avenger in all these things, as we also have forewarned you and testified. For God has not called us to uncleanness, but to holiness.

—1 Thessalonians 4:6–7

In all things presenting yourself as an example of good works: in doctrine, showing integrity, seriousness, sincerity, and sound speech that cannot be condemned, so that the one who opposes you may be ashamed, having nothing evil to say of you.

—Titus 2:7–8

Pray for us. For we trust that we have a good conscience and in all things are willing to live honestly.

—Hebrews 13:18

HOPE

Uphold me according to Your word, that I may live, and let me not be ashamed with my hope.

—Psalm 119:116

Hope deferred makes the heart sick, but when the desire comes, it is a tree of life.

—Proverbs 13:12

So shall the knowledge of wisdom be to your soul; when you have found it, then there will be a reward, and your expectation will not be cut off.

—Proverbs 24:14

Blessed is the man who trusts in the Lord, and whose hope is the Lord. For he shall be as a tree planted by the waters, and that spreads out its roots by the river, and shall not fear when heat comes, but its leaf shall be green. And it shall not be anxious in the year of drought, neither shall cease from yielding fruit.

—Jeremiah 17:7–8

Therefore my heart was glad, and my tongue rejoiced. Moreover my flesh will dwell in hope, for You will not abandon my soul to Hades, nor will You allow Your Holy One to see corruption. You have made known to me the ways of life. You will make me full of joy with Your presence.

—Acts 2:26–28

Now to Him who is able to do exceedingly abundantly beyond all that we ask or imagine, according to the power that works in us, to Him be the glory in the church and in Christ Jesus throughout all generations, forever and ever. Amen.

—Ephesians 3:20–21

Because of the hope which is laid up for you in heaven, of which you have already heard in the word of the truth of the gospel.

—Colossians 1:5

To them God would make known what is the glorious riches of this mystery among the nations. It is Christ in you, the hope of glory.

—Colossians 1:27

Now may our Lord Jesus Christ Himself, and God our Father, who has loved us and has given us eternal consolation and good hope through grace, comfort your hearts and establish you in every good word and work.

—2 Thessalonians 2:16–17

We have this hope as a sure and steadfast anchor of the soul, which enters the Inner Place behind the veil.

—HEBREWS 6:19

Therefore guard your minds, be sober, and hope to the end for the grace that is to be brought to you at the revelation of Jesus Christ.

—1 PETER 1:13

But sanctify the Lord God in your hearts. Always be ready to give an answer to every man who asks you for a reason for the hope that is in you, with gentleness and fear.

—1 PETER 3:15

HOSPITALITY

When a foreigner sojourns with you in your land, you shall not do him wrong. The foreigner who dwells with you shall be to you as one born among you, and you shall love him as yourself for you were foreigners in the land of Egypt: I am the Lord your God.

—LEVITICUS 19:33–34

Is it not to divide your bread with the hungry and bring the poor who are outcasts into your house? When you see the naked, to cover him and not hide yourself from your own flesh? Then your light shall break forth as the morning, and your recovery shall spring forth speedily, and your righteousness shall go before you. The glory of the LORD shall be your reward.

—ISAIAH 58:7–8

For I was hungry and you gave Me food, I was thirsty and you gave Me drink, I was a stranger and you took Me in. I was naked and you clothed Me, I was sick and you visited Me, I was in prison, and you came to Me.

—MATTHEW 25:35–36

The King will answer, "Truly I say to you, as you have done it for one of the least of these brothers of Mine, you have done it for Me."

—MATTHEW 25:40

Then He said also to the one who invited Him, "When you prepare a dinner or a supper, do not call your friends or your brothers or your kinsmen or your rich neighbors, lest they also invite you in return, and you be repaid. But when you prepare a banquet, call the poor, the maimed, the lame, the blind, and you will be blessed, for they cannot repay you. You shall be repaid at the resurrection of the just."

—LUKE 14:12–14

Contribute to the needs of the saints, practice hospitality.

—ROMANS 12:13

I do not mean that other men have relief, and you be burdened, but for equality, that your abundance now at this time may supply their need, and their abundance may supply your need—that there may be equality.

—2 CORINTHIANS 8:13–14

For the administration of this service not only supplies the need of the saints, but is abundant also through many thanksgivings to God. Meanwhile, through the performance of this ministry, they glorify God for the profession of your faith in the gospel of Christ and for your liberal sharing with them and with all others.

—2 Corinthians 9:12–13

But do not forget to do good and to share. For with such sacrifices God is well pleased.

—Hebrews 13:16

If a brother or sister is naked and lacking daily food, and one of you says to them, "Depart in peace, be warmed and filled," and yet you give them nothing that the body needs, what does it profit?

—James 2:15–16

Show hospitality to one another without complaining. As every one has received a gift, even so serve one another with it, as good stewards of the manifold grace of God.

—1 Peter 4:9–10

Whoever has the world's goods and sees his brother in need, but closes his heart of compassion from him, how can the love of God remain in him?

—1 John 3:17

HUMILITY

Now the man Moses was very humble, more than all the men on the face of the earth.

—Numbers 12:3

He who avenges deaths, remembers them; He does not forget the cry of the humble.

—Psalm 9:12

The desire of the humble You have heard, O Lord; You make their heart attentive. You bend Your ear.

—Psalm 10:17

The fear of the Lord is the instruction of wisdom, and before honor is humility.

—Proverbs 15:33

By humility and the fear of the Lord are riches, and honor, and life.

—Proverbs 22:4

A man's pride will bring him low, but honor will uphold the humble in spirit.

—Proverbs 29:23

For thus says the High and Lofty One who inhabits eternity, whose name is Holy, "I dwell in the high and holy place and also with him who is of a contrite and humble spirit, to revive the spirit of the humble, and to revive the heart of the contrite ones."

—Isaiah 57:15

Therefore whoever humbles himself like this little child is greatest in the kingdom of heaven.

—Matthew 18:4

For he who exalts himself will be humbled, and he who humbles himself will be exalted.

—Matthew 23:12

I tell you, this man went down to his house justified rather than the other. For everyone who exalts himself will be humbled, and he who humbles himself will be exalted.

—Luke 18:14

Let this mind be in you all, which was also in Christ Jesus: Who, being in the form of God, did not consider equality with God something to be grasped. But He emptied Himself, taking upon Himself the form of a servant, and was made in the likeness of men. And being found in the form of a man, He humbled Himself and became obedient to death, even death on a cross.

—Philippians 2:5–8

But He gives more grace. For this reason it says, "God resists the proud, but gives grace to the humble."

—James 4:6

HUSBANDS

Enjoy life with the wife whom you love all the days of your vain life which He has given you under the sun, because that is your reward in life and in your toil because you have labored under the sun.

—Ecclesiastes 9:9

Husbands, love your wives, just as Christ also loved the church and gave Himself for it.

—Ephesians 5:25

In this way, men ought to love their wives as their own bodies. He who loves his wife loves himself.

—Ephesians 5:28

Husbands, love your wives, and do not be bitter toward them.

—Colossians 3:19

But if any do not care for their own, and especially for those of their own house, they have denied the faith and are worse than unbelievers.

—1 Timothy 5:8

Likewise, you husbands, live considerately with your wives, giving honor to the woman as the weaker vessel, since they too are also heirs of the grace of life, so that your prayers will not be hindered.

—1 Peter 3:7

HYPOCRISY

For there is no uprightness in their mouth; destruction is in their midst; their throat is an open tomb; they flatter with their tongue.

—Psalm 5:9

Lord, who will abide in Your tabernacle? Who will dwell in Your holy hill? He who walks uprightly, and does righteousness, and speaks truth in his own heart.

—Psalm 15:1–2

Therefore, the Lord said, "Because this people draw near with their mouths and honor Me with their lips, but have removed their hearts far from Me, and their fear toward Me is tradition by the precept of men."

—Isaiah 29:13

You hypocrite! First take the plank out of your own eye, and then you will see clearly to take the speck out of your brother's eye.

—Matthew 7:5

Woe to you, scribes and Pharisees, hypocrites! You shut the kingdom of heaven against men. For you neither enter yourselves, nor allow those who are entering to go in. Woe to you, scribes and Pharisees, hypocrites! You devour widows' houses and for pretense make long prayers. Therefore you will receive the greater condemnation.

—Matthew 23:13–14

Woe to you, scribes and Pharisees, hypocrites! You tithe mint and dill and cumin, but have neglected the weightier matters of the law: justice and mercy and faith. These you ought to have done without leaving the others undone.

—Matthew 23:23

Woe to you, scribes and Pharisees, hypocrites! You cleanse the outside of the cup and dish, but inside they are full of extortion and greed. You blind Pharisee, first cleanse the inside of the cup and dish, that the outside of them may also be clean.

—Matthew 23:25–26

Woe to you, scribes and Pharisees, hypocrites! You are like whitewashed tombs, which indeed appear beautiful outwardly, but inside are full of dead men's bones and of all uncleanness. So you also outwardly appear righteous to men, but inside you are full of hypocrisy and iniquity.

—Matthew 23:27–28

Why do you see the speck that is in your brother's eye, but do not see the beam that is in your own eye? How can you say to your brother, "Brother, let me remove the speck that is in your eye," when you yourself do not see the beam that is in your own eye? You hypocrite! First remove the beam from your own eye, and then you will see clearly to remove the speck that is in your brother's eye.

—Luke 6:41–42

They profess that they know God, but in their deeds they deny Him, being abominable, disobedient, and worthless for every good work.

—Titus 1:16

If anyone among you seems to be religious and does not bridle his tongue, but deceives his own heart, this man's religion is vain.

—James 1:26

If anyone says, "I love God," and hates his brother, he is a liar. For whoever does not love his brother whom he has seen, how can he love God whom he has not seen?

—1 John 4:20

INCEST

None of you shall approach any of his near relatives to have relations: I am the Lord. You must not have relations with your father or have relations with your mother. She is your mother. You shall not have relations with her.

—Leviticus 18:6–7

You must not have relations with a woman and her daughter, nor shall you have her son's daughter or her daughter's daughter, for this exposes the woman's nakedness. They are all near relatives. It is depravity. And you must not have a woman as a rival wife, who is the sister of your other wife, for this is to expose her nakedness while her sister, your other wife, is still alive.

—Leviticus 18:17–18

For whoever shall commit any of these abominations, those persons who commit them shall be cut off from among their people.

—Leviticus 18:29

If my father and my mother forsake me, then the Lord will take me in.

—Psalm 27:10

"You are My witnesses," says the Lord, "and My servant whom I have chosen that you may know and believe Me, and understand that I am He. Before Me there was no God formed, nor shall there be after Me. I, even I, am the Lord, and besides Me there is no savior."

—Isaiah 43:10–11

Indeed, from eternity I am He, and there is none who can deliver out of My hand. I act, and who shall reverse it?

—Isaiah 43:13

INHERITANCE

The lines have fallen for me in pleasant places; yes, an inheritance is beautiful for me.

—Psalm 16:6

The righteous will inherit the land, and dwell on it forever.

—Psalm 37:29

An inheritance may be gained hastily at the beginning; but the end of it will not be blessed.

—Proverbs 20:21

Now, brothers, I commend you to God and to the word of His grace, which is able to build you up and give you an inheritance among all who are sanctified.

—Acts 20:32

And if children, then heirs: heirs of God and joint-heirs with Christ, if indeed we suffer with Him, that we may also be glorified with Him.

—Romans 8:17

So those who are the children of the flesh are not the children of God, but the children of the promise are counted as descendants.

—Romans 9:8

So that the blessing of Abraham might come on the Gentiles through Jesus Christ, that we might receive the promise of the Spirit through faith.

—Galatians 3:14

Therefore you are no longer a servant, but a son, and if a son, then an heir of God through Christ.

—Galatians 4:7

Blessed be the God and Father of our Lord Jesus Christ, who has blessed us with every spiritual blessing in the heavenly places in Christ.

—Ephesians 1:3

That the eyes of your heart may be enlightened, that you may know what is the hope of His calling and what are the riches of the glory of His inheritance among the saints.

—Ephesians 1:18

And whatever you do, do it heartily, as to the Lord, and not for people, knowing that from the Lord you will receive the reward of the inheritance. For you serve the Lord Christ.

—Colossians 3:23–24

By which He has given to us exceedingly great and precious promises, so that through these things you might become partakers of the divine nature and escape the corruption that is in the world through lust.

—2 Peter 1:4

INTEGRITY

Moreover, you shall choose out of all the people capable men who fear God, men of truth, hating dishonest gain, and place these men over them, to be rulers of thousands, rulers of hundreds, rulers of fifties, and rulers of tens.

—Exodus 18:21

You must not pervert judgment nor show impartiality. You must not accept a bribe, for a bribe blinds the eyes of the wise and perverts the words of the righteous. You must follow that which is altogether just, so that you may live and inherit the land which the LORD your God is giving you.

—DEUTERONOMY 16:19–20

The LORD said to the Adversary, "Have you considered My servant Job, that there is none like him on the earth, a blameless and an upright man, who fears God and avoids evil? He still holds fast his integrity, although you moved Me against him, to destroy him without cause."

—JOB 2:3

God forbid that I should justify you. Until I die I will not put away my integrity from me.

—JOB 27:5

I know, my God, that You test the heart, and with uprightness You are pleased, so in the uprightness of my heart I have offered freely all these things, and now I have seen Your people, those present here, offer freely and joyously to You.

—1 CHRONICLES 29:17

The LORD will judge the peoples. Grant me justice, O LORD, according to my righteousness, and according to my integrity within me.

—PSALM 7:8

Truth and integrity will preserve me while I wait for You.

—PSALM 25:21

He who walks uprightly walks surely, but he who perverts his ways will be known.

—PROVERBS 10:9

The integrity of the upright will guide them, but the perverseness of transgressors will destroy them.

—Proverbs 11:3

Righteousness keeps him who is upright in the way, but wickedness overthrows the sinner.

—Proverbs 13:6

In all things presenting yourself as an example of good works: in doctrine, showing integrity, seriousness, sincerity, and sound speech that cannot be condemned, so that the one who opposes you may be ashamed, having nothing evil to say of you.

—Titus 2:7–8

But whoever keeps His word truly has the love of God perfected in him. By this we know we are in Him.

—1 John 2:5

JEALOUSY

You shall not covet your neighbor's wife, nor shall you covet your neighbor's house, his field, his male servant, his female servant, his ox, his donkey, or anything that belongs to your neighbor.

—Deuteronomy 5:21

Rest in the Lord, and wait patiently for Him; do not fret because of those who prosper in their way, because of those who make wicked schemes.

—Psalm 37:7

Do not envy the oppressor, and choose none of his ways.

—Proverbs 3:31

A sound heart is the life of the flesh, but envy the rottenness of the bones.

—PROVERBS 14:30

Do not be envious against evil men, nor desire to be with them.

—PROVERBS 24:1

Wrath is cruel, and anger is outrageous, but who is able to stand before envy?

—PROVERBS 27:4

Then I observed all labor and skill of work that the envy of a man is toward what his companion has.

—ECCLESIASTES 4:4

Then He said to His disciples, "Therefore I say to you, do not be anxious for your life, what you will eat, nor for your body, what you will wear. Life is more than food, and the body is more than clothes."

—LUKE 12:22–23

Let no one seek his own, but each one the other's well-being.

—1 CORINTHIANS 10:24

Let us not be conceited, provoking one another and envying one another.

—GALATIANS 5:26

But if you have bitter envying and strife in your hearts, do not boast and do not lie against the truth.

—JAMES 3:14

Do you think that the Scripture says in vain, "He yearns jealously for the spirit that lives in us"?

—James 4:5

JESUS

The Word became flesh and dwelt among us, and we saw His glory, the glory as the only Son of the Father, full of grace and truth.

—John 1:14

For God so loved the world that He gave His only begotten Son, that whoever believes in Him should not perish, but have eternal life. For God did not send His Son into the world to condemn the world, but that the world through Him might be saved.

—John 3:16–17

Jesus said to her, "I am the resurrection and the life. He who believes in Me, though he may die, yet shall he live. And whoever lives and believes in Me shall never die. Do you believe this?"

—John 11:25–26

For the wages of sin is death, but the gift of God is eternal life through Jesus Christ our Lord.

—Romans 6:23

That if you confess with your mouth Jesus is Lord, and believe in your heart that God has raised Him from the dead, you will be saved.

—Romans 10:9

For none of us lives for himself, and no one dies for himself. For if we live, we live for the Lord. And if we die, we die for the Lord. So, whether we live or die, we are the Lord's.

—ROMANS 14:7–8

But now is Christ risen from the dead and become the firstfruits of those who have fallen asleep.

—1 CORINTHIANS 15:20

Therefore God highly exalted Him and gave Him the name which is above every name, that at the name of Jesus every knee should bow, of those in heaven and on earth and under the earth, and every tongue should confess that Jesus Christ is Lord, to the glory of God the Father.

—PHILIPPIANS 2:9–11

For if we believe that Jesus died and arose again, so God will bring with Him those who sleep in Jesus.

—1 THESSALONIANS 4:14

He is the brightness of His glory, the express image of Himself, and upholds all things by the word of His power. When He had by Himself purged our sins, He sat down at the right hand of the Majesty on high.

—HEBREWS 1:3

So that by two immutable things, in which it was impossible for God to lie, we who have fled for refuge might have strong encouragement to hold fast to the hope set before us. We have this hope as a sure and steadfast anchor of the soul, which enters the Inner Place behind the veil.

—HEBREWS 6:18–19

And we have seen and testify that the Father sent the Son to be the Savior of the world.

—1 John 4:14

JOINT HEIRS

But you shall receive power when the Holy Spirit comes upon you. And you shall be My witnesses in Jerusalem, and in all Judea and Samaria, and to the ends of the earth.

—Acts 1:8

For you are still worldly. Since there is envy, strife, and divisions among you, are you not worldly and behaving as mere men?

—1 Corinthians 3:3

You were bought with a price. Therefore glorify God in your body and in your spirit, which are God's.

—1 Corinthians 6:20

But that one and very same Spirit works all these, dividing to each one individually as He will.

—1 Corinthians 12:11

Who also has sealed us and established the guarantee with the Spirit in our hearts.

—2 Corinthians 1:22

In whom we have redemption through His blood, the forgiveness of sins.

—Colossians 1:14

In Him you were also circumcised by putting off the body of the sinful nature, not a circumcision performed with hands, but by the circumcision performed by Christ.

—Colossians 2:11

Paul, Silas, and Timothy, to the church of the Thessalonians which is in God the Father and in the Lord Jesus Christ: Grace to you and peace from God our Father and the Lord Jesus Christ.

—1 Thessalonians 1:1

Faithful is He who calls you, who also will do it.

—1 Thessalonians 5:24

To an incorruptible and undefiled inheritance that does not fade away, kept in heaven for you.

—1 Peter 1:4

For you know that you were not redeemed from your vain way of life inherited from your fathers with perishable things, like silver or gold, but with the precious blood of Christ, as of a lamb without blemish and without spot.

—1 Peter 1:18–19

Now the one who keeps His commandments remains in Him, and He in him. And by this we know that He remains in us, through the Spirit whom He has given us.

—1 John 3:24

JOY AND GLADNESS

Until He fills your mouth with laughing, and your lips with rejoicing.

—Job 8:21

Blessed are the people who know the joyful shout. They walk, O Lord, in the light of Your presence. In Your name they rejoice all the day, and in Your righteousness they shall be exalted.

—Psalm 89:15–16

Make a joyful noise unto the Lord, all the earth! Serve the Lord with gladness; come before His presence with singing.

—Psalm 100:1–2

Death and destruction are before the Lord; so how much more the hearts of the children of men?

—Proverbs 15:11

You shall fan them, and the wind shall carry them away, and the whirlwind shall scatter them. And you shall rejoice in the Lord, and shall glory in the Holy One of Israel.

—Isaiah 41:16

And children of Zion, exult and rejoice in the Lord your God, because He has given to you the early rain for vindication. He showers down rains for you, the early rain and the latter rain, as before.

—Joel 2:23

Yet I will rejoice in the Lord; I will exult in the God of my salvation.

—Habakkuk 3:18

I have spoken these things to you, that My joy may remain in you, and that your joy may be full.

—John 15:11

Therefore you now have sorrow. But I will see you again, and your heart will rejoice, and no one will take your joy from you.

—John 16:22

Until now you have asked nothing in My name. Ask, and you will receive, that your joy may be full.

—John 16:24

Rejoice in the Lord always. Again I will say, rejoice!

—Philippians 4:4

My brothers, count it all joy when you fall into diverse temptations, knowing that the trying of your faith develops patience.

—James 1:2–3

Whom, having not seen, you love; and in whom, though you do not see Him now, you believe and you rejoice with joy unspeakable and full of glory.

—1 Peter 1:8

KINDNESS

A good man shows generous favor, and lends; he will guide his affairs with justice.

—Psalm 112:5

A gracious woman retains honor, but ruthless men retain riches.

—Proverbs 11:16

Heaviness in the heart of man makes it droop, but a good word makes it glad.

—Proverbs 12:25

"But let him who glories glory in this, that he understands and knows Me, that I am the LORD who exercises lovingkindness, justice, and righteousness in the earth. For in these things I delight," says the LORD.

—JEREMIAH 9:24

Thus says the LORD of Hosts: "Execute true justice, show mercy and compassion, every man to his brother."

—ZECHARIAH 7:9

Give to him who asks you, and from him who would borrow from you do not turn away.

—MATTHEW 5:42

And whoever gives even a cup of cold water to one of these little ones in the name of a disciple, truly I tell you, he shall in no way lose his reward.

—MATTHEW 10:42

Then the King will say to those at His right hand, "Come, you blessed of My Father, inherit the kingdom prepared for you since the foundation of the world. For I was hungry and you gave Me food, I was thirsty and you gave Me drink, I was a stranger and you took Me in. I was naked and you clothed Me, I was sick and you visited Me, I was in prison, and you came to Me."

—MATTHEW 25:34–36

Be of the same mind toward one another. Do not be haughty, but associate with the lowly. Do not pretend to be wiser than you are.

—ROMANS 12:16

Bear one another's burdens, and so fulfill the law of Christ.

—Galatians 6:2

Therefore, as we have opportunity, let us do good to all people, especially to those who are of the household of faith.

—Galatians 6:10

So embrace, as the elect of God, holy and beloved, a spirit of mercy, kindness, humbleness of mind, meekness, and longsuffering.

—Colossians 3:12

Kingdom Keys

Now then, you kings, be wise. Be admonished, you judges of the earth. Serve the Lord with fear, tremble with trepidation!

—Psalm 2:10–11

All the ends of the world will remember and turn to the Lord; and all the families of the nations will worship before You. For kingship belongs to the Lord, and He rules among the nations.

—Psalm 22:27–28

The Gentiles shall see your righteousness, and all kings your glory. And you shall be called by a new name, which the mouth of the Lord shall name.

—Isaiah 62:2

"But let him who glories glory in this, that he understands and knows Me, that I am the Lord who exercises lovingkindness, justice, and righteousness in the earth. For in these things I delight," says the Lord.

—Jeremiah 9:24

Do not store up for yourselves treasures on earth where moth and rust destroy and where thieves break in and steal.

—MATTHEW 6:19

That if you confess with your mouth Jesus is Lord, and believe in your heart that God has raised Him from the dead, you will be saved, for with the heart one believes unto righteousness, and with the mouth confession is made unto salvation.

—ROMANS 10:9–10

LAZINESS

Go to the ant, you sluggard! Consider her ways and be wise....How long will you sleep, O sluggard? When will you arise out of your sleep?

—PROVERBS 6:6, 9

Yet a little sleep, a little slumber, a little folding of the hands to sleep—so will your poverty come upon you like a stalker, and your need as an armed man.

—PROVERBS 6:10–11

He becomes poor who deals with a slack hand, but the hand of the diligent makes rich. He who gathers in summer is a wise son, but he who sleeps in harvest is a son who causes shame.

—PROVERBS 10:4–5

He who tills his land will be satisfied with bread, but he who follows vain persons is void of understanding.

—PROVERBS 12:11

You will have goats' milk enough for your food, for the food of your household, and for the maintenance of your maidens.
—Proverbs 27:27

He who tills his land will have plenty of bread, but he who follows after vain persons will have poverty enough.
—Proverbs 28:19

Notice, what I have observed to be good and pleasing is to eat and drink and see benefit in all one's labor, which he toils under the sun for the number of the days of his life, which God has given to him, for this is his reward. And also everyone to whom God has given to him wealth and possessions, and the ability to eat from it and to receive his reward and to rejoice in his labor, this is a gift from God.
—Ecclesiastes 5:18–19

The roof beams sink in with slothfulness, and with the idleness of one's hands the house drips.
—Ecclesiastes 10:18

Do not be lazy in diligence, be fervent in spirit, serve the Lord.
—Romans 12:11

Let him who steals steal no more. Instead, let him labor, working with his hands things which are good, that he may have something to share with him who is in need.
—Ephesians 4:28

Besides that, they learn to be idle, and not only idle, wandering around from house to house, but also gossips and busybodies, saying what they ought not.
—1 Timothy 5:13

So that you may not be lazy, but imitators of those who through faith and patience inherit the promises.

—Hebrews 6:12

Lifting the Humble

The meek will He guide in judgment; and the meek He will teach His way.

—Psalm 25:9

God will hear and afflict them, even He who sits enthroned from of old. Selah. Because they do not change, and they do not fear God.

—Psalm 55:19

For the Lord takes pleasure in His people; He will beautify the meek with salvation.

—Psalm 149:4

By humility and the fear of the Lord are riches, and honor, and life.

—Proverbs 22:4

A man's pride will bring him low, but honor will uphold the humble in spirit.

—Proverbs 29:23

For he who exalts himself will be humbled, and he who humbles himself will be exalted.

—Matthew 23:12

LIGHT OF THE WORLD

Send out Your light and Your truth. Let them lead me. Let them bring me to Your holy hill, and to Your dwelling place.

—Psalm 43:3

The day is Yours, the night also is Yours; You have prepared the light and the sun. You have established all the borders of the earth; You have made summer and winter.

—Psalm 74:16–17

The sun shall no longer be your light by day, nor for brightness shall the moon give light to you. But the Lord shall be an everlasting light to you and your God for your glory.

—Isaiah 60:19

You are the light of the world. A city that is set on a hill cannot be hidden.

—Matthew 5:14

Again, Jesus spoke to them, saying, "I am the light of the world. Whoever follows Me shall not walk in the darkness, but shall have the light of life."

—John 8:12

For you were formerly darkness, but now you are light in the Lord. Walk as children of light.

—Ephesians 5:8

LONG LIFE

You shall walk in all the ways which the Lord your God has commanded you, so that you may live and that it may be well with you, and that you may prolong your days in the land which you shall possess.

—Deuteronomy 5:33

So that you might fear the Lord your God in order to keep all His statutes and His commandments which I command you—you, and your son, and your grandson—all the days of your life, so that your days may be prolonged.

—Deuteronomy 6:2

And your life will be brighter than noonday, even your darkness will be as the morning.

—Job 11:17

Wisdom is with the elderly, and understanding comes with long life. With Him are wisdom and strength; He has counsel and understanding.

—Job 12:12–13

"Lord, make me to know my end, and what is the measure of my days, that I may know how transient I am. Indeed, You have made my days as a handbreadth, and my age is as nothing before You; indeed every man at his best is as a breath." Selah.

—Psalm 39:4–5

Do not cast me off in the time of old age; do not forsake me when my strength fails.

—Psalm 71:9

O God, You have taught me from my youth; and until now I have proclaimed Your wondrous works. Now also when I am old and gray, O God, do not forsake me, until I have proclaimed Your strength to this generation, and Your power to everyone who is to come.

—Psalm 71:17–18

With long life I will satisfy him and show him My salvation.

—Psalm 91:16

For by me your days will be multiplied, and the years of your life will be increased.

—Proverbs 9:11

The fear of the LORD prolongs days, but the years of the wicked will be shortened.

—Proverbs 10:27

The glory of young men is their strength, and the beauty of old men is the gray head.

—Proverbs 20:29

But as for you, teach what is fitting of sound doctrine: Older men should be sober, serious, temperate, sound in faith, in love, in patience; likewise, older women should be reverent in behavior, and not be false accusers, not be enslaved to much wine, but teachers of good things, that they may teach the young women to love their husbands, to love their children, and to be self-controlled, pure, homekeepers, good, obedient to their own husbands, that the word of God may not be dishonored.

—Titus 2:1–5

LONELINESS

Then the LORD God said, "It is not good that the man should be alone. I will make him a helper suitable for him."

—GENESIS 2:18

Remember, I am with you, and I will protect you wherever you go, and I will bring you back to this land. For I will not leave you until I have done what I promised you.

—GENESIS 28:15

No man will be able to stand against you all the days of your life. As I was with Moses, I will be with you. I will not abandon you. I will not leave you.

—JOSHUA 1:5

But I am poor and needy; yet the LORD thinks about me; You are my help and my deliverer; do not delay, O my God.

—PSALM 40:17

I will lift up my eyes to the hills, from where comes my help? My help comes from the LORD, who made heaven and earth.

—PSALM 121:1–2

Do not fear, for I am with you. Do not be dismayed, for I am your God. I will strengthen you. Indeed, I will help you. Indeed, I will uphold you with My righteous right hand.

—ISAIAH 41:10

Since you were precious in My sight, you have been honorable, and I have loved you. Therefore, I will give men for you, and people for your life.

—ISAIAH 43:4

Then you shall call, and the Lord shall answer. You shall cry, and He shall say, "Here I am." If you take away the yoke from your midst, the pointing of the finger, and speaking wickedness.

—Isaiah 58:9

I will not leave you fatherless. I will come to you.

—John 14:18

"I will be a Father to you, and you shall be My sons and daughters," says the Lord Almighty.

—2 Corinthians 6:18

And you are complete in Him, who is the head of all authority and power.

—Colossians 2:10

Cast all your care upon Him, because He cares for you.

—1 Peter 5:7

Loose Prisoners of Sin

For You are my lamp, O Lord; the Lord illuminates my darkness.

—2 Samuel 22:29

Some sit in darkness and in the shadow of death, being prisoners in affliction and irons, because they rebelled against the words of God and rejected the counsel of the Most High. Therefore He brought down their hearts with hard toil; they fell down, and there was none to help. Then they cried unto the Lord in their trouble, and He delivered them out of their distress. He brought them out of darkness and the shadow of death and broke apart their bonds.

—Psalm 107:10–14

…and forget the Lord your maker who has stretched forth the heavens and laid the foundations of the earth? And have feared continually every day because of the fury of the oppressor as he makes ready to destroy? Yet where is the fury of the oppressor? The exile shall soon be freed, and shall not die in the dungeon, nor will his bread be lacking. But I am the Lord your God who divided the sea whose waves roared. The Lord of Hosts is His name. I have put My words in your mouth, and I have covered you in the shadow of My hand that I may plant the heavens, and lay the foundations of the earth, and say to Zion, "You are My people."

—Isaiah 51:13–16

Thus says the Lord, "Execute justice and righteousness, and deliver the robbed out of the hand of the oppressor. And do no wrong or violence to the stranger, the fatherless, or the widow, neither shed innocent blood in this place."

—Jeremiah 22:3

I will give you the keys of the kingdom of heaven, and whatever you bind on earth shall be bound in heaven, and whatever you loose on earth shall be loosed in heaven.

—Matthew 16:19

Truly I say to you, whatever you bind on earth will be bound in heaven, and whatever you loose on earth will be loosed in heaven.

—Matthew 18:18

Do not be conformed to this world, but be transformed by the renewing of your mind, that you may prove what is the good and acceptable and perfect will of God.

—Romans 12:2

For our fight is not against flesh and blood, but against principalities, against powers, against the rulers of the darkness of this world, and against spiritual forces of evil in the heavenly places.

—Ephesians 6:12

As the body without the spirit is dead, so faith without works is dead.

—James 2:26

For Christ also has once suffered for sins, the just for the unjust, so that He might bring us to God, being put to death in the flesh, but made alive by the Spirit.

—1 Peter 3:18

If we confess our sins, He is faithful and just to forgive us our sins and cleanse us from all unrighteousness.

—1 John 1:9

I am He who lives, though I was dead. Look! I am alive forevermore. Amen. And I have the keys of Hades and of Death.

—Revelation 1:18

LORD OF ALL

The Lord stood above it and said, "I am the Lord God of Abraham your father and the God of Isaac. The land on which you lie, to you will I give it and to your descendants."

—Genesis 28:13

"Arise and thresh, daughter of Zion, for I will make your horn iron, your hoofs I will make bronze, and you will shatter many peoples." I will devote their pillage to the LORD, their wealth to the LORD of all the earth.

—MICAH 4:13

Yet to all who received Him, He gave the power to become sons of God, to those who believed in His name.

—JOHN 1:12

For, "Everyone one who calls on the name of the Lord shall be saved."

—ROMANS 10:13

For by one Spirit we are all baptized into one body, whether we are Jews or Gentiles, whether we are slaves or free, and we have all been made to drink of one Spirit.

—1 CORINTHIANS 12:13

On His robe and on His thigh He has a name written: KING OF KINGS AND LORD OF LORDS.

—REVELATION 19:16

LOVE

You shall not take vengeance, nor bear any grudge against the children of your people, but you shall love your neighbor as yourself: I am the LORD.

—LEVITICUS 19:18

I love those who love me, and those who seek me early will find me.

—PROVERBS 8:17

Jesus said to him, "'You shall love the Lord your God with all your heart, and with all your soul, and with all your mind.' This is the first and great commandment."

—Matthew 22:37–38

A new commandment I give to you, that you love one another, even as I have loved you, that you also love one another. By this all men will know that you are My disciples, if you have love for one another.

—John 13:34–35

You, brothers, have been called to liberty. Only do not use liberty to give an opportunity to the flesh, but by love, serve one another. For the entire law is fulfilled in one word, even in this: "You shall love your neighbor as yourself."

—Galatians 5:13–14

But God, being rich in mercy, because of His great love with which He loved us, even when we were dead in sins, made us alive together with Christ (by grace you have been saved), and He raised us up and seated us together in the heavenly places in Christ Jesus.

—Ephesians 2:4–6

Walk in love, as Christ loved us and gave Himself for us as a fragrant offering and a sacrifice to God.

—Ephesians 5:2

As concerning brotherly love, you do not need me to write to you. For you yourselves are taught by God to love one another.

—1 Thessalonians 4:9

Let brotherly love continue.

—Hebrews 13:1

Since your souls have been purified by obedience to the truth through the Spirit unto a genuine brotherly love, love one another deeply with a pure heart.

—1 Peter 1:22

Consider how much love the Father has given to us, that we should be called children of God. Therefore the world does not know us, because it did not know Him.

—1 John 3:1

No one has seen God at any time. If we love one another, God dwells in us, and His love is perfected in us.

—1 John 4:12

LOVE ONE ANOTHER

You shall not take vengeance, nor bear any grudge against the children of your people, but you shall love your neighbor as yourself: I am the Lord.

—Leviticus 19:18

The foreigner who dwells with you shall be to you as one born among you, and you shall love him as yourself for you were foreigners in the land of Egypt: I am the Lord your God.

—Leviticus 19:34

Behold, how good and how pleasant it is for brothers to dwell together in unity!

—Psalm 133:1

Let love be without hypocrisy. Hate what is evil. Cleave to what is good. Be devoted to one another with brotherly love; prefer one another in honor.

—Romans 12:9–10

Love suffers long and is kind; love envies not; love flaunts not itself and is not puffed up, does not behave itself improperly, seeks not its own, is not easily provoked, thinks no evil; rejoices not in iniquity, but rejoices in the truth; bears all things, believes all things, hopes all things, and endures all things. Love never fails. But if there are prophecies, they shall fail; if there are tongues, they shall cease; and if there is knowledge, it shall vanish.

—1 Corinthians 13:4–8

For in Christ Jesus neither circumcision nor uncircumcision means anything, but faith which works through love.

—Galatians 5:6

You, brothers, have been called to liberty. Only do not use liberty to give an opportunity to the flesh, but by love, serve one another. For the entire law is fulfilled in one word, even in this: "You shall love your neighbor as yourself."

—Galatians 5:13–14

Walk in love, as Christ loved us and gave Himself for us as a fragrant offering and a sacrifice to God.

—Ephesians 5:2

As concerning brotherly love, you do not need me to write to you. For you yourselves are taught by God to love one another.

—1 Thessalonians 4:9

Whoever loves his brother lives in the light, and in him there is no cause for stumbling.

—1 John 2:10

My little children, let us love not in word and speech, but in action and truth.

—1 John 3:18

Beloved, if God so loved us, we must also love one another.

—1 John 4:11

Love, God's

He will love you and bless you and multiply you. He will also bless the fruit of your womb and the fruit of your land, your corn, and your wine, and your oil, the increase of your herd and the young of your flock, in the land which He swore to your fathers to give you.

—Deuteronomy 7:13

The Lord opens the eyes of the blind; the Lord raises those who are brought down; the Lord loves the righteous.

—Psalm 146:8

The way of the wicked is an abomination unto the Lord, but He loves him who follows after righteousness.

—Proverbs 15:9

For as a young man marries a virgin, so your sons shall marry you. And as the bridegroom rejoices over the bride, so your God shall rejoice over you.

—Isaiah 62:5

The Lord has appeared to him from afar, saying, "Indeed, I have loved you with an everlasting love. Therefore with lovingkindness I have drawn you."

—Jeremiah 31:3

Indeed, I will rejoice over them to do them good, and I will plant them in this land assuredly with My whole heart and with My whole soul.

—Jeremiah 32:41

I will heal their backsliding, I will love them freely, for My anger has turned away from him.

—Hosea 14:4

The Lord your God is in your midst, a Mighty One, who will save. He will rejoice over you with gladness; He will quiet you with His love; He will rejoice over you with singing.

—Zephaniah 3:17

For the Father Himself loves you, because you have loved Me, and have believed that I came from God.

—John 16:27

I in them and You in Me, that they may be perfect in unity, and that the world may know that You have sent Me, and have loved them as You have loved Me.

—John 17:23

I have declared Your name to them, and will declare it, that the love with which You loved Me may be in them, and I in them.

—John 17:26

But God, being rich in mercy, because of His great love with which He loved us, even when we were dead in sins, made us alive together with Christ (by grace you have been saved), and He raised us up and seated us together in the heavenly places in Christ Jesus.

—Ephesians 2:4-6

LOVING GOD

Know therefore that the LORD your God, He is God, the faithful God, who keeps covenant and mercy with them who love Him and keep His commandments to a thousand generations.

—DEUTERONOMY 7:9

It will be, if you will diligently obey My commandments which I am commanding you today, to love the LORD your God, and to serve Him with all your heart and with all your soul, then I will give you the rain of your land in its season, the early rain and the latter rain, that you may gather in your grain and your wine and your oil. I will provide grass in your fields for your cattle, that you may eat and be full.

—DEUTERONOMY 11:13–15

Delight yourself in the LORD, and He will give you the desires of your heart.

—PSALM 37:4

Because he has set his love upon me, therefore I will deliver him; I will set him on high, because he has known My name.

—PSALM 91:14

The LORD preserves all those who love Him, but all the wicked He will destroy.

—PSALM 145:20

I love those who love me, and those who seek me early will find me.

—PROVERBS 8:17

That I may cause those who love me to inherit wealth, and I will fill their treasuries.

—Proverbs 8:21

He answered, "'You shall love the Lord your God with all your heart, and with all your soul, and with all your strength, and with all your mind' and 'your neighbor as yourself.'"

—Luke 10:27

He who has My commandments and keeps them is the one who loves Me. And he who loves Me will be loved by My Father. And I will love him and will reveal Myself to him.

—John 14:21

If you keep My commandments, you will remain in My love, even as I have kept My Father's commandments and remain in His love.

—John 15:10

But as it is written, "Eye has not seen, nor ear heard, neither has it entered into the heart of man, the things which God has prepared for those who love Him."

—1 Corinthians 2:9

Grace be with all those who love our Lord Jesus Christ in sincerity. Amen.

—Ephesians 6:24

LOYALTY

You shall have no other gods before Me.... You shall not bow down to them or serve them; for I, the Lord your God, am a jealous God, visiting the iniquity of the fathers on the children to the third and fourth generation of them who hate Me.

—Exodus 20:3–5

But Ruth said, "Do not urge me to leave you or to turn back from following you. For wherever you go, I will go, and wherever you stay, I will stay. Your people shall be my people and your God my God. Where you die, I will die, and there I will be buried. May the Lord do thus to me, and worse, if anything but death separates you and me!"

—Ruth 1:16–17

O Lord, the God of Abraham, Isaac, and Israel, our fathers, keep this forever in the thoughts and intentions of the heart of Your people and direct their heart to You.

—1 Chronicles 29:18

That they might set their hope in God and not forget the works of God, but keep His commandments, and they might not be as their fathers, a stubborn and rebellious generation, a generation that did not set their heart steadfast, and whose spirit was not faithful to God.

—Psalm 78:7–8

A man who has friends must show himself friendly, and there is a friend who sticks closer than a brother.

—Proverbs 18:24

If it be so, our God whom we serve is able to deliver us from the burning fiery furnace, and He will deliver us out of your hand, O king. But even if He does not, be it known to you,

O king, that we will not serve your gods, nor worship the golden image which you have set up.

—Daniel 3:17–18

LUST

And it will be for you a tassel, and you will see it, and you will remember all the commandments of the Lord, and you will do them, and you will not follow the lust of your own heart and your own eyes.

—Numbers 15:39

Do not lust after her beauty in your heart, nor let her allure you with her eyelids. For by means of a harlot a man is reduced to a piece of bread, and the adulteress will prey upon his precious life. Can a man take fire in his bosom, and his clothes not be burned? Can one walk upon hot coals, and his feet not be burned? So he who goes in to his neighbor's wife; whoever touches her will not be innocent.

—Proverbs 6:25–29

Likewise, you also consider yourselves to be dead to sin, but alive to God through Jesus Christ our Lord. Therefore do not let sin reign in your mortal body, that you should obey it in its lusts.... For sin shall not have dominion over you, for you are not under the law, but under grace.

—Romans 6:11–12, 14

But put on the Lord Jesus Christ, and make no provision for the flesh to fulfill its lusts.

—Romans 13:14

Those who are Christ's have crucified the flesh with its passions and lusts.

—Galatians 5:24

Among them we all also once lived in the lusts of our flesh, doing the desires of the flesh and of the mind, and we were by nature children of wrath, even as the rest. But God, being rich in mercy, because of His great love with which He loved us, even when we were dead in sins, made us alive together with Christ (by grace you have been saved), and He raised us up and seated us together in the heavenly places in Christ Jesus.

—Ephesians 2:3–6

That each one of you should know how to possess his own vessel in sanctification and honor.

—1 Thessalonians 4:4

Let no man say when he is tempted, "I am tempted by God," for God cannot be tempted with evil; neither does He tempt anyone.

—James 1:13

As obedient children do not conduct yourselves according to the former lusts in your ignorance. But as He who has called you is holy, so be holy in all your conduct, because it is written, "Be holy, for I am holy."

—1 Peter 1:14–16

By which He has given to us exceedingly great and precious promises, so that through these things you might become partakers of the divine nature and escape the corruption that is in the world through lust.

—2 Peter 1:4

For all that is in the world—the lust of the flesh, the lust of the eyes, and the pride of life—is not of the Father, but is of the world. The world and its desires are passing away, but the one who does the will of God lives forever.

—1 John 2:16–17

They said to you, "In the last days there will be scoffers who will walk after their own ungodly desires." These are the worldly people, devoid of the Spirit, who cause division. But you, beloved, build yourselves up in your most holy faith. Pray in the Holy Spirit. Keep yourselves in the love of God while you are waiting for the mercy of our Lord Jesus Christ, which leads to eternal life.

—Jude 18–21

LYING

You must not give a false report. Do not join your hand with the wicked to be a malicious witness.

—Exodus 23:1

You shall not swear falsely by My name, and so defile the name of your God: I am the Lord.

—Leviticus 19:12

If a false witness rises up against any man to testify against him to accuse him of doing wrong, then both the men between whom the controversy is must stand before the Lord, before the priests and the judges, who are in office those days. The judges will thoroughly investigate, and if the witness is a false witness and has testified falsely against his brother, then you must do to him as he conspired to have done to his brother. In this way you must remove the evil from among you.

—Deuteronomy 19:16–19

The wicked are estranged from the womb onward; those who speak lies go astray from birth.

—Psalm 58:3

The truthful lip will be established forever, but a lying tongue is but for a moment.

—Proverbs 12:19

A faithful witness will not lie, but a false witness will utter lies.

—Proverbs 14:5

A false witness will not be unpunished, and he who speaks lies will not escape.

—Proverbs 19:5

A false witness will not be unpunished, and he who speaks lies will perish.

—Proverbs 19:9

Do not be a witness against your neighbor without cause, and do not deceive with your lips.

—Proverbs 24:28

A man who bears false witness against his neighbor is like a club, a sword, and a sharp arrow.

—Proverbs 25:18

But if you have bitter envying and strife in your hearts, do not boast and do not lie against the truth.

—James 3:14

But the cowardly, the unbelieving, the abominable, the murderers, the sexually immoral, the sorcerers, the idolaters, and all liars shall have their portion in the lake which burns with fire and brimstone. This is the second death.

—Revelation 21:8

MANHOOD

Then God said, "Let Us make man in Our image, after Our likeness, and let them have dominion over the fish of the sea, and over the birds of the air, and over the cattle, and over all the earth, and over every creeping thing that creeps on the earth." So God created man in His own image, in the image of God He created him; male and female He created them.

—Genesis 1:26–27

This is the book of the generations of Adam. In the day when God created man, He made him in the likeness of God.

—Genesis 5:1

The angel of the Lord appeared and said to him, "The Lord is with you, O mighty man of valor."

—Judges 6:12

You grant him dominion over the works of Your hands; You have put all things under his feet, all sheep and oxen, also the beasts of the field, the birds of the sky, and the fish of the sea, and whatever passes through the paths of the seas. O Lord our Lord, how excellent is Your name in all the earth!

—Psalm 8:6–9

A man's heart devises his way, but the LORD directs his steps.
—PROVERBS 16:9

But now, O LORD, You are our Father. We are the clay, and You are our potter. And we all are the work of Your hand.
—ISAIAH 64:8

He has told you, O man, what is good—and what does the LORD require of you, but to do justice and to love kindness, and to walk humbly with your God?
—MICAH 6:8

For a man indeed ought not to cover his head, because he is the image and glory of God. But the woman is the glory of the man. The man is not from the woman, but the woman from the man. The man was not created for the woman, but the woman for the man.
—1 CORINTHIANS 11:7–9

Does even nature itself not teach you that if a man has long hair it is a shame to him? But if a woman has long hair, it is a glory to her, for her hair is given her for a covering.
—1 CORINTHIANS 11:14–15

But when the fullness of time came, God sent forth His Son, born from a woman, born under the law, to redeem those who were under the law, that we might receive the adoption as sons. And because you are sons, God has sent forth into our hearts the Spirit of His Son, crying, "Abba, Father!" Therefore you are no longer a servant, but a son, and if a son, then an heir of God through Christ.
—GALATIANS 4:4–7

If there is any encouragement in Christ, if any comfort of love, if any fellowship of the Spirit, if any compassion and mercy, then fulfill my joy and be like-minded, having the same love, being in unity with one mind. Let nothing be done out of strife or conceit, but in humility let each esteem the other better than himself. Let each of you look not only to your own interests, but also to the interests of others.

—Philippians 2:1–4

But someone in a certain place testified, saying, "What is man that You are mindful of him, or the son of man that You care for him? You made him a little lower than the angels. You crowned him with glory and honor and set him over the works of Your hands. You have put all things in subjection under his feet." For in subjecting all things under him, He left nothing that is not subjected to him. Yet now we do not see all things subject to him.

—Hebrews 2:6–8

MARRIAGE

Then the Lord God said, "It is not good that the man should be alone. I will make him a helper suitable for him."

—Genesis 2:18

Then Adam said, "This is now bone of my bones and flesh of my flesh. She will be called Woman, for she was taken out of Man." Therefore a man will leave his father and his mother and be joined to his wife, and they will become one flesh. They were both naked, the man and his wife, and were not ashamed.

—Genesis 2:23–25

Let your fountain be blessed, and rejoice with the wife of your youth. Let her be as the loving deer and pleasant doe; let her breasts satisfy you at all times; and always be enraptured with her love. Why should you, my son, be intoxicated by an immoral woman, and embrace the bosom of a seductress?

—PROVERBS 5:18–20

Whoever finds a wife finds a good thing, and obtains favor of the LORD.

—PROVERBS 18:22

Enjoy life with the wife whom you love all the days of your vain life which He has given you under the sun, because that is your reward in life and in your toil because you have labored under the sun.

—ECCLESIASTES 9:9

Let the husband render to the wife due affection, and likewise the wife to the husband.

—1 CORINTHIANS 7:3

Wives, be submissive to your own husbands as unto the Lord. For the husband is the head of the wife, just as Christ is the head and Savior of the church, which is His body.

—EPHESIANS 5:22–23

For this reason a man shall leave his father and mother and shall be joined to his wife, and the two shall be one flesh.

—EPHESIANS 5:31

However, let each one of you love his wife as himself, and let the wife see that she respects her husband.

—EPHESIANS 5:33

Wives, submit yourselves to your own husbands, as it is fitting in the Lord. Husbands, love your wives, and do not be bitter toward them.

—Colossians 3:18–19

That they may teach the young women to love their husbands, to love their children, and to be self-controlled, pure, homekeepers, good, obedient to their own husbands, that the word of God may not be dishonored.

—Titus 2:4–5

Marriage is to be honored among everyone, and the bed undefiled. But God will judge the sexually immoral and adulterers.

—Hebrews 13:4

Meekness

The meek will eat and be satisfied; those who seek Him will praise the Lord. May your hearts live forever.

—Psalm 22:26

The meek will He guide in judgment; and the meek He will teach His way.

—Psalm 25:9

But the meek will inherit the earth, and will delight themselves in the abundance of peace.

—Psalm 37:11

The Lord lifts up the meek; He casts the wicked down to the ground.

—Psalm 147:6

For the LORD takes pleasure in His people; He will beautify the meek with salvation.

—PSALM 149:4

A soft answer turns away wrath, but grievous words stir up anger.

—PROVERBS 15:1

But with righteousness he shall judge the poor, and reprove with fairness for the meek of the earth. And he shall strike the earth with the rod of his mouth, and with the breath of his lips he shall slay the wicked.

—ISAIAH 11:4

The meek also shall increase their joy in the LORD, and the poor among men shall rejoice in the Holy One of Israel.

—ISAIAH 29:19

Seek the LORD, all you humble of the land, who carry out His judgment; seek righteousness, seek humility. Perhaps you will be hidden on the day of LORD's anger.

—ZEPHANIAH 2:3

Blessed are the meek, for they shall inherit the earth.

—MATTHEW 5:5

To speak evil of no one, not to be contentious, but gentle, showing all humility toward everyone.

—TITUS 3:2

But let it be the hidden nature of the heart, that which is not corruptible, even the ornament of a gentle and quiet spirit, which is very precious in the sight of God.

—1 PETER 3:4

MERCY

But the mercy of the Lord is from everlasting to everlasting upon those who fear Him, and His righteousness to children's children.

—Psalm 103:17

He who covers his sins will not prosper, but whoever confesses and forsakes them will have mercy.

—Proverbs 28:13

Therefore, the Lord longs to be gracious to you, and therefore, He waits on high to have mercy on you. For the Lord is a God of justice. How blessed are all who long for Him.

—Isaiah 30:18

For My name's sake I will defer My anger, and for My praise I will restrain it for you so that you are not cut off.

—Isaiah 48:9

Then I will sow her for Myself in the earth. I will have mercy upon Lo-ruhamah, and I will say to Lo-ammi, "You are My people," and they will say, "You are my God."

—Hosea 2:23

For I desired mercy, and not sacrifice, and the knowledge of God more than burnt offerings.

—Hosea 6:6

He prayed to the Lord and said, "O Lord! Is this not what I said while I was still in my own land? This is the reason that I fled before to Tarshish, because I knew that You are a gracious God and merciful, slow to anger, abundant in faithfulness, and ready to relent from punishment."

—Jonah 4:2

Who is a God like You, bearing iniquity and passing over transgression for the remnant of His inheritance? He does not remain angry forever, because He delights in benevolence.

—Micah 7:18

His mercy is on those who fear Him from generation to generation.

—Luke 1:50

Be therefore merciful, even as your Father is merciful.

—Luke 6:36

For he who has shown no mercy will have judgment without mercy, for mercy triumphs over judgment.

—James 2:13

Keep yourselves in the love of God while you are waiting for the mercy of our Lord Jesus Christ, which leads to eternal life. On some have compassion, using discernment.

—Jude 21–22

MIRACLES

You are the God who can do wonders. You have declared Your strength among the nations.

—Psalm 77:14

Seek the Lord and His strength; seek His presence continuously. Remember His marvelous works that He has done; His wonders and the judgments from His mouth.

—Psalm 105:4–5

He could not do any miracles there, except that He laid His hands on a few sick people and healed them. And He was amazed because of their unbelief.

—Mark 6:5–6

In that same hour He cured many of their infirmities and afflictions and evil spirits. And to many who were blind He gave sight. So Jesus answered them, "Go and tell John what you have seen and heard: that the blind see, the lame walk, the lepers are cleansed, the deaf hear, the dead are raised, and the gospel is preached to the poor."

—Luke 7:21–22

When the crowds pressed upon Him, He began to say, "This is an evil generation. It looks for a sign, but no sign will be given it except the sign of Jonah the prophet. For as Jonah was a sign to the Ninevites, so will the Son of Man be to this generation."

—Luke 11:29–30

Still, many of the people believed in Him, and said, "When the Christ comes, will He do more signs than these which this Man has done?"

—John 7:31

Jesus answered them, "I told you, and you did not believe. The works that I do in My Father's name bear witness of Me."

—John 10:25

Though He had done so many signs before them, yet they did not believe in Him.

—John 12:37

Truly, truly I say to you, he who believes in Me will do the works that I do also. And he will do greater works than these, because I am going to My Father.

—John 14:12

Jesus performed many other signs in the presence of His disciples, which are not written in this book. But these are written that you might believe that Jesus is the Christ, the Son of God, and that believing you may have life in His name.

—John 20:30–31

Fear came to every soul. And many wonders and signs were done through the apostles.

—Acts 2:43

For the Jews require a sign, and the Greeks seek after wisdom. But we preach Christ crucified, a stumbling block to the Jews and foolishness to the Greeks. But to those who are called, both Jews and Greeks, we preach Christ as the power of God and the wisdom of God.

—1 Corinthians 1:22–24

MONEY

But you must remember the Lord your God, for it is He who gives you the ability to get wealth, so that He may establish His covenant which He swore to your fathers, as it is today.

—Deuteronomy 8:18

If they obey and serve Him, they will spend their days in prosperity, and their years in pleasures.

—Job 36:11

"Because the poor are plundered, because the needy sigh, now I will arise," says the LORD. "I will place him in the safety for which he yearns."

—PSALM 12:5

There is one who makes himself rich, yet has nothing; there is one who makes himself poor, yet has great riches.

—PROVERBS 13:7

Better is little with the fear of the LORD than great treasure with trouble.

—PROVERBS 15:16

The one who loves silver will not be satisfied with silver. And who loves money and does not desire revenue in abundance? This is also vanity.

—ECCLESIASTES 5:10

They shall cast their silver in the streets, and their gold shall become abhorrent. Their silver and their gold shall not be able to deliver them in the day of the wrath of the LORD. They shall not satisfy their souls or fill their stomachs, for their iniquity has become a stumbling block.

—EZEKIEL 7:19

"Will a man rob God? Yet you have robbed Me. But you say, 'How have we robbed You?' In tithes and offerings. You are cursed with a curse, your whole nation, for you are robbing Me. Bring all the tithes into the storehouse, that there may be food in My house, and test Me now in this," says the LORD of Hosts, "if I will not open for you the windows of heaven and pour out for you a blessing, that there will not be room enough to receive it."

—Malachi 3:8–10

Then Jesus, looking upon him, loved him and said to him, "You lack one thing: Go your way, sell whatever you have and give to the poor, and you will have treasure in heaven. And come, take up the cross and follow Me." He was saddened by that word, and he went away grieving. For he had many possessions.

—Mark 10:21–22

But my God shall supply your every need according to His riches in glory by Christ Jesus.

—Philippians 4:19

For the love of money is the root of all evil. While coveting after money, some have strayed from the faith and pierced themselves through with many sorrows.

—1 Timothy 6:10

Listen, my beloved brothers. Has God not chosen the poor of this world to be rich in faith and heirs of the kingdom which He has promised to those who love Him?

—James 2:5

MORAL PURITY

And you shall love the LORD your God, with all your heart and with all your soul and with all your might. These words, which I am commanding you today, shall be in your heart. You shall teach them diligently to your children and shall talk of them when you sit in your house, and when you walk by the way and when you lie down and when you rise up. You shall bind them as a sign on your hand, and they shall be as frontlets between your eyes. You shall write them on the doorposts of your house and on your gates.

—Deuteronomy 6:5–9

They have acted corruptly to Him. They are not His children, but blemished. They are a perverse and crooked generation. Is this how you repay the Lord, you foolish and unwise people? Is He not your father who has bought you? Has He not made you, and established you?

—Deuteronomy 32:5–6

In pride the wicked one is in hot pursuit of the poor. May they be caught in the devices they have planned.

—Psalm 10:2

They sit in the lurking places of the villages; in the secret places they murder the innocent; their eyes lurk against the unfortunate....Break the arm of the wicked and the evil ones; seek out their wickedness until You find none.

—Psalm 10:8, 15

Have mercy on me, O God, according to Your lovingkindness; according to the abundance of Your compassion, blot out my transgressions. Wash me thoroughly from my iniquity, and cleanse me from my sin. For I acknowledge my transgressions, and my sin is ever before me.

—Psalm 51:1–3

I will set no wicked thing before my eyes. I hate the work of those who turn aside; it shall not have part of me. A perverted heart shall be far from me; I will not know anything wicked.

—Psalm 101:3–4

Why do you all scheme against the Lord? He will bring it to an end. It will not rise up a second time. Because they are like interwoven thorns and as drunkards imbibing, they are consumed like completely dry stubble. Out of you, O Nineveh, comes one, a worthless counselor, who devises evil against the Lord.

—Nahum 1:9–11

But Jesus said, "Let the little children come to Me, and do not forbid them. For to such belongs the kingdom of heaven."
—Matthew 19:14

Who know the righteous requirement of God, that those who commit such things are worthy of death. They not only do them, but also give hearty approval to those who practice them.

—Romans 1:32

Do not be conformed to this world, but be transformed by the renewing of your mind, that you may prove what is the good and acceptable and perfect will of God.

—Romans 12:2

But the fruit of the Spirit is love, joy, peace, patience, gentleness, goodness, faith, meekness, and self-control; against such there is no law. Those who are Christ's have crucified the flesh with its passions and lusts. If we live in the Spirit, let us also walk in the Spirit.

—GALATIANS 5:22–25

Fathers, do not provoke your children to anger, lest they be discouraged.

—COLOSSIANS 3:21

MUSIC

Hear, O kings! Listen, O rulers! I will sing to the LORD. I will sing praise to the LORD God of Israel.

—JUDGES 5:3

At the dedication of the wall of Jerusalem they sought to bring the Levites from all their places to Jerusalem to celebrate the dedication appropriately with thanksgiving songs and singing, accompanied by cymbals, harps, and lyres.

—NEHEMIAH 12:27

Let the words of my mouth and the meditation of my heart be acceptable in Your sight, O LORD, my strength, and my redeemer.

—PSALM 19:14

Now my head will be lifted up above my enemies encircling me; therefore I will offer sacrifices of joy in His tabernacle; I will sing, yes, I will sing praises to the LORD.

—PSALM 27:6

Give thanks to the LORD with the harp; make music to Him with an instrument of ten strings. Sing to Him a new song; play an instrument skillfully with a joyful shout.

—PSALM 33:2–3

Speak to one another in psalms, hymns and spiritual songs, singing and making melody in your heart to the Lord. Give thanks always for all things to God the Father in the name of our Lord Jesus Christ.

—Ephesians 5:19–20

OBEDIENCE

See, I am setting before you today a blessing and a curse: The blessing if you obey the commandments of the Lord your God, which I am commanding you today, and the curse, if you will not obey the commandments of the Lord your God, but turn from the way which I am commanding you today, to go after other gods which you have not known.

—Deuteronomy 11:26–28

Therefore, keep the words of this covenant and do them, so that you may prosper in all you do.

—Deuteronomy 29:9

Blessed are those who keep justice and who do righteousness at all times.

—Psalm 106:3

Whoever, therefore, breaks one of the least of these commandments and teaches others to do likewise shall be called the least in the kingdom of heaven. But whoever does and teaches them shall be called great in the kingdom of heaven.

—Matthew 5:19

Not everyone who says to Me, "Lord, Lord," shall enter the kingdom of heaven, but he who does the will of My Father who is in heaven.

—Matthew 7:21

If you know these things, blessed are you if you do them.
—John 13:17

For the hearers of the law are not justified before God, but the doers of the law will be justified.
—Romans 2:13

And being found in the form of a man, He humbled Himself and became obedient to death, even death on a cross.
—Philippians 2:8

Be doers of the word and not hearers only, deceiving yourselves.
—James 1:22

Therefore, to him who knows to do good and does not do it, it is sin.
—James 4:17

And whatever we ask, we will receive from Him, because we keep His commandments and do the things that are pleasing in His sight.
—1 John 3:22

For this is the love of God, that we keep His commandments. And His commandments are not burdensome.
—1 John 5:3

OCCULT

There must not be found among you anyone who makes his son or his daughter pass through the fire, or who uses divination, or uses witchcraft, or an interpreter of omens, or a sorcerer, or one who casts spells, or a spiritualist, or an occultist, or a necromancer. For all that do these things are an abomination to the LORD, and because of these abominations the LORD your God will drive them out from before you.

—Deuteronomy 18:10–12

So Saul died because of his unfaithful deeds against the LORD, because of his failure to keep the word of the LORD, and because he sought to consult a spirit of divination but did not seek the LORD. So He killed him and turned the kingdom over to David the son of Jesse.

—1 Chronicles 10:13–14

You are wearied in the multitude of your counsels. Let now the astrologers, the stargazers, the monthly prognosticators stand up and save you from these things that shall come upon you. Surely they shall be as stubble. The fire shall burn them. They shall not deliver themselves from the power of the flame. There shall not be coal to warm by nor a fire to sit before.

—Isaiah 47:13–14

He has delivered us from the power of darkness and has transferred us into the kingdom of His dear Son, in whom we have redemption through His blood, the forgiveness of sins.

—Colossians 1:13–14

You are of God, little children, and have overcome them, because He who is in you is greater than he who is in the world.

—1 John 4:4

But the cowardly, the unbelieving, the abominable, the murderers, the sexually immoral, the sorcerers, the idolaters, and all liars shall have their portion in the lake which burns with fire and brimstone. This is the second death.

—REVELATION 21:8

OPPRESSION

From the wicked who bring ruin to me, from my deadly enemies who surround me.

—PSALM 17:9

Because of the voice of the enemy, because of the pressure of the wicked, for they cause trouble to drop on me, and in wrath they have animosity against me.

—PSALM 55:3

Yet He raises up the poor from affliction and cares for their families like flocks of sheep. The righteous shall see it and rejoice, and all evil people shall stop their mouth. Whoever is wise let him observe these things; let them consider the lovingkindness of the LORD.

—PSALM 107:41–43

Who executes justice for the oppressed, who gives food to the hungry; the LORD releases the prisoners.

—PSALM 146:7

If you observe in a district an oppression of the poor and a robbing of justice and righteous, do not be astounded at this matter. For the high official is watched over by an even higher official, and there are even higher officials over them.

—ECCLESIASTES 5:8

Let my outcasts dwell with you, Moab. Be a hiding place to them from the face of the destroyer. For the extortioner has come to an end. The destroyer ceases. The oppressors are consumed out of the land.

—Isaiah 16:4

Like a crane or a swallow, so I twitter. I mourn as a dove. My eyes look wistfully upward. O Lord, I am oppressed. Undertake for me.

—Isaiah 38:14

O house of David, thus says the Lord, "Execute justice each morning, and deliver him who has been robbed from the hand of the oppressor, lest My fury go out like fire and burn so that no one can quench it, because of the evil of your deeds."

—Jeremiah 21:12

I will seek that which was lost and bring back that which was driven away and bind up that which was broken and will strengthen that which was sick. But I will destroy the fat and the strong. I will feed them with judgment.

—Ezekiel 34:16

At that time I will deal with all who oppresses you; I will save the lame and gather the outcast; I will give them praise and fame in every land where they have been put to shame.

—Zephaniah 3:19

Then I will make camp at My house with a garrison so that no one can pass back and forth, and no oppressor will pass through them, for now I see with My eyes.

—Zechariah 9:8

How God anointed Jesus of Nazareth with the Holy Spirit and with power, who went about doing good and healing all who were oppressed by the devil, for God was with Him.

—Acts 10:38

OVERCOMING

He removed the high places, broke down the sacred pillars, cut down the Asherah poles, and crushed the bronze serpent that Moses had made, for until those days the Israelites had made offerings to it. They called it Nehushtan.

—2 Kings 18:4

Then the Ammonites and Moabites stood up against those dwelling from Mount Seir to destroy and finish them. Then when they finished the Edomites, each man attacked his companion to destroy each other.

—2 Chronicles 20:23

So pursue them with Your storm, and make them afraid with Your hurricane.

—Psalm 83:15

Let them be confounded and troubled forever; yes, let them be put to shame and perish.

—Psalm 83:17

The ram which you saw having two horns represent the kings of Media and Persia.

—Daniel 8:20

Beloved, do not believe every spirit, but test the spirits to see whether they are from God, because many false prophets have gone out into the world.

—1 John 4:1

OVERTAKING THE ENEMY

I will give peace in the land, and you shall lie down for sleep, and none shall make you afraid; I will remove harmful beasts from the land, and the sword shall not go through your land. You shall chase your enemies, and they shall fall before you by the sword. Five of you shall chase a hundred, and a hundred of you shall put ten thousand to flight, and your enemies shall fall before you by the sword.

—Leviticus 26:6–8

The Lord said to Joshua, "Do not be afraid of them, for I have given them into your hand. Not a single man can stand before you."

—Joshua 10:8

As for you, do not stop pursuing your enemies, but attack them from behind. Do not let them go back to their cities, for the Lord your God has given them into your hand.

—Joshua 10:19

He delivers me from my enemies. You lift me up above those who rise up against me. You have delivered me from the violent one.

—Psalm 18:48

But I trusted in You, O Lord, I said, "You are my God." My times are in Your hand. Deliver me from the hand of my enemies and my pursuers.

—Psalm 31:14–15

You will hide them in the secret of Your presence from conspirators; You will keep them secretly in a shelter from the strife of tongues.

—Psalm 31:20

PARENTAL RESPONSIBILITIES

You shall declare to your son on that day, saying, "This is done because of that which the Lord did for me when I came forth out of Egypt."

—Exodus 13:8

Every person among you shall revere his mother and his father, and you will keep My Sabbaths: I am the Lord your God.

—Leviticus 19:3

Only give heed to yourself and keep your soul diligently, lest you forget the things which your eyes have seen and lest they depart from your heart all the days of your life; but teach them to your sons, and your grandsons. Especially concerning the day you stood before the Lord your God at Horeb, when the Lord said to me, "Gather the people together to Me, so that I will let them hear My words so that they may learn to fear Me all the days they shall live on the earth, and so that they may teach their children."

—Deuteronomy 4:9–10

You shall teach them to your children, speaking of them when you sit in your house and when you walk by the way, when you lie down, and when you rise up.

—Deuteronomy 11:19

We will not hide them from their children, but will tell the coming generation the praises of the Lord, and His strength, and the wonderful works that He has done. For He established a rule in Jacob, and appointed a law in Israel, which He commanded our fathers that they should make them known to their children, that the generation to come might know them, even the children who are not yet born, who will arise and declare them to their children: That they might set their hope in God and not forget the works of God, but keep His commandments.

—Psalm 78:4–7

He who mistreats his father, and chases away his mother, is a son who causes shame and brings reproach.

—Proverbs 19:26

Whoever curses his father or his mother, his lamp will be put out in obscure darkness.

—Proverbs 20:20

The father of the righteous will greatly rejoice, and he who fathers a wise child will have joy of him.

—Proverbs 23:24

Whoever robs his father or his mother and says, "It is no transgression," the same is the companion of a destroyer.

—Proverbs 28:24

Correct your son, and he will give you rest; yes, he will give delight to your soul.

—Proverbs 29:17

You know the commandments: "Do not commit adultery," "Do not kill," "Do not steal," "Do not bear false witness," "Honor your father and your mother."

—Luke 18:20

Fathers, do not provoke your children to anger, lest they be discouraged.

—Colossians 3:21

PATIENCE

Rest in the Lord, and wait patiently for Him; do not fret because of those who prosper in their way, because of those who make wicked schemes.

—Psalm 37:7

The end of a matter is better than the beginning of it, and the patient in spirit than the haughty in spirit.

—Ecclesiastes 7:8

But he who endures to the end shall be saved.

—Matthew 24:13

But the fruit of the Spirit is love, joy, peace, patience, gentleness, goodness, faith.

—Galatians 5:22

And let us not grow weary in doing good, for in due season we shall reap, if we do not give up.

—Galatians 6:9

Now we exhort you, brothers, warn those who are unruly, comfort the faint-hearted, support the weak, and be patient toward everyone. See that no one renders evil for evil to anyone. But always seek to do good to one another and to all.

—1 Thessalonians 5:14–15

So that you may not be lazy, but imitators of those who through faith and patience inherit the promises.

—Hebrews 6:12

For you need patience, so that after you have done the will of God, you will receive the promise.

—Hebrews 10:36

My brothers, count it all joy when you fall into diverse temptations, knowing that the trying of your faith develops patience. But let patience perfect its work, that you may be perfect and complete, lacking nothing.

—James 1:2–4

Therefore be patient, brothers, until the coming of the Lord. Notice how the farmer waits for the precious fruit of the earth and is patient with it until he receives the early and late rain. You also be patient. Establish your hearts, for the coming of the Lord is drawing near.

—James 5:7–8

For what credit is it if when you are being beaten for your sins you patiently endure? But if when doing good and suffering for it, you patiently endure, this is excellence before God.

—1 Peter 2:20

PEACE

Now acquaint yourself with Him and be at peace. Thereby good will come to you.

—Job 22:21

I will both lie down in peace and sleep; for You, Lord, make me dwell safely and securely.

—Psalm 4:8

Turn away from evil, and do good; seek peace, and pursue it.
—Psalm 34:14

I will hear what God the Lord will speak, for He will speak peace to His people and to His saints, but let them not turn again to folly.

—Psalm 85:8

Lord, You will ordain peace for us, for You also have done all our works for us.

—Isaiah 26:12

Salt is good. But if the salt loses its saltiness, how will you season it? Have salt in yourselves, and have peace with one another.

—Mark 9:50

He said to the woman, "Your faith has saved you. Go in peace."

—Luke 7:50

Will be tribulation and anguish, upon every soul of man who does evil, to the Jew first, and then to the Gentile. But glory, honor, and peace will be to every man who does good work—to the Jew first, and then to the Gentile.

—Romans 2:9–10

If it is possible, as much as it depends on you, live peaceably with all men.

—Romans 12:18

For He is our peace, who has made both groups one and has broken down the barrier of the dividing wall.

—Ephesians 2:14

And to reconcile all things to Himself by Him, having made peace through the blood of His cross, by Him, I say, whether they are things in earth, or things in heaven.

—Colossians 1:20

But the wisdom that is from above is first pure, then peaceable, gentle, open to reason, full of mercy and good fruits, without partiality, and without hypocrisy. And the fruit of righteousness is sown in peace by those who make peace.

—James 3:17–18

PEER PRESSURE

"So come out from among them and be separate," says the Lord. "Do not touch what is unclean, and I will receive you. I will be a Father to you, and you shall be My sons and daughters," says the Lord Almighty.

—2 Corinthians 6:17–18

Since we have these promises, beloved, let us cleanse ourselves from all filthiness of the flesh and spirit, perfecting holiness in the fear of God.

—2 Corinthians 7:1

That you would walk in a manner worthy of God, who has called you to His kingdom and glory.

—1 Thessalonians 2:12

Examine all things. Firmly hold onto what is good. Abstain from all appearances of evil.

—1 Thessalonians 5:21–22

As obedient children do not conduct yourselves according to the former lusts in your ignorance. But as He who has called you is holy, so be holy in all your conduct, because it is written, "Be holy, for I am holy."

—1 Peter 1:14–16

But sanctify the Lord God in your hearts. Always be ready to give an answer to every man who asks you for a reason for the hope that is in you, with gentleness and fear. Have a good conscience so that evildoers who speak evil of you and falsely accuse your good conduct in Christ may be ashamed.

—1 Peter 3:15–16

PERSECUTION

All Your commandments are faithful; the proud persecute me wrongfully; help me!

—Psalm 119:86

Blessed are those who are persecuted for righteousness' sake, for theirs is the kingdom of heaven. Blessed are you when men revile you, and persecute you, and say all kinds of evil against you falsely for My sake. Rejoice and be very glad, because great is your reward in heaven, for in this manner they persecuted the prophets who were before you.

—MATTHEW 5:10–12

You will be hated by all men for My name's sake. But he who endures to the end will be saved.

—MATTHEW 10:22

Bless those who persecute you; bless, and do not curse.

—ROMANS 12:14

We labor, working with our own hands. Being reviled, we bless. Being persecuted, we endure. Being slandered, we encourage. We are made as the filth of the world, and are the refuse of all things to this day.

—1 CORINTHIANS 4:12–13

Yes, and all who desire to live a godly life in Christ Jesus will suffer persecution.

—2 TIMOTHY 3:12

PERSEVERANCE IN ADVERSITY

Before I was afflicted I wandered, but now I keep Your word.

—PSALM 119:67

See, I have refined you, but not with silver. I have chosen you in the furnace of affliction.

—ISAIAH 48:10

For a small moment I have forsaken you, but with great mercies I will gather you.

—ISAIAH 54:7

Do not rejoice over me, my enemy! Although I have fallen, I will rise. Although I dwell in darkness, the LORD is my light!

—MICAH 7:8

In your endurance you will gain your souls.

—LUKE 21:19

Not only so, but we also boast in tribulation, knowing that tribulation produces patience, Patience produces character, and character produces hope. And hope does not disappoint, because the love of God is shed abroad in our hearts by the Holy Spirit who has been given to us.

—ROMANS 5:3–5

For I consider that the sufferings of this present time are not worthy to be compared with the glory which shall be revealed to us.

—ROMANS 8:18

Our light affliction, which lasts but for a moment, works for us a far more exceeding and eternal weight of glory.

—2 CORINTHIANS 4:17

My brothers, count it all joy when you fall into diverse temptations, knowing that the trying of your faith develops patience. But let patience perfect its work, that you may be perfect and complete, lacking nothing. If any of you lacks wisdom, let him ask of God, who gives to all men liberally and without criticism, and it will be given to him. But let him ask in faith, without wavering. For he who wavers is like a wave of the sea, driven and tossed with the wind. Let not that man think that he will receive anything from the Lord. A double-minded man is unstable in all his ways.

—James 1:2–8

Is anyone among you suffering? Let him pray. Is anyone merry? Let him sing psalms.

—James 5:13

But rejoice in so far as you share in Christ's sufferings, so that you may rejoice and be glad also in the revelation of His glory.

—1 Peter 4:13

PERSPECTIVE

But the LORD said to Samuel, "Do not look on his appearance or on the height of his stature, because I have rejected him. For the LORD sees not as man sees. For man looks on the outward appearance, but the LORD looks on the heart."

—1 Samuel 16:7

The counsel of the LORD stands forever, the purposes of His heart to all generations.

—Psalm 33:11

Your mercy, O LORD, is in the heavens, and Your faithfulness reaches to the clouds.

—Psalm 36:5

I will remember the works of the LORD; surely I will remember Your wonders of old.... Your way is through the sea, and Your path in the great waters, and Your footsteps are not seen.

—Psalm 77:11, 19

For I have said, "Mercy shall be built up forever; Your faithfulness shall be established in the heavens."

—Psalm 89:2

O Lord, how great are Your works! Your thoughts are very deep!

—Psalm 92:5

For as the heavens are high above the earth, so great is His mercy toward those who fear Him.

—Psalm 103:11

Have you not known? Have you not heard, that the everlasting God, the Lord, the Creator of the ends of the earth, does not faint, nor is He weary? His understanding is inscrutable. He gives power to the faint, and to those who have no might He increases strength.

—Isaiah 40:28–29

"For My thoughts are not your thoughts, nor are your ways My ways," says the Lord. "For as the heavens are higher than the earth, so are My ways higher than your ways, and My thoughts than your thoughts."

—Isaiah 55:8–9

Now I, Nebuchadnezzar, praise and extol and honor the King of heaven, for all His works are true and His ways just, and those who walk in pride He is able to abase.

—Daniel 4:37

If you then, being evil, know how to give good gifts to your children, how much more will your Father who is in heaven give good things to those who ask Him?

—Matthew 7:11

O the depth of the riches and wisdom and knowledge of God! How unsearchable are His judgments and unfathomable are His ways! "For who has known the mind of the Lord? Or who has become His counselor?" "Or who has first given to Him, and it shall be repaid to Him?" For from Him and through Him and to Him are all things. To Him be glory forever. Amen.

—Romans 11:33–36

PORNOGRAPHY

Turn away my eyes from beholding worthlessness, and revive me in Your way.

—Psalm 119:37

But I say to you that whoever looks on a woman to lust after her has committed adultery with her already in his heart.

—Matthew 5:28

Do you not know that the unrighteous will not inherit the kingdom of God? Do not be deceived. Neither the sexually immoral, nor idolaters, nor adulterers, nor male prostitutes, nor homosexuals, nor thieves, nor covetous, nor drunkards, nor revilers, nor extortioners will inherit the kingdom of God.

—1 Corinthians 6:9–10

Escape from sexual immorality. Every sin that a man commits is outside the body. But he who commits sexual immorality sins against his own body. What? Do you not know that your body is the temple of the Holy Spirit, who is in you, whom you have received from God, and that you are not your own? You were bought with a price. Therefore glorify God in your body and in your spirit, which are God's.

—1 Corinthians 6:18–20

No temptation has taken you except what is common to man. God is faithful, and He will not permit you to be tempted above what you can endure, but will with the temptation also make a way to escape, that you may be able to bear it.

—1 Corinthians 10:13

Now the works of the flesh are revealed, which are these: adultery, sexual immorality, impurity, lewdness.

—Galatians 5:19

Therefore this I say and testify in the Lord, that from now on you walk not as other Gentiles walk, in the vanity of their minds, having their understanding darkened, excluded from the life of God through the ignorance that is within them, due to the hardness of their hearts. Being calloused, they have given themselves over to sensuality for the practice of every kind of impurity with greediness. But you did not learn about Christ in this manner.

—Ephesians 4:17–20

And do not have fellowship with the unfruitful works of darkness; instead, expose them. For it is shameful even to speak of those things which are done by them in secret.

—Ephesians 5:11–12

Finally, brothers, whatever things are true, whatever things are honest, whatever things are just, whatever things are pure, whatever things are lovely, whatever things are of good report, if there is any virtue, and if there is any praise, think on these things.

—Philippians 4:8

For God has not given us the spirit of fear, but of power, and love, and self-control.

—2 Timothy 1:7

Marriage is to be honored among everyone, and the bed undefiled. But God will judge the sexually immoral and adulterers.

—Hebrews 13:4

For all that is in the world—the lust of the flesh, the lust of the eyes, and the pride of life—is not of the Father, but is of the world.

—1 John 2:16

POSITION IN GOD

I am the true vine, and My Father is the vinedresser....I am the vine, you are the branches. He who remains in Me, and I in him, bears much fruit. For without Me you can do nothing.

—John 15:1, 5

To the church of God which is at Corinth, to those who are sanctified in Christ Jesus, called to be saints, with all who in every place call on the name of Jesus Christ our Lord, both their Lord and ours.

—1 Corinthians 1:2

Do you not know that you are the temple of God, and that the Spirit of God dwells in you?

—1 Corinthians 3:16

But he who is joined to the Lord becomes one spirit with Him.

—1 Corinthians 6:17

Now you are the body of Christ and members individually.

—1 Corinthians 12:27

All this is from God, who has reconciled us to Himself through Jesus Christ and has given to us the ministry of reconciliation.

—2 Corinthians 5:18

Paul, an apostle of Jesus Christ by the will of God, to the saints who are at Ephesus and to the faithful in Christ Jesus.

—Ephesians 1:1

For through Him we both have access by one Spirit to the Father.

—Ephesians 2:18

Paul and Timothy, servants of Jesus Christ, to all the saints in Christ Jesus who are at Philippi, with the overseers and deacons.

—Philippians 1:1

For you are dead, and your life is hidden with Christ in God.

—Colossians 3:3

You are all the sons of light and the sons of the day. We are not of the night nor of darkness.

—1 Thessalonians 5:5

For we have become partakers of Christ if we hold the beginning of our confidence firmly to the end.

—Hebrews 3:14

POVERTY

For the LORD hears the poor, and does not despise His prisoners.

—PSALM 69:33

Indeed, may he deliver the needy when he cries; the poor also, and him who has no helper. May he have compassion on the poor and needy, and save the lives of the needy.

—PSALM 72:12–13

He will regard the prayer of the destitute and will not despise their prayer.

—PSALM 102:17

He raises up the poor out of the dust and lifts the needy out of the ash heap.

—PSALM 113:7

I will abundantly bless her provisions; I will satisfy her poor with bread.

—PSALM 132:15

Sing to the LORD, praise the LORD. For He has delivered the soul of the poor from the hand of evildoers.

—JEREMIAH 20:13

POWER

But, indeed, for this cause I have raised you up, in order to show in you My power and so that My name may be declared throughout all the earth.

—EXODUS 9:16

See now that I, even I, am He, and there is no god besides Me. I kill, and I make alive. I wound, and I heal. There is no one who can deliver out of My hand.

—DEUTERONOMY 32:39

To You, O LORD, is the greatness, and the power, and the glory, and the victory, and the majesty, for everything in the heavens and the earth is Yours. Yours is the kingdom, O LORD, and You exalt Yourself as head above all.

—1 CHRONICLES 29:11

He is wise in heart and mighty in strength. Who has hardened himself against Him and prospered?

—JOB 9:4

Great is our Lord and great in power; His understanding is without measure.

—PSALM 147:5

A wise man is strong; yes, a man of knowledge increases strength.

—PROVERBS 24:5

Behold, I am the LORD, the God of all flesh. Is anything too hard for Me?

—JEREMIAH 32:27

And all the inhabitants of the earth are reputed as nothing. And He does according to His will in the army of heaven and among the inhabitants of the earth. And no one can stay His hand or say to Him, "What have You done?"

—DANIEL 4:35

The Lord is slow to anger and great in power, and the Lord will in no way acquit the guilty. In gale winds and a storm is His way, and clouds are the dust of His feet.

—Nahum 1:3

And he said, "This is the word of the Lord to Zerubbabel, saying, 'Not by might nor by power, but by My Spirit,' says the Lord of Hosts."

—Zechariah 4:6

But Jesus looked at them and said, "With men this is impossible, but with God all things are possible."

—Matthew 19:26

Strengthened with all might according to His glorious power, enduring everything with perseverance and patience joyfully.

—Colossians 1:11

POWER OF GOD'S WORD

Your right hand, O Lord, is glorious in power. Your right hand, O Lord, shatters the enemy.

—Exodus 15:6

Riches and honor flow from You, and You rule over all. In Your hand are power and might, and in Your hand it is to make great and to strengthen all.

—1 Chronicles 29:12

He rules by His power forever; His eyes keep watch on the nations; do not let the rebellious exalt themselves. Selah.

—Psalm 66:7

Who knows the power of Your anger? Or Your wrath according to Your fear?

—Psalm 90:11

Sanctify them by Your truth. Your word is truth.

—John 17:17

To open their eyes and to turn them from darkness to light, and from the power of Satan to God, that they may receive forgiveness of sins and an inheritance among those who are sanctified by faith in Me.

—Acts 26:18

So then faith comes by hearing, and hearing by the word of God.

—Romans 10:17

By the power of signs and wonders, by the power of the Spirit of God, so that from Jerusalem and as far around as Illyricum, I have fully preached the gospel of Christ.

—Romans 15:19

My speech and my preaching was not with enticing words of man's wisdom, but in demonstration of the Spirit and of power.

—1 Corinthians 2:4

For God, who commanded the light to shine out of darkness, has shone in our hearts to give the light of the knowledge of the glory of God in the face of Jesus Christ.

—2 Corinthians 4:6

For the word of God is alive, and active, and sharper than any two-edged sword, piercing even to the division of soul and spirit, of joints and marrow, and able to judge the thoughts and intents of the heart.

—Hebrews 4:12

Whereas angels, who are greater in power and might, do not bring slanderous accusations against them before the Lord.

—2 Peter 2:11

POWER OF JESUS'S NAME

Then Jesus came and spoke to them saying, "All authority has been given to Me in heaven and on earth."

—Matthew 28:18

Look, I give you authority to trample on serpents and scorpions, and over all the power of the enemy. And nothing shall by any means hurt you.

—Luke 10:19

On that day you will ask Me nothing. Truly, truly I say to you, whatever you ask the Father in My name, He will give it to you.

—John 16:23

Then Peter said, "I have no silver and gold, but I give you what I have. In the name of Jesus Christ of Nazareth, rise up and walk."

—Acts 3:6

Now, Lord, look on their threats and grant that Your servants may speak Your word with great boldness, by stretching out Your hand to heal and that signs and wonders may be performed in the name of Your holy Son Jesus.

—Acts 4:29–30

Whoever practices sin is of the devil, for the devil has been sinning from the beginning. For this purpose the Son of God was revealed, that He might destroy the works of the devil.

—1 John 3:8

POWER OF PRAISE

Sing to the Lord, O you saints of His, and give thanks at the remembrance of His holiness.

—Psalm 30:4

Whoever sacrifices a thank offering glorifies Me and makes a way; I will show him the salvation of God.

—Psalm 50:23

O come, let us worship and bow down; let us kneel before the Lord, our Maker. For He is our God, and we are the people of His pasture and the sheep of His hand.

—Psalm 95:6–7

Praise the Lord! Praise God in His sanctuary; praise Him in the firmament of His power. Praise Him for His mighty acts; praise Him according to His excellent greatness. Praise Him with the sound of the trumpet; praise Him with the lyre and harp. Praise Him with the tambourine and dancing; praise Him with stringed instruments and flute. Praise Him with loud cymbals; praise Him with the clanging cymbals. Let everything that has breath praise the Lord. Praise the Lord!

—Psalm 150:1–6

Without question, great is the mystery of godliness: God was revealed in the flesh, justified in the Spirit, seen by angels, preached to the Gentiles, believed on in the world, and taken up into glory.

—1 Timothy 3:16

Through Him, then, let us continually offer to God the sacrifice of praise, which is the fruit of our lips, giving thanks to His name.

—Hebrews 13:15

POWER OF THE BLOOD

And there was a man whose hand had withered. They asked Him, "Is it lawful to heal on the Sabbath?" that they might accuse Him.

—Matthew 12:10

For this is My blood of the new covenant, which is shed for many for the remission of sins.

—Matthew 26:28

When Jesus had stood up and saw no one but the woman, He said to her, "Woman, where are your accusers? Did no one condemn you?"

—John 8:10

In Him we have redemption through His blood and the forgiveness of sins according to the riches of His grace.

—Ephesians 1:7

And to reconcile all things to Himself by Him, having made peace through the blood of His cross, by Him, I say, whether they are things in earth, or things in heaven.

—Colossians 1:20

Then He says, "Their sins and iniquities will I remember no more."

—Hebrews 10:17

Therefore, brothers, we have confidence to enter the Most Holy Place by the blood of Jesus.

—Hebrews 10:19

You have not yet resisted to bloodshed while striving against sin.

—Hebrews 12:4

And to Jesus, the Mediator of a new covenant; and to the sprinkled blood that speaks better than that of Abel.

—Hebrews 12:24

Now may the God of peace, who through the blood of the eternal covenant brought again from the dead our Lord Jesus, the Great Shepherd of the sheep, make you perfect in every good work to do His will, working in you that which is pleasing in His sight, through Jesus Christ, to whom be glory forever and ever. Amen.

—Hebrews 13:20–21

Then I heard a loud voice in heaven, saying, "Now the salvation and the power and the kingdom of our God and the authority of His Christ have come. For the accuser of our brothers, who accused them before our God day and night, has been cast down."

—Revelation 12:10

They overcame him by the blood of the Lamb and by the word of their testimony. They loved not their lives unto the death.

—REVELATION 12:11

POWER OF THE HOLY SPIRIT

And he said, "This is the word of the LORD to Zerubbabel, saying, 'Not by might nor by power, but by My Spirit,' says the LORD of Hosts."

—ZECHARIAH 4:6

And when Jesus was baptized, He came up immediately out of the water. And suddenly the heavens were opened to Him, and He saw the Spirit of God descending on Him like a dove.

—MATTHEW 3:16

If you then, being evil, know how to give good gifts to your children, how much more will your heavenly Father give the Holy Spirit to those who ask Him?

—LUKE 11:13

But you shall receive power when the Holy Spirit comes upon you. And you shall be My witnesses in Jerusalem, and in all Judea and Samaria, and to the ends of the earth.

—ACTS 1:8

Now may the God of hope fill you with all joy and peace in believing, so that you may abound in hope, through the power of the Holy Spirit.

—ROMANS 15:13

I say then, walk in the Spirit, and you shall not fulfill the lust of the flesh....If we live in the Spirit, let us also walk in the Spirit.

—GALATIANS 5:16, 25

POWER OF THE TONGUE

In the multitude of words sin is not lacking, but he who restrains his lips is wise.

—PROVERBS 10:19

A soft answer turns away wrath, but grievous words stir up anger.

—PROVERBS 15:1

Death and life are in the power of the tongue, and those who love it will eat its fruit.

—PROVERBS 18:21

And he said, "This is the word of the LORD to Zerubbabel, saying, 'Not by might nor by power, but by My Spirit,' says the LORD of Hosts."

—ZECHARIAH 4:6

Let no unwholesome word proceed out of your mouth, but only that which is good for building up, that it may give grace to the listeners.

—EPHESIANS 4:29

If anyone among you seems to be religious and does not bridle his tongue, but deceives his own heart, this man's religion is vain.

—JAMES 1:26

PRAYER

The Lord is far from the wicked, but He hears the prayer of the righteous.

—Proverbs 15:29

O people in Zion, inhabitant in Jerusalem, you shall weep no more. He will be very gracious to you at the sound of your cry. When He hears it, He will answer you.

—Isaiah 30:19

Then you shall call upon Me and you shall come and pray to Me, and I will listen to you.

—Jeremiah 29:12

And I will bring this one third left into the fire and will refine them as the refinement of silver and will test them as the testing of gold. They will call on My name, and I will answer them. I will say, "They are My people," and they will say, "The Lord is my God."

—Zechariah 13:9

Again I say to you, that if two of you agree on earth about anything they ask, it will be done for them by My Father who is in heaven. For where two or three are assembled in My name, there I am in their midst.

—Matthew 18:19–20

Therefore I say to you, whatever things you ask when you pray, believe that you will receive them, and you will have them.

—Mark 11:24

And I tell you, ask, and it will be given to you; seek, and you will find; knock, and it will be opened to you.

—Luke 11:9

Pray in the Spirit always with all kinds of prayer and supplication. To that end be alert with all perseverance and supplication for all the saints.

—Ephesians 6:18

Be anxious for nothing, but in everything, by prayer and supplication with gratitude, make your requests known to God.

—Philippians 4:6

Pray without ceasing.

—1 Thessalonians 5:17

Therefore I exhort first of all that you make supplications, prayers, intercessions, and thanksgivings for everyone.

—1 Timothy 2:1

Let us then come with confidence to the throne of grace, that we may obtain mercy and find grace to help in time of need.

—Hebrews 4:16

Praying for Our Nation

Do not defile yourselves in any of these ways, for in these practices the nations I am casting out before you have defiled themselves.

—Leviticus 18:24

Because if you return to the Lord, your brothers and children will find compassion before those who have taken them captive, in order to return you to this land. For the Lord your God is gracious and compassionate. He will not turn His face from you if you all return to Him.

—2 Chronicles 30:9

All who serve graven images are ashamed, who boast in worthless idols; worship Him, all you gods.

—Psalm 97:7

The Lord reigns; let the peoples tremble! He sits enthroned between the cherubim; let the earth shake.

—Psalm 99:1

But the wicked will be cut off from the earth, and the transgressors will be rooted out of it.

—Proverbs 2:22

The king's heart is in the hand of the Lord, as the rivers of water; He turns it to any place He will.

—Proverbs 21:1

See, a king shall reign in righteousness, and princes shall rule justly.

—Isaiah 32:1

And I will give you shepherds according to My heart, who shall feed you with knowledge and understanding.

—Jeremiah 3:15

It shall come to pass that every living creature which moves to any place the rivers shall come, shall live. And there shall be a very great multitude of fish, because these waters shall come there and the others become healed. Thus everything shall live wherever the river comes.

—Ezekiel 47:9

For the earth will be filled with the knowledge of the glory of the Lord, as the waters cover the seas.

—Habakkuk 2:14

And I will pour out on the house of David and over those dwelling in Jerusalem a spirit of favor and supplication so that they look to Me, whom they have pierced through. And they will mourn over Him as one mourns for an only child and weep bitterly over Him as a firstborn.

—Zechariah 12:10

No unclean thing shall ever enter it, nor shall anyone who commits abomination or falsehood, but only those whose names are written in the Lamb's Book of Life.

—Revelation 21:27

PRIDE

Look on every one who is proud and bring him low, and tread down the wicked in their place.

—Job 40:12

You have rebuked the proud, those cursed, who depart from Your commandments.

—Psalm 119:21

The fear of the Lord is to hate evil; pride and arrogance and the evil way and the perverse mouth I hate.

—Proverbs 8:13

Only by pride comes contention, but with the well-advised is wisdom.

—Proverbs 13:10

Everyone who is proud in heart is an abomination to the Lord; be assured, he will not be unpunished.

—Proverbs 16:5

A high look, a proud heart, and the plowing of the wicked are sin.

—Proverbs 21:4

Let another man praise you, and not your own mouth; a stranger, and not your own lips.

—Proverbs 27:2

The lofty looks of man shall be humbled, and the haughtiness of men shall be bowed down, and the Lord alone shall be exalted in that day.

—Isaiah 2:11

Woe to those who are wise in their own eyes and prudent in their own sight!

—Isaiah 5:21

He sat down and called the twelve. And He said to them, "If anyone desires to be first, he must be last of all and servant of all."

—Mark 9:35

How can you believe, who receive glory from one another and do not seek the glory that comes from the only God?

—John 5:44

But, "Let him who boasts, boast in the Lord." For it not he who commends himself who is approved, but he whom the Lord commends.

—2 Corinthians 10:17–18

PRISONERS

If any of you are driven out to the outmost parts of heaven, from there will the LORD your God gather you, and from there He will get you.

—DEUTERONOMY 30:4

God sets the deserted in families; He brings out prisoners into prosperity, but the rebellious dwell in a dry land.

—PSALM 68:6

He brought them out of darkness and the shadow of death and broke apart their bonds.

—PSALM 107:14

Who executes justice for the oppressed, who gives food to the hungry; the LORD releases the prisoners.

—PSALM 146:7

Indeed, thus says the LORD, "Even the captives of the mighty shall be taken away, and the prey of the tyrant shall be delivered. For I will contend with him who contends with you, and I will save your sons."

—ISAIAH 49:25

Remember those who are in chains, as if imprisoned with them, and those who are ill treated, since you are also in the body.

—HEBREWS 13:3

PROPHECY

I saw in the night visions, and there was one like a Son of Man coming with the clouds of heaven. He came to the Ancient of Days and was presented before Him. There was given to him dominion, and glory, and a kingdom, that all peoples, nations, and languages should serve him. His dominion is an everlasting dominion, which shall not pass away, and his kingdom that which shall not be destroyed.

—Daniel 7:13–14

Then the sign of the Son of Man will appear in heaven, and then all the tribes of the earth will mourn, and they will see the Son of Man coming on the clouds of heaven with power and great glory.

—Matthew 24:30

But he who prophesies speaks to men for their edification and exhortation and comfort.

—1 Corinthians 14:3

While you are waiting for and desiring the coming of the day of God, in which the heavens will be destroyed by fire and the elements will be consumed by intense heat? But, according to His promise, we are waiting for new heavens and a new earth, in which righteousness dwells.

—2 Peter 3:12–13

Look! He is coming with clouds, and every eye will see Him, even those who pierced Him. And all the tribes of the earth will mourn because of Him. Even so, Amen.

—Revelation 1:7

I fell at his feet to worship him. But he said to me, "See that you not do that. I am your fellow servant, and of your brothers who hold the testimony of Jesus. Worship God! For the testimony of Jesus is the spirit of prophecy."

—Revelation 19:10

PROTECTION

For the eyes of the LORD move about on all the earth to strengthen the heart that is completely toward Him. You have acted foolishly in this, and from this point forward you will have wars.

—2 CHRONICLES 16:9

The LORD is my light and my salvation; whom will I fear? The LORD is the strength of my life; of whom will I be afraid?

—PSALM 27:1

Because you have made the LORD, who is my refuge, even the Most High, your dwelling, there shall be no evil befall you, neither shall any plague come near your tent.

—PSALM 91:9–10

The name of the LORD is a strong tower; the righteous run into it and are safe.

—PROVERBS 18:10

But now, thus says the LORD who created you, O Jacob, and He who formed you, O Israel, "Do not fear, for I have redeemed you. I have called you by your name. You are Mine. When you pass through the waters, I will be with you. And through the rivers, they shall not overflow you. When you walk through the fire, you shall not be burned. Neither shall the flame kindle on you."

—ISAIAH 43:1–2

Who is he who will harm you if you follow that which is good?

—1 PETER 3:13

PUNISHMENT

My son, do not despise the chastening of the LORD, nor be weary of His correction. For whom the LORD loves He corrects, even as a father the son in whom he delights.

—PROVERBS 3:11–12

"Your own wickedness will correct you, and your backslidings will reprove you. Know therefore and see that it is an evil thing and bitter for you to have forsaken the LORD your God, and the fear of Me is not in you," says the Lord GOD of Hosts.

—JEREMIAH 2:19

But he who does wrong will receive for the wrong which he has done, and there is no partiality.

—COLOSSIANS 3:25

And to give you who are troubled rest with us when the Lord Jesus is revealed from heaven with His mighty angels, In flaming fire taking vengeance on those who do not know God and do not obey the gospel of our Lord Jesus Christ.

—2 THESSALONIANS 1:7–8

For if the word spoken by angels was true, and every sin and disobedience received a just recompense, how shall we escape if we neglect such a great salvation, which was first declared by the Lord, and was confirmed to us by those who heard Him?

—HEBREWS 2:2–3

Anyone who despised Moses' law died without mercy in the presence of two or three witnesses. How much more severe a punishment do you suppose he deserves, who has trampled under foot the Son of God, and has regarded the blood of the covenant that sanctified him to be a common thing, and has insulted the Spirit of grace?...It is a fearful thing to fall into the hands of the living God.

—Hebrews 10:28–29, 31

PURPOSE

The Lord will fulfill His purpose for me; Your mercy, O Lord, endures forever. Do not forsake the works of Your hands.

—Psalm 138:8

The Lord has made all things for Himself, yes, even the wicked for the day of evil.

—Proverbs 16:4

"For I know the plans that I have for you," says the Lord, "plans for peace and not for evil, to give you a future and a hope."

—Jeremiah 29:11

We know that all things work together for good to those who love God, to those who are called according to His purpose.

—Romans 8:28

For from Him and through Him and to Him are all things. To Him be glory forever. Amen.

—Romans 11:36

But you are a chosen people, a royal priesthood, a holy nation, a people for God's own possession, so that you may declare the goodness of Him who has called you out of darkness into His marvelous light.

—1 Peter 2:9

REBELLION

But they rebelled and grieved His Holy Spirit. Therefore, He turned Himself to be their enemy, and He fought against them.

—Isaiah 63:10

If you love Me, keep My commandments.

—John 14:15

You stiff-necked people, uncircumcised in heart and ears! You always resist the Holy Spirit. As your fathers did, so do you.

—Acts 7:51

Now may the God of hope fill you with all joy and peace in believing, so that you may abound in hope, through the power of the Holy Spirit.

—Romans 15:13

Follow the pattern of sound teaching which you have heard from me in the faith and love that is in Christ Jesus.

—2 Timothy 1:13

The Lord is not slow concerning His promise, as some count slowness. But He is patient with us, because He does not want any to perish, but all to come to repentance.

—2 Peter 3:9

REBUKING THE ENEMY

Rebuke the animals that live among the reeds, the herd of bulls, with the calves of the people, until everyone submits himself with pieces of silver; scatter peoples who delight in war.

—Psalm 68:30

At Your rebuke they fled; at the sound of Your thunder they departed away.

—Psalm 104:7

He rebuked the Red Sea, and it was dried up, so He led them through the depths as through the wilderness.

—Psalm 106:9

You have rebuked the proud, those cursed, who depart from Your commandments.

—Psalm 119:21

The nations rumble like the rumbling of many waters. But God shall rebuke them, and they shall flee far off, and shall be chased as the chaff of the mountains before the wind, and like rolling dust before the whirlwind.

—Isaiah 17:13

For the Lord shall come with fire and with His chariots like a whirlwind, to render His anger with fury and His rebuke with flames of fire.

—Isaiah 66:15

I will execute great vengeance upon them with furious rebukes. And they shall know that I am the Lord when I lay My vengeance upon them.

—Ezekiel 25:17

"I will rebuke the devourer for your sakes, so that it will not destroy the fruit of your ground, and the vines in your field will not fail to bear fruit," says the Lord of Hosts.

—Malachi 3:11

Jesus rebuked him, saying, "Be silent and come out of him!"

—Mark 1:25

He rose and rebuked the wind, and said to the sea, "Peace, be still!" Then the wind ceased and there was a great calm.

—Mark 4:39

While he was coming, the demon threw him down and convulsed him. But Jesus rebuked the unclean spirit, and healed the child, and returned him to his father.

—Luke 9:42

Be sober and watchful, because your adversary the devil walks around as a roaring lion, seeking whom he may devour.

—1 Peter 5:8

Redemption

But He was wounded for our transgressions. He was bruised for our iniquities. The chastisement of our peace was upon Him, and by His stripes we are healed. All of us like sheep have gone astray. Each of us has turned to his own way, but the Lord has laid on Him the iniquity of us all.

—Isaiah 53:5–6

She will bear a Son, and you shall call His name JESUS, for He will save His people from their sins.

—Matthew 1:21

The next day John saw Jesus coming toward him and said, "Look, the Lamb of God, who takes away the sin of the world."

—John 1:29

Therefore, brothers, let it be known to you that through this Man forgiveness of sins is proclaimed to you.

—Acts 13:38

Who gave Himself for our sins, that He might deliver us from this present evil age, according to the will of our God and Father.

—Galatians 1:4

In Him we have redemption through His blood and the forgiveness of sins according to the riches of His grace.

—Ephesians 1:7

This is a faithful saying and worthy of all acceptance, that Christ Jesus came into the world to save sinners, of whom I am the worst.

—1 Timothy 1:15

So Christ was offered once to bear the sins of many, and He will appear a second time, not to bear sin but to save those who eagerly wait for Him.

—Hebrews 9:28

For by one offering He has forever perfected those who are sanctified.

—Hebrews 10:14

He Himself bore our sins in His own body on the tree, that we, being dead to sins, should live unto righteousness. "By His wounds you were healed."

—1 Peter 2:24

My little children, I am writing these things to you, so that you do not sin. But if anyone does sin, we have an Advocate with the Father, Jesus Christ the Righteous One. He is the atoning sacrifice for our sins, and not for ours only, but also for the sins of the whole world.

—1 John 2:1–2

You know that He was revealed to take away our sins, and in Him there is no sin.

—1 John 3:5

RELATIONSHIPS

Iron sharpens iron, so a man sharpens the countenance of his friend.

—Proverbs 27:17

See that you do not despise one of these little ones. For I say to you that in heaven their angels always see the face of My Father who is in heaven.

—Matthew 18:10

Jesus said to him, "'You shall love the Lord your God with all your heart, and with all your soul, and with all your mind.' This is the first and great commandment. And the second is like it: 'You shall love your neighbor as yourself.'"

—Matthew 22:37–39

Then Peter began to speak, saying, "Truthfully, I perceive that God is no respecter of persons. But in every nation he who fears Him and works righteousness is accepted by Him."

—Acts 10:34–35

Render to all what is due them: taxes to whom taxes are due, respect to whom respect is due, fear to whom fear is due, and honor to whom honor is due. Owe no one anything, except to love one another, for he who loves another has fulfilled the law.

—Romans 13:7–8

Do not be unequally yoked together with unbelievers. For what fellowship has righteousness with unrighteousness?…"So come out from among them and be separate," says the Lord. "Do not touch what is unclean, and I will receive you."

—2 Corinthians 6:14, 17

Be eager to keep the unity of the Spirit in the bond of peace. There is one body and one Spirit, even as you were called in one hope of your calling.

—Ephesians 4:3–4

Bear with one another and forgive one another. If anyone has a quarrel against anyone, even as Christ forgave you, so you must do.

—Colossians 3:13

We ask you, brothers, to acknowledge those who labor among you, and are appointed over you in the Lord, and instruct you. Esteem them very highly in love for their work's sake. And be at peace among yourselves.

—1 Thessalonians 5:12–13

The servant of the Lord must not quarrel, but must be gentle toward all people, able to teach, patient, in gentleness instructing those in opposition. Perhaps God will grant them repentance to know the truth.

—2 Timothy 2:24–25

My brothers, have faith in our Lord Jesus Christ, the Lord of glory, without partiality.

—James 2:1

And the fruit of righteousness is sown in peace by those who make peace.

—James 3:18

Releasing the Spoilers

Who leads away priests stripped, and overthrows the mighty.

—Job 12:19

Woe to you, O destroyer, though you were not destroyed, and he who is treacherous though others did not deal treacherously with you! When you cease destroying, you shall be destroyed. And when you finish dealing treacherously, others shall deal treacherously with you.

—Isaiah 33:1

The destroyers have come upon all high places through the wilderness, for the sword of the Lord shall devour from the one end of the land even to the other end of the land. No one shall have peace.

—Jeremiah 12:12

Therefore a tumult will arise among your people, and all your fortresses will be destroyed, as Shalman destroyed Betharbel in the day of battle—mothers were dashed to pieces upon their children.

—Hosea 10:14

There is the sound of wailing shepherds, because their glory is ruined. There is the sound of roaring lions, because the pride of Jordan is ruined.

—ZECHARIAH 11:3

But when a stronger man than he attacks and overpowers him, he seizes all the armor in which the man trusted and divides his spoils.

—LUKE 11:22

RENOUNCE SEXUAL SIN

I urge you therefore, brothers, by the mercies of God, that you present your bodies as a living sacrifice, holy, and acceptable to God, which is your reasonable service of worship. Do not be conformed to this world, but be transformed by the renewing of your mind, that you may prove what is the good and acceptable and perfect will of God.

—ROMANS 12:1–2

Do you not know that the unrighteous will not inherit the kingdom of God? Do not be deceived. Neither the sexually immoral, nor idolaters, nor adulterers, nor male prostitutes, nor homosexuals, nor thieves, nor covetous, nor drunkards, nor revilers, nor extortioners will inherit the kingdom of God.

—1 CORINTHIANS 6:9–10

Escape from sexual immorality. Every sin that a man commits is outside the body. But he who commits sexual immorality sins against his own body.

—1 CORINTHIANS 6:18

I say then, walk in the Spirit, and you shall not fulfill the lust of the flesh.

—GALATIANS 5:16

Therefore put to death the parts of your earthly nature: sexual immorality, uncleanness, inordinate affection, evil desire, and covetousness, which is idolatry.

—COLOSSIANS 3:5

For this is the will of God, your sanctification: that you should abstain from sexual immorality, that each one of you should know how to possess his own vessel in sanctification and honor, not in the lust of depravity, even as the Gentiles who do not know God, and that no man take advantage of and defraud his brother in any matter, because the Lord is the avenger in all these things, as we also have forewarned you and testified. For God has not called us to uncleanness, but to holiness.

—1 THESSALONIANS 4:3–7

REPENTANCE

The LORD is near to the brokenhearted, and saves the contrite of spirit.

—PSALM 34:18

In Your mercy cut off my enemies, and destroy all them who afflict my soul, for I am Your servant.

—PSALM 143:12

But if the wicked turns from all his sins that he has committed, and keeps all My statutes, and does that which is lawful and right, he shall surely live. He shall not die. All his transgressions that he has committed, they shall not be remembered against him. Because of his righteousness that he has done, he shall live.

—Ezekiel 18:21–22

But go and learn what this means, "I desire mercy, and not sacrifice." For I have not come to call the righteous, but sinners, to repentance.

—Matthew 9:13

Saying, "The time is fulfilled, and the kingdom of God is at hand. Repent and believe the gospel."

—Mark 1:15

So they went out and preached that men should repent.

—Mark 6:12

I tell you, no! But unless you repent you will all likewise perish.

—Luke 13:3

Peter said to them, "Repent and be baptized, every one of you, in the name of Jesus Christ for the forgiveness of sins, and you shall receive the gift of the Holy Spirit."

—Acts 2:38

Therefore repent and be converted, that your sins may be wiped away, that times of refreshing may come from the presence of the Lord.

—Acts 3:19

God overlooked the times of ignorance, but now He commands all men everywhere to repent.

—Acts 17:30

Draw near to God, and He will draw near to you. Cleanse your hands, you sinners, and purify your hearts, you double-minded. Grieve and mourn and weep. Let your laughter be turned to mourning, and your joy to dejection. Humble yourselves in the sight of the Lord, and He will lift you up.

—James 4:8–10

Remember therefore from where you have fallen. Repent, and do the works you did at first, or else I will come to you quickly and remove your candlestick from its place, unless you repent.

—Revelation 2:5

RESPECT

Honor your father and your mother, that your days may be prolonged in the land which the Lord your God is giving you.

—Exodus 20:12

You shall rise up before a grey head, and honor the face of an old man, and fear your God: I am the Lord.

—Leviticus 19:32

Therefore the Lord God of Israel says, "I surely said that your house, and the house of your father, should walk before Me forever, but now the Lord says, Far be it from Me to do so, for those who honor Me, I will honor, and those that despise Me will be humbled."

—1 Samuel 2:30

That all men should honor the Son, just as they honor the Father. He who does not honor the Son does not honor the Father who sent Him.

—John 5:23

However, let each one of you love his wife as himself, and let the wife see that she respects her husband.

—Ephesians 5:33

Honor all people. Love the brotherhood. Fear God. Honor the king.

—1 Peter 2:17

REST

Remember the Sabbath day and keep it holy. Six days you shall labor and do all your work, but the seventh day is a Sabbath to the Lord your God. On it you shall not do any work, you, or your son, or your daughter, or your male servant, or your female servant, or your livestock, or your sojourner who is within your gates. For in six days the Lord made heaven and earth, the sea, and all that is in them, and rested on the seventh day. Therefore the Lord blessed the Sabbath day and made it holy.

—Exodus 20:8–11

And He said, "My presence will go with you, and I will give you rest."

—Exodus 33:14

Of Benjamin he said, "The beloved of the Lord will dwell in safety by Him, and the Lord will protect him all day long. He will dwell between His shoulders."

—Deuteronomy 33:12

He makes me lie down in green pastures; He leads me beside restful waters. He restores my soul; He guides me in paths of righteousness for His name's sake.

—Psalm 23:2–3

O God, You are awesome from Your sanctuaries; the God of Israel is He who gives strength and power to people. Blessed be God!

—Psalm 68:35

He who dwells in the shelter of the Most High shall abide under the shadow of the Almighty.

—Psalm 91:1

It is in vain for you to rise up early, to stay up late, and to eat the bread of hard toil, for He gives sleep to His beloved.

—Psalm 127:2

For thus says the Lord God, the Holy One of Israel, "In returning and rest you shall be saved. In quietness and in confidence shall be your strength." Yet you were not willing.

—Isaiah 30:15

He gives power to the faint, and to those who have no might He increases strength. Even the youths shall faint and be weary, and the young men shall utterly fall. But those who wait upon the LORD shall renew their strength. They shall mount up with wings as eagles. They shall run, and not be weary. And they shall walk, and not faint.

—Isaiah 40:29–31

Come to Me, all you who labor and are heavily burdened, and I will give you rest. Take My yoke upon you, and learn from

Me. For I am meek and lowly in heart, and you will find rest for your souls. For My yoke is easy, and My burden is light.

—Matthew 11:28–30

Then He said to them, "Come away by yourselves to a remote place and rest a while," for many were coming and going, and they had no leisure even to eat.

—Mark 6:31

Therefore a rest remains for the people of God. For whoever enters His rest will also cease from his own works, as God did from His. Let us labor therefore to enter that rest, lest anyone fall by the same pattern of unbelief.

—Hebrews 4:9–11

RESTITUTION

If the sun has risen on him, then there is blood guilt for him. He must make full restitution. If he has nothing, then he will be sold for his theft. If the stolen item is in fact found alive in his possession, whether it be an ox, or donkey, or sheep, then he shall repay double.

—Exodus 22:3–4

When a person sins and acts unfaithfully against the Lord by lying to another concerning something left in storage, or entrusted to him, or theft, or by extorting his neighbor...or about which he swore falsely, then he shall repay it in full and shall add one fifth to it. He shall give it to whom it belongs on the day that he is found guilty.

—Leviticus 6:2, 5

Men do not despise a thief if he steals to satisfy himself when he is hungry. But if he is found, he will restore sevenfold; he will give all the substance of his house.

—Proverbs 6:30–31

Whoever, therefore, breaks one of the least of these commandments and teaches others to do likewise shall be called the least in the kingdom of heaven. But whoever does and teaches them shall be called great in the kingdom of heaven.

—Matthew 5:19

But Zacchaeus stood and said to the Lord, "Look, Lord, I give half of my possessions to the poor. And if I have taken anything from anyone by false accusation, I will repay him four times as much." Jesus said to him, "Today salvation has come to this house, because he also is a son of Abraham."

—Luke 19:8–9

Beloved, do not avenge yourselves, but rather give place to God's wrath, for it is written: "Vengeance is Mine. I will repay," says the Lord.

—Romans 12:19

RESURRECTION

O Lord, You have brought up my soul from the grave; You have kept me alive, that I should not go down to the pit.

—Psalm 30:3

But You, O Lord, be gracious to me, and raise me up, that I may repay them.

—Psalm 41:10

He said to them, "Do not be frightened. You are looking for Jesus of Nazareth, who was crucified. He is risen. He is not here. See the place where they laid Him. But go your way, tell His disciples and Peter that He is going before you to Galilee. There you will see Him, as He told you."

—Mark 16:6–7

Jesus said to her, "I am the resurrection and the life. He who believes in Me, though he may die, yet shall he live. And whoever lives and believes in Me shall never die. Do you believe this?"

—John 11:25–26

Yet a little while and the world will see Me no more. But you will see Me. Because I live, you will live also.

—John 14:19

With great power the apostles testified to the resurrection of the Lord Jesus, and great grace was on them all.

—Acts 4:33

I have hope in God that there will be a resurrection of the dead, both of the just and the unjust, which they also expect.

—Acts 24:15

Do you not know that we who were baptized into Jesus Christ were baptized into His death? Therefore we were buried with Him by baptism into death, that just as Christ was raised up from the dead by the glory of the Father, even so, we also should walk in newness of life.

—Romans 6:3–4

For I delivered to you first of all that which I also received: how Christ died for our sins according to the Scriptures, was buried, rose again the third day according to the Scriptures, and was seen by Cephas, and then by the twelve. Then He was seen by over five hundred brothers at once, of whom the greater part remain to this present time, though some have passed away. Then He was seen by James and then by all the apostles. Last of all, He was seen by me also, as by one born at the wrong time.

—1 Corinthians 15:3–8

If Christ has not risen, then our preaching is vain, and your faith is also vain....If Christ is not raised, your faith is vain; you are still in your sins.

—1 Corinthians 15:14, 17

If in this life only we have hope in Christ, we are of all men most miserable. But now is Christ risen from the dead and become the firstfruits of those who have fallen asleep.

—1 Corinthians 15:19–20

But the day of the Lord will come like a thief in the night, in which the heavens will pass away with a loud noise, and the elements will be destroyed with intense heat. The earth also and the works that are in it will be burned up.

—2 Peter 3:10

REVENGE

You shall not take vengeance, nor bear any grudge against the children of your people, but you shall love your neighbor as yourself: I am the Lord.

—Leviticus 19:18

Vengeance is Mine, and recompense. Their foot will slip in due time, for the day of their calamity is at hand, and the things to come hasten upon them.

—Deuteronomy 32:35

I will make My arrows drunk with blood, and My sword will devour flesh—the blood of the slain and of the captives, from the heads of the leaders of the enemies.

—Deuteronomy 32:42

Do not rejoice when your enemy falls, and do not let your heart be glad when he stumbles.

—Proverbs 24:17

You have heard that it was said, "An eye for an eye, and a tooth for a tooth." But I say to you, do not resist an evil person. But whoever strikes you on your right cheek, turn to him the other as well. And if anyone sues you in a court of law and takes away your tunic, let him have your cloak also. And whoever compels you to go a mile, go with him two.

—Matthew 5:38–41

See that no one renders evil for evil to anyone. But always seek to do good to one another and to all.

—1 Thessalonians 5:15

RIGHTEOUSNESS

And you shall love the Lord your God, with all your heart and with all your soul and with all your might.

—Deuteronomy 6:5

Salvation belongs to the LORD: Your blessing is on Your people. Selah.

—PSALM 3:8

You desire truth in the inward parts, and in the hidden part You make me to know wisdom.

—PSALM 51:6

And people will say, "Surely there is a reward for the righteous; surely there is a God who judges on the earth."

—PSALM 58:11

A good man obtains favor of the LORD, but a man of wicked devices will He condemn.

—PROVERBS 12:2

Evil pursues sinners, but to the righteous good will be repaid.

—PROVERBS 13:21

Say to the righteous that it shall be well with them. For they shall eat the fruit of their deeds.

—ISAIAH 3:10

Blessed are those who hunger and thirst for righteousness, for they shall be filled.

—MATTHEW 5:6

He said this to test him, for He Himself knew what He would do.

—JOHN 6:6

Whether Paul or Apollos or Cephas or the world or life or death or things present or things to come, all are yours, And you are Christ's, and Christ is God's.

—1 CORINTHIANS 3:22–23

I am confident of this very thing, that He who began a good work in you will perfect it until the day of Jesus Christ.

—Philippians 1:6

If you then were raised with Christ, desire those things which are above, where Christ sits at the right hand of God. Set your affection on things above, not on things on earth.

—Colossians 3:1–2

Role Models

Hear, you children, the instruction of a father, and attend to know understanding.

—Proverbs 4:1

My son, keep my words, and lay up my commandments within you. Keep my commandments and live, and my teaching as the apple of your eye. Bind them on your fingers, write them on the tablet of your heart.

—Proverbs 7:1–3

He will turn the hearts of the fathers to their children, and the hearts of the children to their fathers, lest I come and strike the earth with a curse.

—Malachi 4:6

But it shall not be so among you. Whoever would be great among you must be your servant, and whoever among you would be greatest must be servant of all.

—Mark 10:43–44

If anyone hears My words and does not believe, I do not judge him. For I did not come to judge the world, but to save the world. He who rejects Me, and does not receive My words, has that which judges him. The word I have spoken will judge him on the last day.

—John 12:47–48

For I have given you an example, that you should do as I have done to you.

—John 13:15

Jesus said to him, "I am the way, the truth, and the life. No one comes to the Father except through Me."

—John 14:6

Therefore be imitators of God as beloved children. Walk in love, as Christ loved us and gave Himself for us as a fragrant offering and a sacrifice to God.

—Ephesians 5:1–2

Let no one despise your youth, but be an example to the believers in speech, in conduct, in love, in spirit, in faith and in purity.

—1 Timothy 4:12

Remembering the genuine faith that first lived in your grandmother Lois and your mother Eunice and that I am persuaded lives in you also.

—2 Timothy 1:5

For to this you were called, because Christ suffered for us, leaving us an example, that you should follow His steps.

—1 Peter 2:21

Shepherd the flock of God that is among you, take care of them, not by constraint, but willingly, not for dishonest gain, but eagerly. Do not lord over those in your charge, but be examples to the flock.

—1 Peter 5:2–3

Safety in Him

The desire of the humble You have heard, O Lord; You make their heart attentive. You bend Your ear to judge the orphan and the oppressed. Man on earth no longer trembles.

—Psalm 10:17–18

"Because the poor are plundered, because the needy sigh, now I will arise," says the Lord. "I will place him in the safety for which he yearns."

—Psalm 12:5

Then He led out His own people like sheep and guided them in the wilderness like a flock.

—Psalm 78:52

Great is our Lord and great in power; His understanding is without measure. The Lord lifts up the meek; He casts the wicked down to the ground.

—Psalm 147:5–6

For thus says the High and Lofty One who inhabits eternity, whose name is Holy, "I dwell in the high and holy place and also with him who is of a contrite and humble spirit, to revive the spirit of the humble, and to revive the heart of the contrite ones."

—Isaiah 57:15

Likewise you younger ones, submit yourselves to the elders. Yes, all of you be submissive one to another and clothe yourselves with humility, because "God resists the proud, and gives grace to the humble." Humble yourselves under the mighty hand of God, that He may exalt you in due time.

—1 Peter 5:5–6

SALVATION

The Lord is my strength and song, and He has become my salvation. He is my God, and I will praise Him, my father's God, and I will exalt Him.

—Exodus 15:2

Now say, "Save us, O God of our salvation, and gather us and deliver us from the nations, that we may give thanks to Your holy name, to glory in Your praise."

—1 Chronicles 16:35

Nevertheless He saved them for His name's sake, that He might make His mighty power known.

—Psalm 106:8

Seek the Lord while He may be found, call you upon Him while He is near.

—Isaiah 55:6

Jesus answered him, "Truly, truly I say to you, unless a man is born again, he cannot see the kingdom of God." Nicodemus said to Him, "How can a man be born when he is old? Can he enter a second time into his mother's womb and be born?" Jesus answered, "Truly, truly I say to you, unless a man is born of water and the Spirit, he cannot enter the kingdom of God. That which is born of the flesh is flesh, and that which is born of the Spirit is spirit. Do not marvel that I said to you, 'You must be born again.'"

—John 3:3–7

On the last and greatest day of the feast, Jesus stood and cried out, "If anyone is thirsty, let him come to Me and drink. He who believes in Me, as the Scripture has said, out of his heart shall flow rivers of living water."

—John 7:37–38

But the free gift is not like the trespass. For if through the trespass of one man many died, then how much more has the grace of God and the free gift by the grace of the one Man, Jesus Christ, abounded to many.

—Romans 5:15

And you were dead in your trespasses and sins.

—Ephesians 2:1

And you, being dead in your sins and the uncircumcision of your flesh, He has resurrected together with Him, having forgiven you all sins.

—Colossians 2:13

For this is good and acceptable in the sight of God our Savior. Who desires all men to be saved and to come to the knowledge of the truth.

—1 Timothy 2:3–4

Therefore, as the Holy Spirit says, "Today, if you hear His voice, do not harden your hearts as in the rebellion, on the day of temptation in the wilderness."

—Hebrews 3:7–8

They cried out with a loud voice, "Salvation belongs to our God who sits on the throne, and to the Lamb!"

—Revelation 7:10

SATAN, FATHER OF LIES

Let God arise, let His enemies be scattered; let those who hate Him flee before Him.

—Psalm 68:1

How are you fallen from heaven, O Lucifer, son of the morning! How you are cut down to the ground, you who weaken the nations! For you have said in your heart, "I will ascend into heaven, I will exalt my throne above the stars of God. I will sit also on the mount of the congregation, in the recesses of the north. I will ascend above the heights of the clouds, I will be like the Most High." Yet you shall be brought down to hell, to the sides of the pit.

—Isaiah 14:12–15

You were the anointed cherub that covers, and I set you there. You were upon the holy mountain of God. You walked up and down in the midst of the stones of fire. You were perfect in your ways from the day that you were created until iniquity was found in you.

—Ezekiel 28:14–15

Then Jesus said to him, "Get away from here, Satan! For it is written, 'You shall worship the Lord your God, and Him only shall you serve.'"

—Matthew 4:10

You are of your father the devil, and you want to do the desires of your father. He was a murderer from the beginning, and does not stand in the truth, because there is no truth in him. When he lies, he speaks from his own nature, for he is a liar and the father of lies. Yet because I tell the truth, you do not believe Me. Which of you convicts Me of sin? If I speak the truth, why do you not believe Me? He who is of God hears God's words. Therefore, you do not hear them, because you are not of God.

—John 8:44–47

But if our gospel is hidden, it is hidden to those who are lost. The god of this world has blinded the minds of those who do not believe, lest the light of the glorious gospel of Christ, who is the image of God, should shine on them.

—2 Corinthians 4:3–4

And no wonder! For even Satan disguises himself as an angel of light.

—2 Corinthians 11:14

Put on the whole armor of God that you may be able to stand against the schemes of the devil.

—Ephesians 6:11

Now the Spirit clearly says that in the last times some will depart from the faith and pay attention to seducing spirits and doctrines of devils.

—1 Timothy 4:1

But we see Jesus, who was made a little lower than the angels to suffer death, crowned with glory and honor, so that He, by the grace of God, should experience death for everyone.

—Hebrews 2:9

The great dragon was cast out, that ancient serpent called the Devil, or Satan, who deceives the whole world. He was cast down to the earth, and his angels were cast down with him. Then I heard a loud voice in heaven, saying, "Now the salvation and the power and the kingdom of our God and the authority of His Christ have come. For the accuser of our brothers, who accused them before our God day and night, has been cast down."

—Revelation 12:9–10

The devil, who deceived them, was cast into the lake of fire and brimstone where the beast and the false prophet were. They will be tormented day and night forever and ever.

—Revelation 20:10

Savior

And did not know her until she had given birth to her first-born Son. And he called His name JESUS.

—Matthew 1:25

Is He not the carpenter's son? Is His mother not called Mary? And are not His brothers James and Joseph and Simon and Judas?

—Matthew 13:55

And my spirit rejoices in God my Savior.

—Luke 1:47

For God so loved the world that He gave His only begotten Son, that whoever believes in Him should not perish, but have eternal life.

—John 3:16

Peter said to them, "Repent and be baptized, every one of you, in the name of Jesus Christ for the forgiveness of sins, and you shall receive the gift of the Holy Spirit."

—Acts 2:38

There is no salvation in any other, for there is no other name under heaven given among men by which we must be saved.

—Acts 4:12

But God demonstrates His own love toward us, in that while we were yet sinners, Christ died for us.

—Romans 5:8

Do you not know that we who were baptized into Jesus Christ were baptized into His death? Therefore we were buried with Him by baptism into death, that just as Christ was raised up from the dead by the glory of the Father, even so, we also should walk in newness of life.

—Romans 6:3–4

For the wages of sin is death, but the gift of God is eternal life through Jesus Christ our Lord.

—Romans 6:23

But the firm foundation of God stands, having this seal, "The Lord knows those who are His," and, "Let every one who calls on the name of Christ depart from iniquity."

—2 Timothy 2:19

The Lord is not slow concerning His promise, as some count slowness. But He is patient with us, because He does not want any to perish, but all to come to repentance.

—2 Peter 3:9

He is the atoning sacrifice for our sins, and not for ours only, but also for the sins of the whole world.

—1 John 2:2

SECURITY

Therefore You delivered them into the hand of their enemies, who afflicted them. When they cried to You in the time of their affliction, You heard from heaven, and, according to Your abundant mercy, You gave them deliverers who delivered them out of the hand of their enemies.

—Nehemiah 9:27

I for my part confide in Your kindness. May my heart exult in Your salvation!

—Psalm 13:5

I have set the Lord always before me; because He is at my right hand, I will not be moved.

—Psalm 16:8

You are my hiding place; You will preserve me from trouble; You will surround me with shouts of deliverance. Selah.

—Psalm 32:7

But the salvation of the righteous is from the Lord; He is their refuge in the time of distress.

—Psalm 37:39

And the peace of God, which surpasses all understanding, will protect your hearts and minds through Christ Jesus.

—Philippians 4:7

Seeking God

But if from there you will seek the LORD your God, you will find Him, if you seek Him with all your heart and with all your soul.

—Deuteronomy 4:29

For I was ashamed to ask the king for an escort of foot and horse soldiers to help us against the enemy on the way, because we had spoken to the king, saying, "The hand of our God is upon all who seek Him for good, but His power and His wrath are against all who forsake Him."

—Ezra 8:22

As for you, Solomon my son, know the God of your fathers and serve Him with a whole heart and with a willing spirit, for the LORD searches every heart and understands the intent of every thought. If you seek Him, He will be found by you, but if you abandon Him, He will reject you utterly.

—1 Chronicles 28:9

And he went out to meet Asa and said to him, "Listen to me, Asa, and all Judah and Benjamin: The LORD is with you while you are with Him. If you all seek Him, He will be found with you. But if you forsake Him, He will forsake you."

—2 Chronicles 15:2

Those who know Your name will put their trust in You, for You, LORD, have not forsaken those who seek You.

—Psalm 9:10

I love those who love me, and those who seek me early will find me.

—Proverbs 8:17

"You shall seek Me and find Me, when you shall search for Me with all your heart. I will be found by you," says the LORD, "and I will turn away your captivity and gather you from all the nations and from all the places where I have driven you," says the LORD, "and I will bring you back into the place from where I caused you to be carried away captive."

—JEREMIAH 29:13–14

The LORD is good to those who wait for Him, to the soul that seeks Him.

—LAMENTATIONS 3:25

Sow to yourselves righteousness; reap mercy; break up your fallow ground, for it is time to seek the LORD, until He comes and rains righteousness upon you.

—HOSEA 10:12

Indeed, thus says the LORD to the house of Israel: "Seek Me and live!"

—AMOS 5:4

So that they should seek the Lord to perhaps that they might reach for Him and find Him, though He is not far from each one of us.

—ACTS 17:27

And without faith it is impossible to please God, for he who comes to God must believe that He exists and that He is a rewarder of those who diligently seek Him.

—HEBREWS 11:6

SELF-CONTROL

Judge me, O Lord, for I have walked in my integrity. I have trusted in the Lord; I will not slip. Examine me, O Lord, and test me; try my affections and my heart.

—Psalm 26:1–2

A fool utters all his mind, but a wise man keeps it in until afterwards.

—Proverbs 29:11

But I bring and keep my body under subjection, lest when preaching to others I myself should be disqualified.

—1 Corinthians 9:27

Put on the whole armor of God that you may be able to stand against the schemes of the devil. For our fight is not against flesh and blood, but against principalities, against powers, against the rulers of the darkness of this world, and against spiritual forces of evil in the heavenly places.

—Ephesians 6:11–12

But refuse profane and foolish myths. Instead, exercise in the ways of godliness. For bodily exercise profits a little, but godliness is profitable in all things, holding promise for the present life and also for the life to come.

—1 Timothy 4:7–8

Blessed is the man who endures temptation, for when he is tried, he will receive the crown of life, which the Lord has promised to those who love Him.

—James 1:12

SELF-DENIAL

You have heard that it was said, "An eye for an eye, and a tooth for a tooth." But I say to you, do not resist an evil person. But whoever strikes you on your right cheek, turn to him the other as well. And if anyone sues you in a court of law and takes away your tunic, let him have your cloak also. And whoever compels you to go a mile, go with him two.

—Matthew 5:38–41

Then Jesus said to His disciples, "If anyone will come after Me, let him deny himself, and take up his cross, and follow Me. For whoever would save his life will lose it, and whoever loses his life for My sake will find it. For what will it profit a man if he gains the whole world and loses his own soul? Or what shall a man give in exchange for his soul?"

—Matthew 16:24–26

He said to them, "Truly, I tell you, there is no man who has left his home or parents or brothers or wife or children, for the sake of the kingdom of God, who shall not receive many times more in this age and, in the age to come, eternal life."

—Luke 18:29–30

Therefore, brothers, we are debtors not to the flesh, to live according to the flesh. For if you live according to the flesh, you will die, but if through the Spirit you put to death the deeds of the body, you will live.

—Romans 8:12–13

Those who are Christ's have crucified the flesh with its passions and lusts.

—Galatians 5:24

For the grace of God that brings salvation has appeared to all men, teaching us that, denying ungodliness and worldly desires, we should live soberly, righteously, and in godliness in this present world.

—Titus 2:11–12

SELF-IMAGE

For the Lord will be your confidence, and will keep your foot from being caught.

—Proverbs 3:26

For as he thinks in his heart, so is he. "Eat and drink," he says to you, but his heart is not with you.

—Proverbs 23:7

I am the vine, you are the branches. He who remains in Me, and I in him, bears much fruit. For without Me you can do nothing.

—John 15:5

I have spoken these things to you, that My joy may remain in you, and that your joy may be full.

—John 15:11

For those whom He foreknew, He predestined to be conformed to the image of His Son, so that He might be the firstborn among many brothers.

—Romans 8:29

For we are His workmanship, created in Christ Jesus for good works, which God prepared beforehand, so that we should walk in them.

—Ephesians 2:10

SELF-PITY

But he went a day's journey into the wilderness and came and sat down under a juniper tree and asked that he might die, saying, "It is enough! Now, O Lord, take my life, for I am not better than my fathers."

—1 Kings 19:4

After this Job opened his mouth, and cursed the day of his birth.

—Job 3:1

For I was envious at the boastful, I saw the prosperity of the wicked.

—Psalm 73:3

When I thought to understand this, it was troublesome in my eyes, until I went into the sanctuary of God; then I understood their end.

—Psalm 73:16–17

For who makes you differ from another? And what do you have that you did not receive? Now if you received it, why do you boast as if you had not received it?

—1 Corinthians 4:7

For you know that you were not redeemed from your vain way of life inherited from your fathers with perishable things, like silver or gold, but with the precious blood of Christ, as of a lamb without blemish and without spot.

—1 Peter 1:18–19

SELF-RIGHTEOUSNESS

The way of a fool is right in his own eyes, but he who listens to counsel is wise.

—PROVERBS 12:15

Do you see a man wise in his own conceit? There is more hope for a fool than for him.

—PROVERBS 26:12

Let another man praise you, and not your own mouth; a stranger, and not your own lips.

—PROVERBS 27:2

He who is of a proud heart stirs up strife, but he who puts his trust in the LORD will prosper. He who trusts in his own heart is a fool, but whoever walks wisely will be delivered.

—PROVERBS 28:25–26

There is a generation that is pure in its own eyes, and yet is not washed from its filthiness. There is a generation, O how lofty are their eyes! And their eyelids are lifted up.

—PROVERBS 30:12–13

Woe to those who are wise in their own eyes and prudent in their own sight!

—ISAIAH 5:21

But we all are as an unclean thing, and all our righteousness is as filthy rags. And we all fade as a leaf. And our iniquities, like the wind, have taken us away.

—ISAIAH 64:6

Yet you say, "Because I am innocent, surely His anger shall turn away from me." Now I will plead with you, because you say, "I have not sinned."

—Jeremiah 2:35

He said to them, "You are those who justify yourselves before men, but God knows your hearts. For that which is highly esteemed before men is an abomination before God."

—Luke 16:15

Jesus said, "If you were blind, you would have no sin. But now you say, 'We see.' Therefore your sin remains."

—John 9:41

But, "Let him who boasts, boast in the Lord." For it not he who commends himself who is approved, but he whom the Lord commends.

—2 Corinthians 10:17–18

For if someone thinks himself to be something when he is nothing, he deceives himself.

—Galatians 6:3

SELF-WORTH

What is man that You are mindful of him, or his descendants that You attend to them? For You have made him a little lower than God, and crowned him with glory and honor. You grant him dominion over the works of Your hands; You have put all things under his feet.

—Psalm 8:4–6

You brought my inner parts into being; You wove me in my mother's womb. I will praise you, for You made me with fear and wonder; marvelous are Your works, and You know me completely.

—Psalm 139:13–14

How precious also are Your thoughts to me, O God! How great is the sum of them! If I should count them, they are more in number than the sand; when I awake, I am still with You.

—Psalm 139:17–18

Better is the poor who walks in his uprightness, than he who is perverse in his ways, though he be rich.

—Proverbs 28:6

Before I formed you in the womb I knew you. And before you came forth out of the womb I sanctified you, and I ordained you a prophet to the nations.

—Jeremiah 1:5

Are not five sparrows sold for two pennies? Yet not one of them is forgotten by God. Indeed, even the hairs of your head are all numbered. Therefore do not fear. You are more valuable than many sparrows.

—Luke 12:6–7

He has made from one every nation of men to live on the entire face of the earth, having appointed fixed times and the boundaries of their habitation.

—Acts 17:26

"For in Him we live and move and have our being." As some of your own poets have said, "We are His offspring."

—Acts 17:28

Do not be conformed to this world, but be transformed by the renewing of your mind, that you may prove what is the good and acceptable and perfect will of God.

—Romans 12:2

What? Do you not know that your body is the temple of the Holy Spirit, who is in you, whom you have received from God, and that you are not your own? You were bought with a price. Therefore glorify God in your body and in your spirit, which are God's.

—1 Corinthians 6:19–20

For we are His workmanship, created in Christ Jesus for good works, which God prepared beforehand, so that we should walk in them.

—Ephesians 2:10

Not by works of righteousness which we have done, but according to His mercy He saved us, through the washing of rebirth and the renewal of the Holy Spirit.

—Titus 3:5

SERVANTHOOD

Only carefully obey the commandment and the law that Moses the servant of the Lord commanded you: to love the Lord your God, to walk in all His ways, to obey His commandments, to cling to Him, and to serve Him with all your heart and soul.

—Joshua 22:5

Fear the Lord: serve Him in truth with all your heart, and consider what great things He has done for you.

—1 Samuel 12:24

For whoever would save his life will lose it, and whoever loses his life for My sake will find it.

—Matthew 16:25

He who is greatest among you shall be your servant.

—Matthew 23:11

And said to them, "Whoever receives this child in My name receives Me, and whoever receives Me receives Him who sent Me. For he who is least among you all will be great."

—Luke 9:48

But you are not so. Instead, let him who is greatest among you be as the younger, and he who rules as he who serves. For who is greater: he who sits at the table, or he who serves? Is it not he who sits at the table? But I am among you as He who serves.

—Luke 22:26–27

He who loves his life will lose it. And he who hates his life in this world will keep it for eternal life. If anyone serves Me, he must follow Me. Where I am, there will My servant be also. If anyone serves Me, the Father will honor him.

—John 12:25–26

Be devoted to one another with brotherly love; prefer one another in honor, do not be lazy in diligence, be fervent in spirit, serve the Lord.

—Romans 12:10–11

There are differences of administrations, but the same Lord.

—1 Corinthians 12:5

You, brothers, have been called to liberty. Only do not use liberty to give an opportunity to the flesh, but by love, serve one another.

—Galatians 5:13

Let this mind be in you all, which was also in Christ Jesus: Who, being in the form of God, did not consider equality with God something to be grasped. But He emptied Himself, taking upon Himself the form of a servant, and was made in the likeness of men. And being found in the form of a man, He humbled Himself and became obedient to death, even death on a cross.

—Philippians 2:5–8

If anyone speaks, let him speak as the oracles of God. If anyone serves, let him serve with the strength that God supplies, so that God in all things may be glorified through Jesus Christ, to whom be praise and dominion forever and ever.

—1 Peter 4:11

Sexual Immorality

You have heard that it was said by the ancients, "You shall not commit adultery." But I say to you that whoever looks on a woman to lust after her has committed adultery with her already in his heart.

—Matthew 5:27–28

"Food is for the belly, and the belly is for food," but God will destroy both of them. Now the body is not for sexual immorality, but for the Lord, and the Lord is for the body.

—1 Corinthians 6:13

Do you not know that your bodies are the parts of Christ? Shall I then take the parts of Christ and make them the parts of a harlot? God forbid!

—1 Corinthians 6:15

Escape from sexual immorality. Every sin that a man commits is outside the body. But he who commits sexual immorality sins against his own body. What? Do you not know that your body is the temple of the Holy Spirit, who is in you, whom you have received from God, and that you are not your own? You were bought with a price. Therefore glorify God in your body and in your spirit, which are God's.

—1 Corinthians 6:18–20

Now concerning the things about which you wrote to me: "It is good for a man not to touch a woman." Nevertheless, because of sexual immorality, let every man have his own wife, and let every woman have her own husband.

—1 Corinthians 7:1–2

I say to the unmarried and widows that it is good for them if they live even as I am. But if they cannot restrain themselves, let them marry. For it is better to marry than to burn with passion.

—1 Corinthians 7:8–9

Nevertheless he who stands steadfast in his heart without necessity, and has power over his own will, and has so decreed in his heart that he will keep his virgin, does well.

—1 Corinthians 7:37

Now the works of the flesh are revealed, which are these: adultery, sexual immorality, impurity, lewdness....Envy, murders, drunkenness, carousing, and the like. I warn you, as I previously warned you, that those who do such things shall not inherit the kingdom of God.

—GALATIANS 5:19, 21

For this is the will of God, your sanctification: that you should abstain from sexual immorality.

—1 THESSALONIANS 4:3

Then the Lord knows how to rescue the godly from trial, and to keep the unrighteous under punishment for the Day of Judgment.

—2 PETER 2:9

For since He Himself suffered while being tempted, He is able to help those who are being tempted.

—HEBREWS 2:18

These are those who were not defiled with women, for they are virgins. These are those who follow the Lamb wherever He goes. These were redeemed from among men, as first-fruits to God and to the Lamb.

—REVELATION 14:4

SEXUAL INTIMACY

I made a covenant with my eyes; why then should I look upon a young woman?

—JOB 31:1

Turn away my eyes from beholding worthlessness, and revive me in Your way.

—PSALM 119:37

Let your eyes look right on, and let your eyelids look straight before you. Ponder the path of your feet, and let all your ways be established. Do not turn to the right or to the left; remove your foot from evil.

—Proverbs 4:25–27

For the ways of man are before the eyes of the Lord, and He ponders all his goings.

—Proverbs 5:21

What? Do you not know that your body is the temple of the Holy Spirit, who is in you, whom you have received from God, and that you are not your own? You were bought with a price. Therefore glorify God in your body and in your spirit, which are God's.

—1 Corinthians 6:19–20

The wife does not have authority over her own body, but the husband does. Likewise, the husband does not have authority over his own body, but the wife does. Do not deprive one another except with consent for a time, that you may give yourselves to fasting and prayer. Then come together again, so that Satan does not tempt you for lack of self-control.

—1 Corinthians 7:4–5

And do not let sexual immorality, or any impurity, or greed, be named among you, as these are not proper among saints.

—Ephesians 5:3

In this way, men ought to love their wives as their own bodies. He who loves his wife loves himself. For no one ever hated his own flesh, but nourishes and cherishes it, just as the Lord cares for the church.

—Ephesians 5:28–29

For this is the will of God, your sanctification: that you should abstain from sexual immorality, that each one of you should know how to possess his own vessel in sanctification and honor, not in the lust of depravity, even as the Gentiles who do not know God.

—1 Thessalonians 4:3–5

For God has not called us to uncleanness, but to holiness.

—1 Thessalonians 4:7

But each man is tempted when he is drawn away by his own lust and enticed. Then, when lust has conceived, it brings forth sin; and when sin is finished, it brings forth death. Do not err, my beloved brothers.

—James 1:14–16

For all that is in the world—the lust of the flesh, the lust of the eyes, and the pride of life—is not of the Father, but is of the world. The world and its desires are passing away, but the one who does the will of God lives forever.

—1 John 2:16–17

SHAME

At the evening sacrifice I rose up from my heaviness and, despite having my clothes and my robe torn, I knelt on my knees and stretched out my hands in prayer to the Lord my God, and said, "O my God, I am ashamed and embarrassed to lift up my face to You, my God, because our iniquities have expanded over our heads and our wrongdoing has grown up to the heavens."

—Ezra 9:5–6

O my God, I trust in You; may I not be ashamed, may my enemies not triumph over me. Yes, let none who wait on You be ashamed; let them be ashamed who transgress without cause.

—Psalm 25:2–3

Then I shall not be ashamed, when I have my focus on all Your commandments.

—Psalm 119:6

Let my heart be blameless in Your statutes, that I may not be ashamed.

—Psalm 119:80

But He was wounded for our transgressions. He was bruised for our iniquities. The chastisement of our peace was upon Him, and by His stripes we are healed.

—Isaiah 53:5

Do not fear, for you shall not be ashamed nor be humiliated; for you shall not be put to shame, for you shall forget the shame of your youth and shall not remember the reproach of your widowhood anymore. For your Maker is your husband. The Lord of Hosts is His name. And your Redeemer is the Holy One of Israel. He shall be called the God of the whole earth.

—Isaiah 54:4–5

And hope does not disappoint, because the love of God is shed abroad in our hearts by the Holy Spirit who has been given to us.

—Romans 5:5

As it is written, "Look! I lay in Zion a stumbling stone and rock of offense, and whoever believes in Him will not be ashamed."

—Romans 9:33

For the Scripture says, "Whoever believes in Him will not be ashamed."

—Romans 10:11

For these things I suffer, but I am not ashamed, for I know whom I have believed, and am persuaded that He is able to keep that which was committed to me until that Day.

—2 Timothy 1:12

Study to show yourself approved by God, a workman who need not be ashamed, rightly dividing the word of truth.

—2 Timothy 2:15

Yet if anyone suffers as a Christian, let him not be ashamed, but let him glorify God because of it.

—1 Peter 4:16

SICKNESS AND DISEASE

When the wicked came against me to eat my flesh—my enemies and my foes—they stumbled and fell.

—Psalm 27:2

The mountains melt like wax at the presence of the Lord, at the presence of the Lord of the earth.

—Psalm 97:5

For they are life to those who find them, and health to all their body.

—Proverbs 4:22

…until a dart struck through his liver. As a bird hastens to the snare, and knows not that it is for his life.

—Proverbs 7:23

The hand of the Lord was upon me, and He carried me out in the Spirit of the Lord and set me down in the midst of the valley which was full of bones, and He caused me to pass among them round about. And there were very many in the open valley. And they were very dry. He said to me, "Son of man, can these bones live?" And I answered, "O Lord God, You know." Again He said to me, "Prophesy over these bones and say to them, 'O dry bones, hear the word of the Lord.'"

—Ezekiel 37:1–4

From there, I will give her vineyards to her, and the valley of Achor as a door of hope. She will respond there, as in the days of her youth, and as in the day when she came up out of the land of Egypt.

—Hosea 2:15

And it will be that in that day the mountains will drip sweet wine, and the hills will flow with milk, and all the streambeds of Judah will flow with water. A spring will proceed from the house of the Lord and will water the valley of Shittim.

—Joel 3:18

Jesus went throughout all Galilee teaching in their synagogues, preaching the gospel of the kingdom, and healing all kinds of sickness and all sorts of diseases among the people. His fame went throughout all Syria. And they brought to Him all sick people who were taken with various diseases and tormented with pain, those who were possessed with demons, those who had seizures, and those who had paralysis, and He healed them.

—Matthew 4:23–24

"But that you may know that the Son of Man has authority on earth to forgive sins"—then He said to the paralytic, "Arise, pick up your bed, and go into your house." And he rose and departed to his house.

—Matthew 9:6–7

And they were all amazed at the mighty power of God.

—Luke 9:43

Peter said to him, "Aeneas, Jesus the Christ heals you. Rise up and make your bed." And immediately he rose up.

—Acts 9:34

Is anyone sick among you? Let him call for the elders of the church, and let them pray over him, anointing him with oil in the name of the Lord. And the prayer of faith will save the sick, and the Lord will raise him up. And if he has committed any sins, he will be forgiven. Confess your faults to one another and pray for one another, that you may be healed. The effective, fervent prayer of a righteous man accomplishes much.

—James 5:14–16

SIN, FREEDOM FROM

Then I will sprinkle clean water upon you, and you shall be clean. From all your filthiness and from all your idols, I will cleanse you. Also, I will give you a new heart, and a new spirit I will put within you. And I will take away the stony heart out of your flesh, and I will give you a heart of flesh.

—EZEKIEL 36:25–26

I am the vine, you are the branches. He who remains in Me, and I in him, bears much fruit. For without Me you can do nothing.

—JOHN 15:5

To Him all the prophets bear witness that whoever believes in Him will receive remission of sins through His name.

—ACTS 10:43

What shall we say then? Shall we continue in sin that grace may increase? God forbid! How shall we who died to sin live any longer in it?

—ROMANS 6:1–2

Knowing this, that our old man has been crucified with Him, so that the body of sin might be destroyed, and we should no longer be slaves to sin. For the one who has died is freed from sin.

—ROMANS 6:6–7

For sin shall not have dominion over you, for you are not under the law, but under grace.

—ROMANS 6:14

Let love be without hypocrisy. Hate what is evil. Cleave to what is good.

—Romans 12:9

Do you not know that the unrighteous will not inherit the kingdom of God? Do not be deceived. Neither the sexually immoral, nor idolaters, nor adulterers, nor male prostitutes, nor homosexuals.

—1 Corinthians 6:9

Awake to righteousness and do not sin, for some do not have the knowledge of God. I say this to your shame.

—1 Corinthians 15:34

I have been crucified with Christ. It is no longer I who live, but Christ who lives in me. And the life I now live in the flesh, I live by faith in the Son of God, who loved me and gave Himself for me.

—Galatians 2:20

Therefore, brothers, diligently make your calling and election sure. For if you do these things, you will never stumble. For in this way, the entrance into the eternal kingdom of our Lord and Savior Jesus Christ will be abundantly provided for you.

—2 Peter 1:10–11

If we say that we have no sin, we deceive ourselves, and the truth is not in us.

—1 John 1:8

SINGLE PARENT

The LORD, He goes before you. He will be with you. He will not fail you nor forsake you. Do not fear, nor be dismayed.

—DEUTERONOMY 31:8

No man will be able to stand against you all the days of your life. As I was with Moses, I will be with you. I will not abandon you. I will not leave you.

—JOSHUA 1:5

My eyes shall be favorable to the faithful in the land, that they may live with me. He who walks in a blameless manner, he shall serve me.

—PSALM 101:6

The LORD is near to all those who call upon Him, to all who call upon Him in truth.

—PSALM 145:18

"Am I a God who is near," says the LORD, "and not a God far off? Can a man hide himself in secret places so that I do not see him?" says the LORD. "Do I not fill heaven and earth?" says the LORD.

—JEREMIAH 23:23–24

But grow in the grace and knowledge of our Lord and Savior Jesus Christ. To Him be glory, both now and forever. Amen.

—2 PETER 3:18

SLANDER

He will bring forth your righteousness as the light, and your judgment as the noonday.

—PSALM 37:6

He will send from heaven and save me from the taunt of the one who crushes me. Selah. God will send forth His mercy and His truth.

—Psalm 57:3

Listen to Me, you who know righteousness, the people in whose heart is My law. Do not fear the reproach of men nor be afraid of their revilings.

—Isaiah 51:7

Blessed are you when men revile you, and persecute you, and say all kinds of evil against you falsely for My sake. Rejoice and be very glad, because great is your reward in heaven, for in this manner they persecuted the prophets who were before you.

—Matthew 5:11–12

You will be hated by all men for My name's sake. But he who endures to the end will be saved.

—Matthew 10:22

If you are reproached because of the name of Christ, you are blessed, because the Spirit of glory and of God rests upon you. On their part He is blasphemed, but on your part He is glorified.

—1 Peter 4:14

SPEAKING TO MOUNTAINS

The mountains quaked before the LORD, this very Sinai, before the LORD God of Israel.

—Judges 5:5

He puts forth his hand upon the rock; he overturns the mountains by the roots.

—Job 28:9

See, I will make you a new sharp threshing instrument with double edges. You shall thresh the mountains, and beat them small, and shall make the hills as chaff.

—Isaiah 41:15

I will lay waste mountains and hills and dry up all their vegetation. And I will make the rivers islands, and I will dry up the pools.

—Isaiah 42:15

"I am against you, O destroying mountain," says the Lord, "who destroys all the earth. And I will stretch out My hand against you, and roll you down from the rocks, and will make you a burnt mountain."

—Jeremiah 51:25

Therefore, O mountains of Israel, hear the word of the Lord God. "Thus says the Lord God to the mountains and to the hills, to the rivers and to the valleys, to the desolate wastes and to the cities that are forsaken, which became a prey and derision to the rest of the nations that are round about."

—Ezekiel 36:4

Listen to what the Lord says: "Arise, plead your case before the mountains, that the hills may hear your voice."

—Micah 6:1

Hear, mountains, the indictment of the LORD, O enduring foundations of the earth—that the LORD has an indictment against His people, and against Israel He will dispute.

—MICAH 6:2

The mountains saw You and trembled; the overflowing water passed by. The deep lifted its voice, and lifted its hands on high.

—HABAKKUK 3:10

Who are you, O great mountain? Before Zerubbabel you will be made level ground, and he will bring out the top stone amidst shouting of "Grace! Grace to the stone!"

—ZECHARIAH 4:7

Jesus said to them, "Because of your unbelief. For truly I say to you, if you have faith as a grain of mustard seed, you will say to this mountain, 'Move from here to there,' and it will move. And nothing will be impossible for you."

—MATTHEW 17:20

For truly I say to you, whoever says to this mountain, "Be removed and be thrown into the sea," and does not doubt in his heart, but believes that what he says will come to pass, he will have whatever he says.

—MARK 11:23

SPEECH

Who is the man who desires life, and loves a long life in order to see good? Keep your tongue from evil, and your lips from speaking deceit. Turn away from evil, and do good; seek peace, and pursue it.

—PSALM 34:12–14

The mouth of the righteous utters wisdom, and their tongue speaks justice.

—Psalm 37:30

My lips shall declare praise, for You have taught me Your statutes. My tongue shall speak of Your word, for all Your commandments are right.

—Psalm 119:171–172

The tongue of the just is as choice silver; the heart of the wicked is worth little.

—Proverbs 10:20

A man has joy by the answer of his mouth, and a word spoken in due season, how good is it!

—Proverbs 15:23

Every man will kiss his lips that gives a right answer.

—Proverbs 24:26

A word fitly spoken is like apples of gold in settings of silver.

—Proverbs 25:11

O generation of vipers, how can you, being evil, speak good things? For out of the abundance of the heart the mouth speaks.

—Matthew 12:34

But, speaking the truth in love, we may grow up in all things into Him, who is the head, Christ Himself.

—Ephesians 4:15

Do all things without murmuring and disputing.

—Philippians 2:14

Let your speech always be with grace, seasoned with salt, that you may know how you should answer everyone.

—Colossians 4:6

We all err in many ways. But if any man does not err in word, he is a perfect man and able also to control the whole body. See how we put bits in the mouths of horses that they may obey us, and we control their whole bodies.

—James 3:2–3

Spiritual Warfare

Your right hand, O Lord, is glorious in power. Your right hand, O Lord, shatters the enemy. In the greatness of Your excellence, You overthrow those who rise up against You. You send out Your wrath; it consumes them like stubble.

—Exodus 15:6–7

The Lord said to Joshua, "Do not be afraid of them, for I have given them into your hand. Not a single man can stand before you."

—Joshua 10:8

As for you, do not stop pursuing your enemies, but attack them from behind. Do not let them go back to their cities, for the Lord your God has given them into your hand.

—Joshua 10:19

For I was ashamed to ask the king for an escort of foot and horse soldiers to help us against the enemy on the way, because we had spoken to the king, saying, "The hand of our God is upon all who seek Him for good, but His power and His wrath are against all who forsake Him."

—Ezra 8:22

Then we began the journey from the Ahava River on the twelfth day of the first month to go to Jerusalem. The hand of our God was upon us, and He delivered us from the hand of the attacker and the ambusher along the way.

—EZRA 8:31

He has torn me in His wrath, and He has carried a grudge against me. He has gnashed me with His teeth; my enemy sharpens His gaze upon me. They have gaped upon me with their mouth; they have struck me upon the cheek with reproach; they have gathered themselves together against me.

—JOB 16:9–10

Surely you have spoken in my hearing, and I have heard the sound of your words saying, "I am clean, without transgression, I am innocent, nor is there iniquity in me."

—JOB 33:8–9

Shall evil be recompensed for good? For they have dug a pit for my soul. Remember that I stood before you to speak good for them, and to turn away Your wrath from them. Therefore, deliver up their children to the famine and pour out their blood by the power of the sword; and let their wives be bereaved of their children and become widows. And let their men be put to death; let their young men be slain by the sword in battle.

—JEREMIAH 18:20–21

He told them another parable, saying, "The kingdom of heaven is like a man who sowed good seed in his field. But while men slept, his enemy came and sowed weeds among the wheat and went away."

—MATTHEW 13:24–25

Look, I give you authority to trample on serpents and scorpions, and over all the power of the enemy. And nothing shall by any means hurt you.

—Luke 10:19

Remind them of these things, commanding them before the Lord that they not argue about words, which leads to nothing of value and to the destruction of those who hear them.

—2 Timothy 2:14

We are of God, and whoever knows God listens to us. Whoever is not of God does not listen to us. This is how we know the spirit of truth and the spirit of error.

—1 John 4:6

STANDING AGAINST SATAN

Then Jesus said to him, "Get away from here, Satan! For it is written, 'You shall worship the Lord your God, and Him only shall you serve.'"

—Matthew 4:10

He said to them, "I saw Satan as lightning fall from heaven."

—Luke 10:18

Then should not this woman, being a daughter of Abraham whom Satan has bound these eighteen years, be loosed from this bondage on the Sabbath?

—Luke 13:16

Then the Lord said, "Simon, Simon, listen! Satan has demanded to have you to sift you as wheat."

—Luke 22:31

The thief does not come, except to steal and kill and destroy. I came that they may have life, and that they may have it more abundantly.

—John 10:10

To open their eyes and to turn them from darkness to light, and from the power of Satan to God, that they may receive forgiveness of sins and an inheritance among those who are sanctified by faith in Me.

—Acts 26:18

The God of peace will soon crush Satan under your feet. The grace of our Lord Jesus Christ be with you.

—Romans 16:20

Do not give place to the devil.

—Ephesians 4:27

Therefore we wished to come to you—even I, Paul, once and again—but Satan hindered us.

—1 Thessalonians 2:18

Be sober and watchful, because your adversary the devil walks around as a roaring lion, seeking whom he may devour.

—1 Peter 5:8

I know your works and where you live, where Satan's throne is. Yet you hold firmly to My name, and did not deny My faith even in the days of Antipas, My faithful martyr, who was killed among you, where Satan dwells.

—Revelation 2:13

Therefore rejoice, you heavens and you who dwell in them! Woe unto the inhabitants of the earth and sea! For the devil has gone down to you with great wrath, because he knows that his time is short.

—REVELATION 12:12

STRENGTH

Riches and honor flow from You, and You rule over all. In Your hand are power and might, and in Your hand it is to make great and to strengthen all.

—1 CHRONICLES 29:12

The righteous also will hold to his way, and he who has clean hands will be stronger and stronger.

—JOB 17:9

The LORD is the strength of His people, and He is the saving strength of His anointed.

—PSALM 28:8

O God, You are awesome from Your sanctuaries; the God of Israel is He who gives strength and power to people. Blessed be God!

—PSALM 68:35

My soul collapses on account of grief; strengthen me according to Your word.

—PSALM 119:28

Surely, one shall say, "Only in the LORD are righteousness and strength." Men shall come to him, and all who are incensed at Him shall be ashamed.

—ISAIAH 45:24

"I will make them strong in the Lord, and they will go to and fro in His name," says the Lord.

—Zechariah 10:12

But He said to me, "My grace is sufficient for you, for My strength is made perfect in weakness." Therefore most gladly I will boast in my weaknesses, that the power of Christ may rest upon me. So I take pleasure in weaknesses, in reproaches, in hardships, in persecutions, and in distresses for Christ's sake. For when I am weak, then I am strong.

—2 Corinthians 12:9–10

That He would give you, according to the riches of His glory, power to be strengthened by His Spirit in the inner man, and that Christ may dwell in your hearts through faith; that you, being rooted and grounded in love…

—Ephesians 3:16–17

I can do all things because of Christ who strengthens me.

—Philippians 4:13

Strengthened with all might according to His glorious power, enduring everything with perseverance and patience joyfully, giving thanks to the Father, who has enabled us to be partakers in the inheritance of the saints in light.

—Colossians 1:11–12

Therefore, since we are encompassed with such a great cloud of witnesses, let us also lay aside every weight and the sin that so easily entangles us, and let us run with endurance the race that is set before us.

—Hebrews 12:1

STRESS

On the seventh day God completed His work which He had done, and He rested on the seventh day from all His work which He had done.

—GENESIS 2:2

Cast your care on the LORD, and He will sustain you; He will not allow the righteous to totter forever.

—PSALM 55:22

Heaviness in the heart of man makes it droop, but a good word makes it glad.

—PROVERBS 12:25

For thus says the Lord GOD, the Holy One of Israel, "In returning and rest you shall be saved. In quietness and in confidence shall be your strength." Yet you were not willing.

—ISAIAH 30:15

For I satiate the weary souls and I replenish every languishing soul.

—JEREMIAH 31:25

The LORD God is my strength; He will make my feet like hinds' feet, and He will make me walk on my high places.

—HABAKKUK 3:19

Come to Me, all you who labor and are heavily burdened, and I will give you rest. Take My yoke upon you, and learn from Me. For I am meek and lowly in heart, and you will find rest for your souls. For My yoke is easy, and My burden is light.

—MATTHEW 11:28–30

Peace I leave with you. My peace I give to you. Not as the world gives do I give to you. Let not your heart be troubled, neither let it be afraid.

—John 14:27

We know that all things work together for good to those who love God, to those who are called according to His purpose.

—Romans 8:28

Be anxious for nothing, but in everything, by prayer and supplication with gratitude, make your requests known to God.

—Philippians 4:6

Therefore, since the promise of entering His rest remains, let us fear lest any of you should seem to come short of it.

—Hebrews 4:1

Therefore a rest remains for the people of God. For whoever enters His rest will also cease from his own works, as God did from His. Let us labor therefore to enter that rest, lest anyone fall by the same pattern of unbelief.

—Hebrews 4:9–11

SUCCESS

His master saw that the Lord was with him and that the Lord made all that he did to prosper. Joseph found favor in his sight and served him. So he made him overseer over his house, and all that he had he put under his charge.

—Genesis 39:3–4

I will provide grass in your fields for your cattle, that you may eat and be full.

—Deuteronomy 11:15

The LORD will make you overflow in prosperity, in the off-spring of your body, in the offspring of your cattle, and in the produce of your ground, in the land which the LORD swore to your fathers to give you. The LORD will open up to you His good treasure, the heavens, to give the rain to your land in its season and to bless all the work of your hand. You will lend to many nations, but you will not borrow.

—DEUTERONOMY 28:11–12

So they rose up early in the morning and went out to the wilderness of Tekoa. And when they went out, Jehoshaphat stood and said, "Listen to me, Judah and those dwelling in Jerusalem. Believe in the LORD your God, and you will be supported. Believe His prophets, and you will succeed."

—2 CHRONICLES 20:20

And in every deed that he undertook in the service of the house of God and with the law and commandment to seek out his God, he did this with all his heart, and he found success.

—2 CHRONICLES 31:21

Wealth and riches shall be in his house; and his righteous-ness endures forever.

—PSALM 112:3

Riches and honor are with me, yes, enduring riches and righteousness. My fruit is better than gold, yes, than fine gold, and my revenue than choice silver.

—PROVERBS 8:18–19

In the house of the righteous is much treasure, but in the revenue of the wicked is trouble.

—PROVERBS 15:6

And also that everyone should eat and drink and experience good in all their labor. This is a gift of God.

—ECCLESIASTES 3:13

Then He shall give you rain for the seed which you shall sow in the ground and bread of the increase of the earth. And it shall be rich and plentiful. On that day your cattle shall feed in large pastures.

—ISAIAH 30:23

TAKE AWAY FEAR

Do not be afraid of sudden terror, nor of trouble from the wicked when it comes. For the LORD will be your confidence, and will keep your foot from being caught.

—PROVERBS 3:25–26

It shall come to pass in the day that the LORD shall give you rest from your sorrow, and from your fear, and from the hard bondage in which you were made to serve.

—ISAIAH 14:3

He shall be the stability of your times, a wealth of salvation, wisdom, and knowledge. The fear of the LORD is His treasure.

—ISAIAH 33:6

That we should be saved from our enemies and from the hand of all who hate us.

—LUKE 1:71

For God has not given us the spirit of fear, but of power, and love, and self-control.

—2 Timothy 1:7

There is no fear in love, but perfect love casts out fear, because fear has to do with punishment. Whoever fears is not perfect in love.

—1 John 4:18

Talents

But you must remember the Lord your God, for it is He who gives you the ability to get wealth, so that He may establish His covenant which He swore to your fathers, as it is today.

—Deuteronomy 8:18

May He grant you according to your own heart, and fulfill all your counsel.

—Psalm 20:4

A man's gift makes room for him, and brings him before great men.

—Proverbs 18:16

For to the person who is pleasing before Him, God gives wisdom, knowledge, and joy, but to the one who sins, He gives the task to gather and collect in order to give to the other person who is pleasing before God. Also this is vanity and chasing the wind.

—Ecclesiastes 2:26

"So I was afraid, and went and hid your talent in the ground. Here you have what is yours." His master answered, "You wicked and slothful servant! You knew that I reap where I have not sown, and gather where I have not winnowed."

—Matthew 25:25–26

So take the talent from him, and give it to him who has ten talents. For to everyone who has will more be given, and he will have an abundance. But from him who has nothing, even what he has will be taken away. And throw the unprofitable servant into outer darkness, where there will be weeping and gnashing of teeth.

—Matthew 25:28–30

But he who unknowingly committed acts worthy of punishment shall be beaten with few stripes. For to whom much is given, of him much shall be required. And from him to whom much was entrusted, much will be asked.

—Luke 12:48

For the gifts and calling of God are irrevocable.

—Romans 11:29

By Him you are enriched in everything, in all speech and in all knowledge.

—1 Corinthians 1:5

There are various gifts, but the same Spirit. There are differences of administrations, but the same Lord. There are various operations, but it is the same God who operates them all in all people.... But that one and very same Spirit works all these, dividing to each one individually as He will.

—1 Corinthians 12:4–6, 11

Let no one despise your youth, but be an example to the believers in speech, in conduct, in love, in spirit, in faith and in purity. Until I come, give attention to reading, exhortation, and doctrine. Do not neglect the gift that is in you, which was given to you by prophecy, with the laying on of hands by the elders.

—1 Timothy 4:12–14

As every one has received a gift, even so serve one another with it, as good stewards of the manifold grace of God.

—1 Peter 4:10

TEARS AND SORROW

And Hannah answered and said, "No, my lord, I am a woman of sorrow. I have drunk neither wine nor strong drink, but have poured out my soul before the Lord."

—1 Samuel 1:15

Then he said to them, "Go your way. Eat the fat, drink the sweet drink, and send portions to those for whom nothing is prepared; for this day is holy to our Lord. Do not be grieved, for the joy of the Lord is your strength."

—Nehemiah 8:10

He restores my soul; He guides me in paths of righteousness for His name's sake.

—Psalm 23:3

Why are you cast down, O my soul? And why are you disquieted in me? Hope in God, for I will yet thank Him for the help of His presence.

—Psalm 42:5

You take account of my wandering; put my tears in Your bottle; are they not in Your book?

—Psalm 56:8

Let the beauty of the Lord our God be upon us, and establish the work of our hands among us; yes, the work of our hands establish it.

—Psalm 90:17

Those who sow in tears shall reap in joy.

—Psalm 126:5

It shall come to pass in the day that the Lord shall give you rest from your sorrow, and from your fear, and from the hard bondage in which you were made to serve.

—Isaiah 14:3

He will swallow up death for all time, and the Lord God will wipe away tears from all faces. And the reproach of His people He shall take away from all the earth, for the Lord has spoken it.

—Isaiah 25:8

Go, and say to Hezekiah, "Thus says the Lord, the God of David your father, 'I have heard your prayer, I have seen your tears. Surely I will add to your days fifteen years.'"

—Isaiah 38:5

Your sun shall no more go down, nor shall your moon wane. For the Lord shall be your everlasting light, and the days of your mourning shall end.

—Isaiah 60:20

Truly, truly I say to you that you will weep and lament, but the world will rejoice. You will be sorrowful, but your sorrow will be turned into joy. When a woman is giving birth, she has pain, because her hour has come. But as soon as she delivers the child, she no longer remembers the anguish for joy that a child is born into the world.

—JOHN 16:20–21

TEMPTATION

My son, if sinners entice you, do not consent.

—PROVERBS 1:10

Watch and pray that you enter not into temptation. The spirit indeed is willing, but the flesh is weak.

—MATTHEW 26:41

And Jesus answered him, "Get behind Me, Satan! For it is written, 'You shall worship the Lord your God, and Him only shall you serve.'"

—LUKE 4:8

When He came there, He said to them, "Pray that you may not fall into temptation."

—LUKE 22:40

I have told you these things so that in Me you may have peace. In the world you will have tribulation. But be of good cheer. I have overcome the world.

—JOHN 16:33

No temptation has taken you except what is common to man. God is faithful, and He will not permit you to be tempted above what you can endure, but will with the temptation also make a way to escape, that you may be able to bear it.

—1 Corinthians 10:13

Put on the whole armor of God that you may be able to stand against the schemes of the devil. For our fight is not against flesh and blood, but against principalities, against powers, against the rulers of the darkness of this world, and against spiritual forces of evil in the heavenly places.

—Ephesians 6:11–12

For we do not have a High Priest who cannot sympathize with our weaknesses, but One who was in every sense tempted like we are, yet without sin.

—Hebrews 4:15

My brothers, count it all joy when you fall into diverse temptations, knowing that the trying of your faith develops patience. But let patience perfect its work, that you may be perfect and complete, lacking nothing.

—James 1:2–4

Blessed is the man who endures temptation, for when he is tried, he will receive the crown of life, which the Lord has promised to those who love Him. Let no man say when he is tempted, "I am tempted by God," for God cannot be tempted with evil; neither does He tempt anyone.... Then, when lust has conceived, it brings forth sin; and when sin is finished, it brings forth death.

—James 1:12–13, 15

Then the Lord knows how to rescue the godly from trial, and to keep the unrighteous under punishment for the Day of Judgment.

—2 Peter 2:9

Because you have kept My word of patience, I also will keep you from the hour of temptation which shall come upon the entire world, to test those who dwell on the earth.

—Revelation 3:10

THANKFULNESS

It happened, when the trumpet players and singers made one sound to praise and give thanks to the Lord, and when they lifted up their voice with the trumpets and cymbals and all the instruments of music and praised the Lord saying, "For He is good and His mercy endures forever," that the house, the house of the Lord, was filled with a cloud.

—2 Chronicles 5:13

He said, "Naked I came from my mother's womb, and naked will I return there. The Lord gave, and the Lord has taken away; blessed be the name of the Lord." In all this Job did not sin, and he did not accuse God of wrongdoing.

—Job 1:21–22

I will thank the Lord according to His righteousness, and will sing praise to the name of the Lord Most High.

—Psalm 7:17

I will bless the Lord at all times; His praise will continually be in my mouth.

—Psalm 34:1

"The voice of joy, and the voice of gladness, the voice of the bridegroom, and the voice of the bride, the voice of those who shall say, 'Give thanks to the LORD of Hosts, for the LORD is good. For His mercy endures forever,' and of those who bring the sacrifice of praise into the house of the LORD. For I will restore the fortunes of the land as at the first," says the LORD.
—JEREMIAH 33:11

Thanks be to God for His indescribable gift.
—2 CORINTHIANS 9:15

Give thanks always for all things to God the Father in the name of our Lord Jesus Christ.
—EPHESIANS 5:20

I thank my God for every reminder of you. In every prayer of mine for you all, I have always made requests with joy, due to your fellowship in the gospel from the first day until now.
—PHILIPPIANS 1:3–5

Rooted and built up in Him and established in the faith, as you have been taught, and abounding with thanksgiving.
—COLOSSIANS 2:7

Continue in prayer, and be watchful with thanksgiving.
—COLOSSIANS 4:2

For everything created by God is good, and not to be refused if it is received with thanksgiving.
—1 TIMOTHY 4:4

Therefore, since we are receiving a kingdom that cannot be moved, let us be gracious, by which we may serve God acceptably with reverence and godly fear.

—Hebrews 12:28

TRANSFORMATION

Truly, truly I say to you, whoever hears My word and believes in Him who sent Me has eternal life and shall not come into condemnation, but has passed from death into life.

—John 5:24

Therefore, since we have been justified by faith, we have peace with God through our Lord Jesus Christ.

—Romans 5:1

For if we have been united with Him in the likeness of His death, so shall we also be united with Him in the likeness of His resurrection, knowing this, that our old man has been crucified with Him, so that the body of sin might be destroyed, and we should no longer be slaves to sin.

—Romans 6:5–6

There is therefore now no condemnation for those who are in Christ Jesus, who walk not according to the flesh, but according to the Spirit.

—Romans 8:1

For "who has known the mind of the Lord that he may instruct Him"? But we have the mind of Christ.

—1 Corinthians 2:16

Therefore, if any man is in Christ, he is a new creature. Old things have passed away. Look, all things have become new.

—2 Corinthians 5:17

I have been crucified with Christ. It is no longer I who live, but Christ who lives in me. And the life I now live in the flesh, I live by faith in the Son of God, who loved me and gave Himself for me.

—Galatians 2:20

For as many of you as have been baptized into Christ have put on Christ.

—Galatians 3:27

To the praise of the glory of His grace which He graciously bestowed on us in the Beloved. In Him we have redemption through His blood and the forgiveness of sins according to the riches of His grace, which He lavished on us in all wisdom and insight.

—Ephesians 1:6–8

Even when we were dead in sins, made us alive together with Christ (by grace you have been saved).

—Ephesians 2:5

For we are His workmanship, created in Christ Jesus for good works, which God prepared beforehand, so that we should walk in them.

—Ephesians 2:10

And you are complete in Him, who is the head of all authority and power.

—Colossians 2:10

TROUBLE

The LORD also will be a refuge for the oppressed, a refuge in times of trouble.

—Psalm 9:9

The LORD is my pillar, and my fortress, and my deliverer; my God, my rock, in whom I take refuge; my shield, and the horn of my salvation, my high tower. I will call on the LORD, who is worthy to be praised, and I will be saved from my enemies.

—Psalm 18:2–3

For in the time of trouble He will hide me in His pavilion; in the shelter of His tabernacle He will hide me; He will set me up on a rock.

—Psalm 27:5

I will be glad and rejoice in Your lovingkindness, for You have seen my trouble; You have known my soul in adversities....Be gracious to me, O LORD, for I am in trouble; my eye wastes away with grief, yes, my soul and my body.

—Psalm 31:7, 9

But the salvation of the righteous is from the LORD; He is their refuge in the time of distress. The LORD will help them and deliver them; He will deliver them from the wicked, and save them, because they take refuge in Him.

—Psalm 37:39–40

God is our refuge and strength, a well-proven help in trouble.

—Psalm 46:1

Cast your care on the LORD, and He will sustain you; He will not allow the righteous to totter forever.

—PSALM 55:22

Remember, O LORD, the people of Edom in the day of Jerusalem, who said, "Raze it, raze it, down to its foundations." O daughter of Babylon, who is to be destroyed, blessed is the one who rewards you as you have done to us.

—PSALM 137:7–8

The righteous is delivered out of trouble, and the wicked comes in his place.

—PROVERBS 11:8

Let not your heart be troubled. You believe in God. Believe also in Me.

—JOHN 14:1

Peace I leave with you. My peace I give to you. Not as the world gives do I give to you. Let not your heart be troubled, neither let it be afraid.

—JOHN 14:27

Blessed be God, the Father of our Lord Jesus Christ, the Father of mercies, and the God of all comfort, who comforts us in all our tribulation, that we may be able to comfort those who are in any trouble by the comfort with which we ourselves are comforted by God.

—2 CORINTHIANS 1:3–4

TRUST

The LORD bless you and keep you; the LORD make His face to shine upon you, and be gracious unto you; the LORD lift His countenance upon you, and give you peace.

—NUMBERS 6:24–26

The God of my strength, in whom I will trust; my shield and the horn of my salvation, my fortress and my sanctuary; my Savior, You save me from violence.

—2 SAMUEL 22:3

He trusted in the LORD God of Israel. Afterwards, there was no one like him among all the kings of Judah or among those who were before him.

—2 KINGS 18:5

To You, O LORD, do I lift up my soul. O my God, I trust in You; may I not be ashamed, may my enemies not triumph over me. Yes, let none who wait on You be ashamed; let them be ashamed who transgress without cause.

—PSALM 25:1–3

Many sorrows come to the wicked, but lovingkindness will surround the man who trusts in the LORD.

—PSALM 32:10

God is our refuge and strength, a well-proven help in trouble. Therefore we will not fear, though the earth be removed, and though the mountains be carried into the midst of the sea.

—PSALM 46:1–2

Those who trust in their wealth, and boast in the multitude of their riches, none of them can by any means redeem the other, nor give to God a ransom for anyone.

—Psalm 49:6–7

Blessed is the one who has the God of Jacob for his help, whose hope is in the Lord his God.

—Psalm 146:5

He who handles a matter wisely will find good, and whoever trusts in the Lord, happy is he.

—Proverbs 16:20

He who is of a proud heart stirs up strife, but he who puts his trust in the Lord will prosper.

—Proverbs 28:25

Then Nebuchadnezzar spoke and said, "Blessed be the God of Shadrach, Meshach, and Abednego, who has sent His angel and delivered His servants who trusted in Him. They have defied the king's word, and yielded their bodies, that they might not serve nor worship any god, except their own God."

—Daniel 3:28

He did not waver at the promise of God through unbelief, but was strong in faith, giving glory to God, and being fully persuaded that what God had promised, He was able to perform.

—Romans 4:20–21

Unbelieving Spouse

Those who know Your name will put their trust in You, for You, Lord, have not forsaken those who seek You.

—Psalm 9:10

But as for me, I will walk in my integrity. Redeem me, and be gracious to me.

—Psalm 26:11

I have been young, and now am old; yet I have not seen the righteous forsaken, nor their offspring begging bread.

—Psalm 37:25

Lest strangers be filled with your wealth, and your labors go to the house of a stranger.

—Proverbs 5:10

And I will give them one heart and one way, that they may fear Me forever, for their good and for their children after them.

—Jeremiah 32:39

"For the Lord, the God of Israel, says that He hates divorce; for it covers one's garment with violence," says the Lord of Hosts. Therefore take heed to your spirit, that you do not deal treacherously.

—Malachi 2:16

But I say to you, whoever divorces his wife, except for sexual immorality, and marries another, commits adultery. And whoever marries her who is divorced commits adultery.

—Matthew 19:9

He said to them, "Whoever divorces his wife and marries another commits adultery against her. And if a woman divorces her husband and marries another, she commits adultery."

—MARK 10:11–12

Now to the married I command, not I, but the Lord, do not let the wife depart from her husband. But if she departs, let her remain unmarried or be reconciled to her husband. And do not let the husband divorce his wife.

—1 CORINTHIANS 7:10–11

To the rest I speak, not the Lord: If any brother has an unbelieving wife who consents to live with him, he should not divorce her. And if the woman has an unbelieving husband who consents to live with her, she should not divorce him. For the unbelieving husband is sanctified by the wife, and the unbelieving wife is sanctified by the husband. Otherwise, your children would be unclean. But now they are holy.

—1 CORINTHIANS 7:12–14

But if the unbeliever departs, let that one depart. A brother or a sister is not bound in such cases. God has called us to peace. For how do you know, O wife, whether you will save your husband? Or how do you know, O husband, whether you will save your wife?

—1 CORINTHIANS 7:15–16

Likewise you wives, be submissive to your own husbands, so that if any do not obey the word, they may be won without a word by the conduct of their wives, as they see the purity and reverence of your lives.

—1 PETER 3:1–2

UNPARDONABLE SIN

Therefore I say to you, all kinds of sin and blasphemy will be forgiven men, but the blasphemy against the Holy Spirit will not be forgiven men. Whoever speaks a word against the Son of Man will be forgiven. But whoever speaks against the Holy Spirit will not be forgiven, neither in this world, nor in the world to come.

—MATTHEW 12:31–32

Truly I say to you, all sins will be forgiven the sons of men, and whatever blasphemies they speak.

—MARK 3:28

For it is impossible for those who were once enlightened, who have tasted the heavenly gift, who shared in the Holy Spirit, and have tasted the good word of God and the powers of the age to come, if they fall away, to be renewed once more to repentance, since they again crucify to themselves the Son of God and subject Him to public shame.

—HEBREWS 6:4–6

How much more severe a punishment do you suppose he deserves, who has trampled under foot the Son of God, and has regarded the blood of the covenant that sanctified him to be a common thing, and has insulted the Spirit of grace?

—HEBREWS 10:29

For if after they have escaped the defilements of the world through the knowledge of the Lord and Savior Jesus Christ, and they are again entangled in them and are overcome, the latter end is worse for them than the beginning.

—2 PETER 2:20

The Lord is not slow concerning His promise, as some count slowness. But He is patient with us, because He does not want any to perish, but all to come to repentance.

—2 PETER 3:9

VALUES

Beware that you do not forget the LORD your God by not keeping His commandments, and His judgments, and His statutes, which I am commanding you today.

—DEUTERONOMY 8:11

The LORD requites to every man his right conduct and loyalty. So the LORD gave you into my hand today, but I am not willing to stretch my hand against the LORD's anointed.

—1 SAMUEL 26:23

Evil men do not understand justice, but those who seek the LORD understand all things.

—PROVERBS 28:5

Better is the poor who walks in his uprightness, than he who is perverse in his ways, though he be rich.

—PROVERBS 28:6

Two things I have required of you; do not deny me them before I die: Remove vanity and lies far from me; give me neither poverty nor riches; feed me with food convenient for me; lest I be full, and deny You, and say, "Who is the LORD?" or lest I be poor, and steal, and take the name of my God in vain.

—PROVERBS 30:7–9

Thus says the LORD, "Stand in the ways and see, and ask for the old paths where the good way is and walk in it, and you shall find rest for your souls." But they said, "We will not walk in it."

—Jeremiah 6:16

Then those who feared the Lord spoke to one another. The Lord listened and heard them, and a book of remembrance was written before Him for those who fear the Lord and who esteem His name. "They shall be Mine," says the Lord of Hosts, "on the day when I make up My jewels. And I will spare them as a man spares his son who serves him."

—Malachi 3:16–17

Jesus said to him, "'You shall love the Lord your God with all your heart, and with all your soul, and with all your mind.' This is the first and great commandment. And the second is like it: 'You shall love your neighbor as yourself.' On these two commandments hang all the Law and the Prophets."

—Matthew 22:37–40

So embrace, as the elect of God, holy and beloved, a spirit of mercy, kindness, humbleness of mind, meekness, and long-suffering. Bear with one another and forgive one another. If anyone has a quarrel against anyone, even as Christ forgave you, so you must do. And above all these things, embrace love, which is the bond of perfection.

—Colossians 3:12–14

Remembering without ceasing your work of faith, labor of love, and patient hope in our Lord Jesus Christ in the sight of God and our Father.

—1 Thessalonians 1:3

For bodily exercise profits a little, but godliness is profitable in all things, holding promise for the present life and also for the life to come.

—1 Timothy 4:8

Pursue peace with all men, and the holiness without which no one will see the Lord, watching diligently so that no one falls short of the grace of God, lest any root of bitterness spring up to cause trouble, and many become defiled by it.

—Hebrews 12:14–15

WAITING ON THE PROMISE

What if God, willing to show His wrath and to make His power known, endured with much patience the vessels of wrath prepared for destruction.

—Romans 9:22

Anyone who competes as an athlete is not rewarded without competing legally. The farmer who labors should be first to partake of the crops.

—2 Timothy 2:5–6

So after Abraham had patiently endured, he obtained the promise.

—Hebrews 6:15

Remember the former days, after you were enlightened, in which you endured a great struggle of afflictions.

—Hebrews 10:32

Indeed we count them happy who endure. You have heard of the patience of Job and have seen the purpose of the Lord, that the Lord is very gracious and merciful.

—James 5:11

For this is commendable, if because of conscience toward God a person endures grief, suffering unjustly. For what credit is it if when you are being beaten for your sins you patiently endure? But if when doing good and suffering for it, you patiently endure, this is excellence before God.

—1 Peter 2:19–20

Walking in God's Ways

From Mount Halak to Seir, and as far as Baal Gad in the Lebanon Valley under Mount Hermon: All their kings he captured, struck down, and killed.

—Joshua 11:17

The Lord is near to the brokenhearted, and saves the contrite of spirit.

—Psalm 34:18

May there be abundance of grain in the earth on the top of the mountains; may its fruit shake like Lebanon; and may those from the city flourish like grass of the earth.

—Psalm 72:16

The righteous shall flourish like the palm tree and grow like a cedar in Lebanon.

—Psalm 92:12

Many people shall go and say, "Come, and let us go up to the mountain of the Lord, to the house of the God of Jacob, and

He will teach us of His ways, and we will walk in His paths."
For out of Zion shall go forth the law, and the word of the
Lord from Jerusalem.

—Isaiah 2:3

But this thing I commanded them, saying, "Obey My voice,
and I will be your God, and you shall be My people. And
walk in all the ways that I have commanded you, that it may
be well with you."

—Jeremiah 7:23

"Bring all the tithes into the storehouse, that there may be
food in My house, and test Me now in this," says the Lord
of Hosts, "if I will not open for you the windows of heaven
and pour out for you a blessing, that there will not be room
enough to receive it."

—Malachi 3:10

Heal the sick, cleanse the lepers, raise the dead, and cast out
demons. Freely you have received, freely give.

—Matthew 10:8

For you were formerly darkness, but now you are light in the
Lord. Walk as children of light.

—Ephesians 5:8

See then that you walk carefully, not as fools, but as wise
men.

—Ephesians 5:15

Walk in wisdom toward those who are outside, wisely using
the opportunity.

—Colossians 4:5

So that you may walk honestly toward those who are outsiders and that you may lack nothing.

—1 Thessalonians 4:12

WAR

To everything there is a season, a time for every purpose under heaven…a time to kill, and a time to heal; a time to break down, and a time to build up…a time to love, and a time to hate; a time of war and a time of peace.

—Ecclesiastes 3:1, 3, 8

He shall judge among the nations, and shall rebuke many people. And they shall beat their swords into ploughshares, and their spears into pruning hooks. Nation shall not lift up sword against nation, nor shall they learn war any more.

—Isaiah 2:4

For even Christ did not please Himself. But as it is written, "The insults of those who insulted You fell on Me."

—Romans 15:3

Therefore I exhort first of all that you make supplications, prayers, intercessions, and thanksgivings for everyone, for kings and for all who are in authority, that we may lead a quiet and peaceful life in all godliness and honesty.

—1 Timothy 2:1–2

Where do wars and fights among you come from? Do they not come from your lusts that war in your body? You lust and do not have, so you kill. You desire to have and cannot obtain. You fight and war. Yet you do not have, because you do not ask. You ask, and do not receive, because you ask amiss, that you may spend it on your passions.

—James 4:1–3

Submit yourselves to every human authority for the Lord's sake, whether it be to the king, as supreme, or to governors, who are sent by him for the punishment of evildoers and for the praise of those who do right.

—1 Peter 2:13–14

WIDOWS

A father of the fatherless, and a protector of the widows, is God in His holy habitation.

—Psalm 68:5

Learn to do good. Seek justice. Relieve the oppressed. Judge the fatherless. Plead for the widow.

—Isaiah 1:17

Do not oppress the widow, orphan, sojourner, or poor. And let none of you contemplate evil deeds in your hearts against his brother.

—Zechariah 7:10

Who devour widows' houses and for a pretense make long prayers. They will receive greater condemnation.

—Luke 20:47

Honor widows that are widows indeed. But if any widow has children or grandchildren, let them learn first to show piety at home and to repay their parents. For this is good and acceptable before God. Now she who is a widow indeed, and desolate, trusts in God, and continues in supplications and prayers night and day. But she who lives in pleasure is dead while she lives.

—1 Timothy 5:3–6

If any believing man or woman has widows, let those assist them. Do not let the church be charged, so that it may relieve those who are widows indeed.

—1 Timothy 5:16

Will of God (How to Find and Know)

And he said, "Blessed be the Lord God of my master Abraham, who has not forsaken His mercy and His truth toward my master. As for me, the Lord led me to the house of my master's relatives."

—Genesis 24:27

Samuel said, "Does the Lord delight in burnt offerings and sacrifices as much as in obeying the voice of the Lord? Obedience is better than sacrifice, a listening ear than the fat of rams."

—1 Samuel 15:22

I will instruct you and teach you in the way which you will go; I will counsel you with my eye on you. Do not be as the horse or as the mule that are without understanding, that must be restrained with bit and bridle, or they will not come near you.

—Psalm 32:8–9

I delight to do Your will, O my God; Your law is within my inward parts.

—Psalm 40:8

Your word is a lamp to my feet, and a light to my path.

—Psalm 119:105

Cause me to hear Your lovingkindness in the morning; for in You I have my trust; cause me to know the way I should walk, for I lift up my soul unto You.

—Psalm 143:8

Commit your works to the Lord, and your thoughts will be established.

—Proverbs 16:3

Your kingdom come. Your will be done on earth, as it is in heaven.

—Matthew 6:10

Not everyone who says to Me, 'Lord, Lord,' shall enter the kingdom of heaven, but he who does the will of My Father who is in heaven.

—Matthew 7:21

"If you love Me, keep My commandments."…Jesus answered him, "If a man loves Me, he will keep My word. My Father will love him, and We will come to him, and make Our home with him."

—John 14:15, 23

But when the Spirit of truth comes, He will guide you into all truth. For He will not speak on His own authority. But He will speak whatever He hears, and He will tell you things that are to come.

—John 16:13

In everything give thanks, for this is the will of God in Christ Jesus concerning you.

—1 Thessalonians 5:18

Wisdom

Man does not know its price, nor is it found in the land of the living.... It cannot be bought for gold, nor can silver be weighed for its price.

—Job 28:13, 15

To man He said: "Look, the fear of the Lord, that is wisdom; and to depart from evil is understanding."

—Job 28:28

The fear of the Lord is the beginning of wisdom; all who live it have insight. His praise endures forever!

—Psalm 111:10

The fear of the Lord is the beginning of knowledge, but fools despise wisdom and instruction.

—Proverbs 1:7

Get wisdom, get understanding. Do not forget it, nor turn away from the words of my mouth.... Wisdom is principal; therefore get wisdom. And with all your getting get understanding.

—Proverbs 4:5, 7

To do mischief is like sport to a fool, but a man of understanding has wisdom.

—Proverbs 10:23

Through wisdom is a house built, and by understanding it is established; and by knowledge the rooms will be filled with all precious and pleasant riches.

—Proverbs 24:3–4

Evil men do not understand justice, but those who seek the Lord understand all things.

—Proverbs 28:5

Have you not known? Have you not heard, that the everlasting God, the Lord, the Creator of the ends of the earth, does not faint, nor is He weary? His understanding is inscrutable. He gives power to the faint, and to those who have no might He increases strength.

—Isaiah 40:28–29

For the foolishness of God is wiser than men, and the weakness of God is stronger than men.

—1 Corinthians 1:25

Let the word of Christ dwell in you richly in all wisdom, teaching and admonishing one another in psalms and hymns and spiritual songs, singing with grace in your hearts to the Lord.

—Colossians 3:16

If any of you lacks wisdom, let him ask of God, who gives to all men liberally and without criticism, and it will be given to him.

—James 1:5

WITCHCRAFT

But this is how you shall deal with them: You shall destroy their altars and break down their images and cut down their Asherim and burn their graven images with fire. For you are a holy people to the LORD your God. The LORD your God has chosen you to be His special people, treasured above all peoples who are on the face of the earth.

—DEUTERONOMY 7:5–6

He built shrines on the mountaintops and made priests from all the people, even those who were not of the tribe of Levi.

—1 KINGS 12:31

When Joram saw Jehu he said, "Is it peace, Jehu?" And he said, "What peace, so long as the harlotries of your mother Jezebel and her sorceries are so many?"

—2 KINGS 9:22

He took down the foreign altars and high places, and he shattered the pillars and cut down the Asherim poles.

—2 CHRONICLES 14:3

Hide me from the secret counsel of the wicked, from the throng of workers of iniquity, who sharpen their tongue like a sword, and bend their bows to shoot their arrows—bitter words, that they may shoot in secret at the person of integrity; suddenly they shoot at him and do not fear.

—PSALM 64:2–4

Let them curse, but You will bless; when they arise, let them be ashamed, but let Your servant rejoice.

—PSALM 109:28

The word of the LORD came to me the second time, saying, "What do you see?" And I said, "I see a boiling pot. And it is facing away from the north." Then the LORD said to me, "Out of the north an evil will break forth upon all the inhabitants of the land."

—JEREMIAH 1:13–14

Therefore thus says the Lord GOD, "Your slain whom you have laid in the midst of it, they are the flesh and this city is the cauldron. But I will bring you forth out of the midst of it."

—EZEKIEL 11:7

When he shall stand up, his kingdom shall be broken and shall be divided toward the four winds of heaven, but not to his posterity, nor according to his dominion which he ruled. For his kingdom shall be plucked up, even for others besides them.

—DANIEL 11:4

Then I will cut off the cities of your land, and I will overthrow your strongholds; then I will cut off sorceries from your hand, and you will no longer have fortune-tellers; then I will cut off your idols and your sacred stones from among you, and you will no longer bow down to the work of your hands; then I will root out your Asherah idols from among you, and I will annihilate your cities. And in anger and wrath I will take vengeance on the nations that have not listened.

—MICAH 5:11–15

"You son of the devil, enemy of all righteousness, full of deceit and of all fraud, will you not cease perverting the right ways of the Lord? Now, look! The hand of the Lord is against you, and you shall be blind, not seeing the sun for a time."

Immediately mist and darkness fell on him, and he went about seeking someone to lead him by the hand.

—Acts 13:10–11

O foolish Galatians! Who has bewitched you that you should not obey the truth? Before your eyes Jesus Christ was clearly portrayed among you as crucified.

—Galatians 3:1

Witnessing

Go therefore and make disciples of all nations, baptizing them in the name of the Father and of the Son and of the Holy Spirit, teaching them to observe all things I have commanded you. And remember, I am with you always, even to the end of the age. Amen.

—Matthew 28:19–20

He said to them, "Go into all the world, and preach the gospel to every creature. He who believes and is baptized will be saved. But he who does not believe will be condemned."

—Mark 16:15–16

Jesus said to him, "I am the way, the truth, and the life. No one comes to the Father except through Me."

—John 14:6

But you shall receive power when the Holy Spirit comes upon you. And you shall be My witnesses in Jerusalem, and in all Judea and Samaria, and to the ends of the earth.

—Acts 1:8

When they saw the boldness of Peter and John and perceived that they were illiterate and uneducated men, they marveled. And they recognized that they had been with Jesus.

—Acts 4:13

For I am not ashamed of the gospel of Christ. For it is the power of God for salvation to everyone who believes, to the Jew first, and also to the Greek.

—Romans 1:16

As it is written, "There is none righteous. No, not one."

—Romans 3:10

That if you confess with your mouth Jesus is Lord, and believe in your heart that God has raised Him from the dead, you will be saved, for with the heart one believes unto righteousness, and with the mouth confession is made unto salvation.

—Romans 10:9–10

For, "Everyone one who calls on the name of the Lord shall be saved." How then shall they call on Him in whom they have not believed? And how shall they believe in Him of whom they have not heard? And how shall they hear without a preacher?

—Romans 10:13–14

Meanwhile, through the performance of this ministry, they glorify God for the profession of your faith in the gospel of Christ and for your liberal sharing with them and with all others.

—2 Corinthians 9:13

Yet, we know that a man is not justified by the works of the law, but through faith in Jesus Christ, even we have believed in Christ Jesus, so that we might be justified by faith in Christ, rather than by the works of the law. For by the works of the law no flesh shall be justified.

—Galatians 2:16

I ask you also, true companion, help those women who labored with me in the gospel, with Clement also, and with my other fellow laborers, whose names are in the Book of Life.

—Philippians 4:3

But be self-controlled in all things, endure afflictions, do the work of an evangelist, and prove your ministry.

—2 Timothy 4:5

Wives

Every wise woman builds her house, but the foolish pulls it down with her hands.

—Proverbs 14:1

A foolish son is the calamity of his father, and the contentions of a wife are a continual dripping of water. House and riches are the inheritance of fathers, and a prudent wife is from the Lord.

—Proverbs 19:13–14

Who can find a virtuous woman? For her worth is far above rubies.

—Proverbs 31:10

But I say to you that whoever divorces his wife, except for marital unfaithfulness, causes her to commit adultery. And whoever marries her who is divorced commits adultery.

—MATTHEW 5:32

Wives, be submissive to your own husbands as unto the Lord. For the husband is the head of the wife, just as Christ is the head and Savior of the Church, which is His body.

—EPHESIANS 5:22–23

Do not let your adorning be the outward adorning of braiding the hair, wearing gold, or putting on fine clothing. But let it be the hidden nature of the heart, that which is not corruptible, even the ornament of a gentle and quiet spirit, which is very precious in the sight of God.

—1 PETER 3:3–4

WORD OF GOD

Therefore you must fix these words of mine in your heart and in your soul, and bind them as a sign on your hand, so that they may be as frontlets between your eyes.

—DEUTERONOMY 11:18

This book of the law must not depart from your mouth. Meditate on it day and night so that you may act carefully according to all that is written in it. For then you will make your way successful, and you will be wise.

—JOSHUA 1:8

The giving of Your words gives light; it grants understanding to the simple.

—PSALM 119:130

For the commandment is a lamp, and the law is light; and reproofs of instruction are the way of life.

—Proverbs 6:23

You search the Scriptures, because you think in them you have eternal life. These are they who bear witness of Me.

—John 5:39

Now, brothers, I commend you to God and to the word of His grace, which is able to build you up and give you an inheritance among all who are sanctified.

—Acts 20:32

And that since childhood you have known the Holy Scriptures, which are able to make you wise unto salvation through the faith that is in Christ Jesus. All Scripture is inspired by God and is profitable for teaching, for reproof, for correction, and for instruction in righteousness.

—2 Timothy 3:15–16

Be doers of the word and not hearers only, deceiving yourselves. For if anyone is a hearer of the word and not a doer, he is like a man viewing his natural face in a mirror.

—James 1:22–23

For you have been born again, not from perishable seed, but imperishable, through the living and eternal word of God.

—1 Peter 1:23

As newborn babies, desire the pure milk of the word, that by it you may grow.

—1 Peter 2:2

And we have a more reliable word of prophecy, which you would do well to follow, as to a light that shines in a dark place, until the day dawns and the morning star arises in your hearts.

—2 Peter 1:19

Blessed is he who reads and those who hear the words of this prophecy and keep those things which are written in it, for the time is near.

—Revelation 1:3

WORK

Then God blessed the seventh day and made it holy, because on it He had rested from all His work which He had created and made.

—Genesis 2:3

Six days you shall labor, and do all your work, but the seventh day is the Sabbath of the Lord your God. On it you shall not do any work, you, nor your son, nor your daughter, nor your male servant, nor your female servant, nor your ox, nor your donkey, nor any of your cattle, nor the foreigner that is within your gates, so that your male servant and your female servant may rest as well as you.

—Deuteronomy 5:13–14

Except the Lord build the house, those who build labor in vain; except the Lord guards the city, the watchman stays awake in vain.

—Psalm 127:1

In all labor there is profit, but mere talk leads only to poverty.

—Proverbs 14:23

He who had received five talents came and brought the other five talents, saying, "Master, you entrusted to me five talents. Look, I have gained five talents more." His master said to him, "Well done, you good and faithful servant. You have been faithful over a few things. I will make you ruler over many things. Enter the joy of your master."

—MATTHEW 25:20–21

Jesus said to them, "My food is to do the will of Him who sent Me, and to finish His work."

—JOHN 4:34

Now to him who works, wages are not given as a gift, but as a debt.

—ROMANS 4:4

Therefore, my beloved brothers, be steadfast, unmovable, always abounding in the work of the Lord, knowing that your labor in the Lord is not in vain.

—1 CORINTHIANS 15:58

Where there is neither Greek nor Jew, circumcision nor uncircumcision, Barbarian, Scythian, slave nor free, but Christ is all and in all. So embrace, as the elect of God, holy and beloved, a spirit of mercy, kindness, humbleness of mind, meekness, and longsuffering.

—COLOSSIANS 3:11–12

And whatever you do in word or deed, do all in the name of the Lord Jesus, giving thanks to God the Father through Him.

—COLOSSIANS 3:17

But if any do not care for their own, and especially for those of their own house, they have denied the faith and are worse than unbelievers.

—1 Timothy 5:8

For God is not unjust so as to forget your work and labor of love that you have shown for His name, in that you have ministered to the saints and continue ministering. We desire that every one of you show the same diligence for the full assurance of hope to the end.

—Hebrews 6:10–11

WORRY

The LORD also will be a refuge for the oppressed, a refuge in times of trouble. Those who know Your name will put their trust in You, for You, LORD, have not forsaken those who seek You.

—Psalm 9:9–10

You are my hiding place; You will preserve me from trouble; You will surround me with shouts of deliverance. Selah.

—Psalm 32:7

God is our refuge and strength, a well-proven help in trouble. Therefore we will not fear, though the earth be removed, and though the mountains be carried into the midst of the sea; though its waters roar and foam, though the mountains shake with its swelling. Selah.

—Psalm 46:1–3

The work of righteousness shall be peace, and the effect of righteousness quietness and assurance forever.

—Isaiah 32:17

For he shall be as a tree planted by the waters, and that spreads out its roots by the river, and shall not fear when heat comes, but its leaf shall be green. And it shall not be anxious in the year of drought, neither shall cease from yielding fruit.

—JEREMIAH 17:8

Therefore, if God so clothes the grass of the field, which today is here and tomorrow is thrown into the oven, will He not much more clothe you, O you of little faith? Therefore, take no thought, saying, 'What shall we eat?' or 'What shall we drink?' or 'What shall we wear?' (For the Gentiles seek after all these things). For your heavenly Father knows that you have need of all these things.

—MATTHEW 6:30–32

Jesus answered her, "Martha, Martha, you are anxious and troubled about many things. But one thing is needed. And Mary has chosen the good part, which shall not be taken from her."

—LUKE 10:41–42

We are troubled on every side, yet not distressed; we are perplexed, but not in despair; persecuted, but not forsaken; cast down, but not destroyed.

—2 CORINTHIANS 4:8–9

Be anxious for nothing, but in everything, by prayer and supplication with gratitude, make your requests known to God. And the peace of God, which surpasses all understanding, will protect your hearts and minds through Christ Jesus.

—PHILIPPIANS 4:6–7

But my God shall supply your every need according to His riches in glory by Christ Jesus.

—PHILIPPIANS 4:19

If you then were raised with Christ, desire those things which are above, where Christ sits at the right hand of God.

—COLOSSIANS 3:1

But let him ask in faith, without wavering. For he who wavers is like a wave of the sea, driven and tossed with the wind.

—JAMES 1:6

WORSHIP

For you must not worship any other god, for the LORD, whose name is Jealous, is a jealous God.

—EXODUS 34:14

Give to the LORD the glory of His name; worship the LORD in holy splendor.

—PSALM 29:2

All the earth will worship You and will sing to You; they will sing to Your name. Selah.

—PSALM 66:4

All nations whom You have made shall come and worship before You, O Lord, and shall glorify Your name.

—PSALM 86:9

O sing unto the LORD a new song; sing unto the LORD, all the earth!...For the LORD is great, and greatly to be praised; He is to be feared above all gods....Honor and majesty are before Him; strength and beauty are in His sanctuary.

—PSALM 96:1, 4, 6

Exalt the LORD our God, and worship at His holy mountain; for the LORD our God is holy!

—PSALM 99:9

Shadrach, Meshach, and Abednego answered and said to the king, "O Nebuchadnezzar, we do not need to give you an answer in this matter. If it be so, our God whom we serve is able to deliver us from the burning fiery furnace, and He will deliver us out of your hand, O king. But even if He does not, be it known to you, O king, that we will not serve your gods, nor worship the golden image which you have set up."

—DANIEL 3:16–18

Now after Jesus was born in Bethlehem of Judea in the days of Herod the king, wise men came from the east to Jerusalem, Saying, "Where is He who was born King of the Jews? For we have seen His star in the east and have come to worship Him."

—MATTHEW 2:1–2

Then Jesus said to him, "Get away from here, Satan! For it is written, 'You shall worship the Lord your God, and Him only shall you serve.'" Then the devil left Him, and immediately angels came and ministered to Him.

—MATTHEW 4:10–11

And then a leper came and worshipped Him, saying, "Lord, if You are willing, You can make me clean." Jesus reached out His hand and touched him, saying, "I will. Be clean." And immediately his leprosy was cleansed.

—MATTHEW 8:2–3

And the devil said to Him, "I will give You all this power and their glory, for it has been delivered to me. And I give it to whomever I will. If You, then, will worship me, all will be Yours." And Jesus answered him, "Get behind Me, Satan! For it is written, 'You shall worship the Lord your God, and Him only shall you serve.'"

—LUKE 4:6–8

God is Spirit and those who worship Him must worship Him in spirit and truth.

—JOHN 4:24

PASSIO

PASSIONATE. AUTHENTIC. MISSIONAL.

Enjoy additional promise books from the
Modern English Version Bible translation.

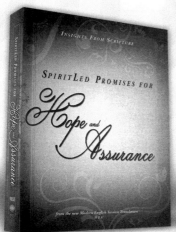

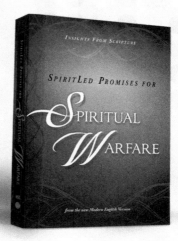

Selected for their power to transform your mind, heart, and soul,
these verses will help you pray with purpose, grow your faith, and
live with joy.

www.MEVBible.com

The MEV Bible is the most modern translation of the King
James Bible in thirty years. The word-for-word translation
accurately communicates God's Word in a way that
combines the beauty of the past with the clarity of today.

Visit the Passio website for additional products and
TO SIGN UP FOR OUR FREE NEWSLETTER
www.PASSIOFAITH.com
www.twitter.com/passiofaith | www.facebook.com/passiofaith

12206

THE ART OF AUTHENTIC FAITH

FREE NEWSLETTERS
TO HELP EMPOWER YOUR LIFE

Why subscribe today?

❏ **DELIVERED DIRECTLY TO YOU.** All you have to do is open your inbox and read.

❏ **EXCLUSIVE CONTENT.** We cover the news overlooked by the mainstream press.

❏ **STAY CURRENT.** Find the latest court rulings, revivals, and cultural trends.

❏ **UPDATE OTHERS.** Easy to forward to friends and family with the click of your mouse.

CHOOSE THE E-NEWSLETTER THAT INTERESTS YOU MOST:

- Christian news
- Daily devotionals
- Spiritual empowerment
- And much, much more

SIGN UP AT: **http://freenewsletters.charismamag.com**

8178